THE PIONEERING GARRETTS

'My strength lies in the extra amount of daring which I have as a family endowment. All Garretts have it.'

Elizabeth Garrett to Harriet Cook, 12 April 1864

GARRETT FAMILY TREE (simplified)

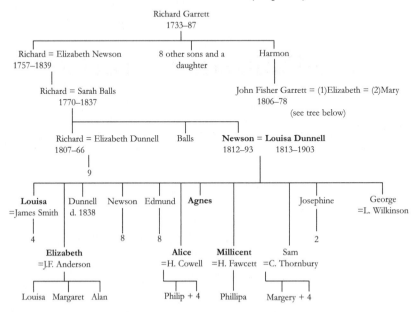

Richard Garrett
1733–87

Richard = Elizabeth Newson
1757–1839

8 other sons and a
daughter

Harmon

Richard = Sarah Balls
1770–1837

John Fisher Garrett = (1)Elizabeth = (2)Mary
1806–78

(see tree below)

Richard = Elizabeth Dunnell
1807–66

Balls

Newson = **Louisa Dunnell**
1812–93   1813–1903

9

Louisa
=James Smith

Dunnell
d. 1838

Newson

Edmund

Agnes

Josephine

George
=L. Wilkinson

4

8

8

2

Elizabeth
=J.F. Anderson

Alice
=H. Cowell

Millicent
=H. Fawcett

Sam
=C. Thornbury

Louisa Margaret Alan

Philip + 4

Phillipa

Margery + 4

THE DERBYSHIRE GARRETTS

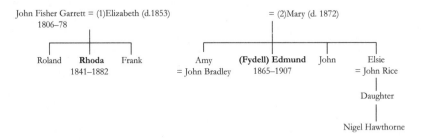

John Fisher Garrett = (1)Elizabeth (d.1853)
1806–78

= (2)Mary (d. 1872)

Roland

Rhoda
1841–1882

Frank

Amy
= John Bradley

(Fydell) Edmund
1865–1907

John

Elsie
= John Rice

Daughter

Nigel Hawthorne

The Pioneering Garretts

Breaking the Barriers for Women

Jenifer Glynn

**hambledon
continuum**

Hambledon Continuum, A Continuum imprint

The Tower Building   80 Maiden Lane, Suite 704
11 York Road   New York, NY 10038
London SE1 7NX

www.continuumbooks.com

First published 2008

British Library Cataloguing-in-Publication Data
A catalogue record for this book is available from the British Library.

ISBN: 978–184725–207–4

Library of Congress Cataloging-in-Publication Data
A catalog record for this book is available from the Library of Congress.

Typeset by YHT Ltd, London
Printed and bound in Great Britain by MPG Books Ltd, Bodmin, Cornwall

Contents

Preface

I have long had a visitors book, kept by my aunt in Mandate Palestine. On March 28th 1928, in firm handwriting, are the names of the leader of the British suffrage movement Millicent Fawcett and her sister Agnes Garrett. They were then aged 81 and 83. I learnt, I admit to my surprise, that they were the sisters of Elizabeth Garrett Anderson, who had been the first woman to qualify as a doctor in Britain. Later I learnt that they were all daughters of Newson Garrett, builder of the Maltings at Snape. I found that I was not alone in being surprised – though many were aware of the individual achievements of Elizabeth and Millicent, few knew their story in its family context. And it is the family context, the interaction of the beliefs and ambitions of the six sisters, four brothers and close community of cousins that make the story so absorbing.

This book makes use of a great many letters, some of them previously unpublished, and it pulls together accounts from a wide variety of sources, including contemporary comments and writings by the Garretts themselves, and. the wonderful collection of letters at the Women's Library. I am very grateful to that Library, and to members of the Garrett family for allowing me to reproduce family letters and photographs; above all to Alice's great grandson, Hew Stevenson, for showing me his family archive, with Alice's letters from India. Elizabeth Crawford's thoroughly researched book *Enterprising Women* has also been invaluable.

There are many others to thank for help and advice; particularly, at Hambledon Continuum, Michael Greenwood and the team of editors and designers; at Newnham, Gillian Sutherland; and from my family, my daughter Judith Glynn, her husband John Twigg, and of course my husband Ian.

List of Illustrations

Alde House, Aldeburgh: the Garrett family home

1

Where it All Began: Snape and Aldeburgh

The most important thing women have to do is to stir up the zeal of women themselves.

John Stuart Mill, 1869

All her life Elizabeth Garrett remembered how she and her elder sister Louie were taken by their father Newson in 1851 to see the Great Exhibition, and how they spent some of the money given them by their Uncle Richard on presents for their young sisters at home – and Millicent remembered that at four years old she had resented being left behind, though the present of a blue velvet bonnet was some consolation. For Louie and Elizabeth were the eldest of the impressive tribe of sisters in Newson Garrett's large family. Louie, who became a source of strength and support to all the rest, died in her forties leaving four young children. Elizabeth grew up to marry James Skelton Anderson, become the first woman doctor to qualify in England, and open up the medical profession to women. Millicent, eleven years younger than Elizabeth, was to marry the blind politician Henry Fawcett and become the leader of the movement for women's suffrage. Another sister, Agnes, together with her cousin Rhoda set up the first architectural decoration business to be run by women; Alice, yet another, had no dramatic achievements herself but, living in India throughout her sisters' formative ten years from 1863, she left a valuable stream of comments on the radical family developments; the youngest, Josephine, was sympathetic but less actively involved.

Many women shared their longing for education and professions and votes, but the Garrett sisters had their own special mixture of vision, energy and practical persistence. All of them, together with siblings and descendants, were working for wider education and opportunities for women. Between them they had huge success in tackling frustrations and knocking down barriers. There are now more women than men in English medical schools; in 1928, in Millicent's lifetime, women achieved the vote on the same terms as men; and it is thanks to the work of pioneers like Agnes and Rhoda that it is now totally accepted that women should run their own businesses, qualify as architects, or advise on interior design. The sisters were brought up, not in any great centre of political life, but as the children of a corn merchant in the little Suffolk seaside town of Aldeburgh and the neighbouring village of Snape.

Snape, to opera-goers around the world, means the Aldeburgh Festival and Benjamin Britten. It is the home of an opera house in the most unexpected of settings – Glyndebourne has its own distinction, the Sydney Opera House soars beside the grand harbour, but there is nothing grand about the rural informality of Snape. The Maltings rise, as if by accident, out of the Suffolk marshes with views spreading over the reed beds, and the Concert Hall itself is among the jumble of buildings. Some of the loyal audience are local, some happen to be holidaying nearby, and many come from London or further. The Aldeburgh Festival moved here in 1967, into a building converted from a grain-drying kiln, the largest of the rambling range. Two years later the Concert Hall was destroyed by a fire; rebuilt, it opened again in 1970.

Now the whole range is busy. There is the music school in the old barley store, the trendy furnishing and food shops, the antiques, the cafés, and – a clue to its history – a sailing barge ready to travel down the river to the sea. For the Maltings, built by Newson Garrett in the middle of the nineteenth century, were well placed on the river Alde so that barley collected from the neighbouring farms could be shipped round the coast to the breweries, either north to Newcastle or south to London. Newson Garrett, who was in so many ways an ambitious man, would have been amazed and delighted to see the present commercial activity, an unpredictable evolution of the buildings he had designed.

It all started in 1841, when Newson bought a corn and coal warehouse at Snape. He had been born nearby in Leiston, the third son of Richard Garrett, a successful manufacturer of agricultural machinery. Since the business was destined for the eldest son, Newson had to make his own way. First this led him to London, where he visited his brother's parents-in-law John and Elizabeth Dunnell, met and married their younger daughter Louisa, and started managing Dunnell's pawnbroker's shop in Whitechapel. In 1916, when Newson's nephew Frank helped V. B. Redstone to write *The Garretts of Suffolk*,[1] Agnes politely pointed out that: 'Millie and I both feel that you might say something about the Dunnells. Both your mother and ours were very remarkable women and all our generation of Garretts owe a great deal to them, don't you think? At the same time I am conscious that perhaps it was not the Dunnell but the Gayford [maternal grandmother] strain that made them what they were – again through the female line you see!'[2] But the strong women in their heritage had remained as influences in the background. It was the growth of the women's movement in the middle of the nineteenth century that encouraged the Garretts to emerge as leaders.

Newson's first two children, Louisa (Louie) and Elizabeth, were born over the Whitechapel shop. Next, Newson progressed to Dunnell's larger shop in Long Acre, becoming both pawnbroker and silversmith. But he had soon had enough of London. With a small inheritance from his father, his own savings, his wife's money and his father-in-law's help, he moved back to Suffolk to buy the corn and coal warehouse that became the foundation of his whole enterprise. By this time he had four living children – there were to be six more – and they settled into the handsome Georgian house opposite Aldeburgh church where the poet George Crabbe had once been an apprentice apothecary, the house which has now become the Uplands Hotel.

The enterprise flourished. In a Directory of Suffolk published only three years after he had started, we read that in Snape 'About 17000 quarters of barley are shipped yearly for London and other markets by Mr Newson Garrett, who has wharehouses, etc., on both sides of the bridge'.[3] He soon owned, or had shares in, about half of Aldeburgh's 22 coasting vessels.[4] He became the local shipping agent for Lloyds, built his own barges and a gasworks, took over a local brickworks and used the bricks for cottages and a row of terrace houses in Aldeburgh, two of them later used by his daughters Alice and Josephine. For himself and his family he built in 1852 a mansion, Alde House,[5] with a grand garden, stables, granaries, piggeries and an ice house; under the influence of news from the Crimea, a Turkish bath was added – 'Master is building hisself a sweatin' house', a groom was heard to mutter, 'if he'd rub the hosses down he wouldn't want no sweatin' house'.[6]

There seemed no limit to Newson's success. In 1854 he introduced a new and profitable industry at Snape, turning the barley into the malt needed for beer before shipping it to London. He had close personal and business relations with several breweries – his father-in-law was among other things a publican in Marylebone, his second cousin Abraham Garrett was similarly (and very successfully) involved in the brewing trade, his brother Richard (of the Leiston works) ran the Camden Brewery, and Newson himself was to become a partner in the Bow Brewery. Malting involves soaking and storing and heating barley grain under special conditions; Newson made his own designs for the necessary new buildings, having them built with his own bricks after reputedly sketching the outline with a stick in the dust. In 1859 he persuaded the East Suffolk Railway to run a short private spur to the complex – speed limit 15 miles an hour. He also built the thatched one-storey Snape Bridge House where the whole family could live in winter while the malting took place.

That was the heyday of the Maltings. In the following generations an assortment of workshops colonized the rambling buildings; in the Second World War there was an air raid siren on the top. Malting did not totally stop until 1964, only two years before work started on the Concert Hall conversion. The family link had gone on to the end, with Newson's great grandson John Wood (Josephine's grandson) as the last chairman and managing director of the company that since 1918 had become S. Swonnell and Son. There are not now many signs of Newson's reign – some dates, an uneven frontage said to follow that uneven line drawn in the dust, and on the stairs in the opera house a row of sturdy Victorian portraits. Painted, his daughter Millicent wrote later, because a 'suitable artist' happened to be 'handy', they show Newson himself, his wife, and maltsters who had worked for them for more than twenty years. It must have been at that same time that the children's (and grandchildren's) friend Barham, the groom and gardener, was painted, carrying a rake because he had refused to be painted with a pot of azaleas. All the portraits are similar in size and style.[7]

Newson loved horses, rode daily, taught all his children to ride, and was, in Millicent's memory, dangerously accident-prone with a horse and trap: 'it was one of our family jokes that he kept up this habit of upsetting himself even when age and infirmity had reduced him to a bathchair: it was a bathchair with a pony to draw it, and he even managed to upset himself in this, and was found laughing to himself, the pony standing close by perfectly quiet, my father still encased in his wrappings, chair and all, like a hermit crab in its shell'.[8]

He was loyal, generous and brave, but he could be, family memoirs admit, intolerant, impulsive, quarrelsome. Periodically he quarrelled with the local clergyman, and for a time would march his family off to the dissenting chapel; his son Sam, born during one of those quarrels, was taken to the church at Snape for his christening. There were serious quarrels too between Newson and his eldest brother Richard. These may have started as rivalry, resentment at Richard inheriting the family business spurring Newson to show he could manage just as well without it. But after Newson changed his politics in the early 1860s, leaving the

Newson in his pony chair, with Louisa

Conservatives to join the Liberals, he and Richard scarcely spoke. In Newson's own family, his son Edmund remained Conservative while all the rest were predictably on the side of reform apart from his increasingly unsatisfactory eldest son, Newson Dunnell.

It seems that his wife Louisa, a strong character in her own way, brought some calm and stability to balance Newson's stormy temperament. She was deeply religious – she was the one who conducted family prayers, having taken over because Newson tried to shorten the ordeal by skipping pages – she kept careful household accounts, she smoothed over his quarrels. Alice, mildly chaotic and forgetful in her demanding Indian housekeeping days, came to admire her mother's calm organization of endless children and grandchildren and visitors. The Garretts' friend and neighbour Edward Fitzgerald wrote of Louisa as 'a Good Motherly Woman', but she was far more than that. She would help her husband at times with difficult letters and, Millicent thought, 'if such things had come her way, she would have proved a very capable organizer of a big business'.[9] Her granddaughter Louisa Garrett Anderson said that such business letters of hers that have survived are excellent, 'but it must be admitted that her letters to her family were dull' – a pity, because there are many of them, but they are conscientiously worthy and gossip-free. Newson, who had been to school only briefly and unenthusiastically at nearby Grundisburgh, stuck to phonetic spelling and had illegible handwriting – 'He wrote with a quill pen and when in doubt for a letter or two, the quill would dart forward in a thick continuous stroke until it reached letters on which he could rely'.[10] But he respected the qualities he lacked, was determined to get good education, by the standards of the time, for all his children, and dutifully went to church even on holiday in Norway with one of his daughters, so that he could please Louisa by telling her when he got home.

While Newson was developing the malting industry, a few miles away in Leiston his eldest brother Richard was bringing new industrial technology to agriculture. It was in a family tradition that went back a long way – and so, confusingly, was the Garretts' limited choice of first names, with many repeats over the generations and with frequent use of their wives' maiden names. The first Richard Garrett, bladesmith and gunsmith, had married Elizabeth Newson of Leiston in 1778 and had taken over the family forge; their son Richard had married Sarah Balls, daughter of the designer of the first effective threshing machine.[11] Richard and Sarah's sons were the Richard we are now concerned with who took over the business; Balls, who moved to Kent to run the Medway Iron Works; and Newson. This third Richard, married to Elizabeth Dunnell, with a family of nine children, was described as 'charitable, industrious, impetuous, impatient of opposition'[12] – in many ways like his brother Newson. He did not try for a private railway line, but he had joined the successful campaign for a branch from Saxmundham to Leiston;[13] he developed the machine works until they covered ten acres and employed 600 men, leading the population of Leiston to double in 30 years.[14] He made seed drills, horseshoes, threshing machines, steam engines, steam rollers. The writer Naomi Mitchison has suggested that a steam roller – steady and unstoppable – might be the right symbol for the Garretts.[15] Between them, in their separate spheres, the brothers dominated the life of the district.

For the Great Exhibition, Messrs Garrett of Leiston 'gave to the persons in their employment – nearly 300 in number – a treat they will not easily forget, in an opportunity of seeing the wonders of the Crystal Palace. Messrs Garrett fitted up and victualled, entirely at their own cost, two schooners, the *Margaret* and the *Jane* of Aldeburgh, and had them towed by the steam-tug *Joseph Soames* to London, where they remained a week; the workmen living on board during their stay'.[16]

The Garrett stand at the Exhibition (where Louie and Elizabeth had such a happy time) was a huge success, and led to so many orders that the following year Richard built the Long Shop,[17] a handsome early example of a flow-line assembly hall, for his portable steam engines. His business developed until he was exporting 90 per cent of his products to Europe, South America, and the colonies.[18] In Leiston, Richard built a Mechanics' Institute with reading room and library, was a Justice of the Peace, and raised money for a new 'College for the education of the middle classes' at nearby Framlingham (with one of his sons-in-law as the first architect and another casting the iron statue of Prince Albert in the front). Newson, also a Justice of the Peace, became Aldeburgh's first mayor and first county councillor and in 1887, for the Queen's Golden Jubilee, gave Aldeburgh the Jubilee Hall, which was to become the first home of the Music Festival in 1948. He was the local chairman of the Royal National Lifeboat Institution, who testified to his bravery on the terrible day in 1855 when seventeen ships were wrecked in a storm off Aldeburgh. He loved the sea, wrote Millicent, 'was a very good sailor himself, and he never quite succeeded in ridding himself of the notion that to be sea-sick was affectation. One day, however, a little party of us, headed by my father and completed by a dog, embarked in a small boat for a sail. Before long the dog was sea-sick. My father was immensely astonished; he said, several times, "God bless my soul, look at that poor thing; then it is *not* affectation, after all." '[19]

But in spite of their similarities there was a divide between the two brothers, deeper than sibling rivalry and political beliefs. The two families had fundamental differences, and one symptom was their different approaches to their children. It is notable that Richard's four sons all followed him, one way or another, into the agricultural machinery business; in the book about the Garretts of Leiston[20] the future of the five daughters is not mentioned. Perhaps this was following the family tradition, since there is hardly anything about earlier generations of daughters. Surprisingly, in her memoir Millicent only writes in passing that Newson and Richard did have a sister (and we hear no more about her), and she does not even mention that her father's grandfather had a sister as well as nine brothers.[21] Anyway, no one could ignore Newson's daughters – his drive and intelligence, mixed with Louisa's firm morality had formidable results, firing his whole family with ambition. The achievements of their astonishing children were greater than even Newson could have imagined. It did not end there – the next generation produced two mathematicians who came top of the Cambridge mathematical tripos[22] (Philippa Fawcett and Philip Cowell), another distinguished pioneering doctor, and a clutch of social reformers.

Ambition, mixed with a confidence in their own ability, lay behind the great changes that Newson's family helped to bring to British life. Yet their radicalism was always combined with a fierce patriotism and a sense of tradition. Millicent remembered how, at the time of the Crimean War when she was eight years old, her father came in to breakfast 'with a newspaper in his hand, looking gay and handsome, and calling out to all his little brood, "Heads up and shoulders down; Sebastopol is taken." '[23] It was a feeling that inspired her and would echo in later troubles, in South Africa or in the 1914 War.

Elizabeth's daughter Louisa tells a famous story of life at Alde House when Elizabeth, then 23, was visited by Emily Davies, the clergyman's daughter from Newcastle who was to become the great campaigner for women's education: 'before the bedroom fire, the girls were brushing their hair. As they brushed they debated. "Women can get nowhere", said Emily, "unless they are as well educated as men. I shall open the universities to them". "Yes", agreed Elizabeth, "We need education but we need an income too and we can't earn that without training and a profession. I shall start women in medicine. But what shall we do with Milly [then aged 13]?" They agreed that she should get the parliamentary vote for women'.[24]

Well, it may or may not have been quite like that, but that was the family tradition of their approach and their confidence. And they did it.

2

Education

The claim of the female mind to instruction in the classics and mathematics will not be again denied by sensible people of either sex. And they have equally firm ground to stand upon in regard to every other kind of knowledge which is open to anybody.

Harriet Martineau in the *Cornhill Magazine*, November 1864

In their early years Newson Garrett's daughters were treated much like their brothers. They were free to explore the coast and marshes of Aldeburgh, to make friends with the fishermen's wives, their father's workmen, the lifeboat crews. One of Millicent's happiest childhood memories was of joining her father in the lifeboat on a 'five shilling' practice day – the crew got three shillings each if it was smooth, and five if it was rough. Their father taught them to ride, took them for picnics, encouraged them to think about the world around them and not to be afraid to discuss and to argue. So incidents connected with world events stuck in young Millicent's mind – her father trying to persuade some of the beachmen to volunteer for the navy for the Crimean War (when she was six), and the announcement on the stage of a London theatre (when she was ten) that Orsini had tried to blow up the French Emperor and Empress.

Their father ran the outings, but it was their mother, running the large household, who gave the children their first lessons. With such a family it was a major undertaking. By 1846, the year before Millicent's birth, even Louisa, struggling to care for six children, was ready to accept help. The relaxed equal treatment of the early days soon ended when the boys, conventionally, were given a tutor; Louie and Elizabeth were a separate problem.

It was all very well to believe in education for daughters as well as sons, but what could be done for middle-class girls in mid-nineteenth-century Suffolk? Elementary schools, if they existed at all, were for working-class boys and girls; the generally unsatisfactory answer for upper- or middle-class families was to employ a governess.[1] There was a scattering of small boarding schools for girls; scarcely any jobs apart from teaching, either in a school or in a family, seemed possible for middle-class unmarried women who needed to earn their living, however slight their qualification. But caught in a peculiar no-man's-land between the servants and the householders, often with no vocation for teaching, governesses were too often inadequate and seldom happy. The most famous reluctant governesses, Anne and Charlotte Brontë, struggled unsympathetically with unruly charges and unfriendly parents: 'I see now more clearly than I have ever done before that a private governess has no existence, is not considered as a living and rational being except as connected with the wearisome duties she has to fulfil', Charlotte wrote to Emily.[2] Yet, of necessity, advertisements brought avalanches of applicants. The 1851 census recorded 24,770 governesses in Britain, either teaching in schools or living with a family, in a total of 67,551 teachers; Bessie Parkes (granddaughter of Joseph Priestley and later the mother of Hilaire Belloc) wrote of one post paying only £15 a year that had 810 candidates.[3]

Amelia Edgeworth, dimly related to the novelist Maria, was, according to Elizabeth's daughter Louisa, chosen to educate the Garrett girls because of 'her poverty, friendlessness and piety'.[4] It was a charitable gesture, but not necessarily the way to find someone suitable for highly intelligent lively children. By the standards of the time she was treated well by her employers, with £25 a year and meals with the family. But with her boring lists of French irregular verbs, 'Mangnall's Historical and Miscellaneous Questions for the Use of Young People', and her dreary regimented walks, she failed to get any respect from the girls, who soon found they could retaliate with questions that were out of her depth. Millicent later heartlessly described her as 'incompetent to the last degree'.[5] Agnes, kinder but perhaps less honest in her recollections, led an interviewer to write that they had had a good grounding in lessons from a governess 'of the good old type';[6] she cannot have been a total failure for the sisters seem to have kept in touch with her, and she re-appeared later at Aldeburgh to help with the grandchildren. Would Charlotte Brontë have responded to Garrett high spirits and intelligence, or would she too have been overwhelmed? Anyway, as the children grew older it clearly became too much for poor Amelia Edgeworth, and in 1849 when the eldest, Louisa, was 15, and Elizabeth was 13, they were sent away to school, to be followed in due course by Alice, Agnes and Millicent.

A year earlier the Christian Socialist Frederick Denison Maurice had founded Queen's College (Harley Street), intending to provide education for girls who planned to become governesses, though it soon turned into a more general institution for higher education; Miss Buss went there before founding the North London Collegiate School in 1850, Miss Beale before becoming the second principal of Cheltenham Ladies' College in 1858.[7] In 1849 Elizabeth Reid started the rather similar but non-sectarian Bedford College. There is no mention of girls in an article on 'Middle Class and Primary Education in England' in the *Cornhill* as late as 1861. Many of Elizabeth Garrett's intellectual contemporaries never went to school – Thackeray's daughters, Charles Darwin's daughters, Florence Nightingale, Emily Davies were all educated at home.

In 1858 a Royal Commission on Popular Education included the views of twelve women in their evidence. One of them, Barbara Bodichon,[8] wrote: 'until the law gives a married woman a right to her own wages, and an independent legal existence, some control over her children, and social arrangements admit a woman's right to more liberty of action, the education of girls will be miserably neglected'.[9] And she contributed a paper 'Middle-class Schools for Girls' to the Social Science Association in 1860. In 1864 the new Schools Enquiry Commission (the Taunton Commission) was persuaded by Emily Davies and her allies to consider the question of education for girls as well as for boys. There were two articles by Harriet Martineau in the November *Cornhill* that year on middle-class education, one on boys and one on girls; for girls, she wrote, 'there is no tradition, no common conviction, no established method, no imperative custom, – nothing beyond a supposition that girls must somehow learn to read and write, and to practise whatever accomplishment may be the fashion at the time'.

Three centuries earlier, she said, girls had learnt some classics; that had gradually disappeared, but throughout the eighteenth century time-honoured general domestic activities had flourished, keeping girls occupied and teaching them how to organize a household; the trouble came when families who had made money in the French wars at the turn of the century had 'an evil emulation ... to rise in gentility ... hence the mushroom "Ladies' Seminaries" which became a byword long ago, – a representative term for false pretension, vulgarity, and cant'. Domestic skills were lost, while nothing worthwhile was learnt. Shortly after the wars, when profits had fallen and there was no longer money to spare, many single women found they were sadly unprepared for the challenge of supporting themselves. And this was of course only one part of the general problem; there was also, overwhelmingly, what

Mrs Gaskell had called 'the feeling of purposelessness'. But Harriet Martineau welcomed the mid-nineteenth-century stirrings of wider education, girls again learning Latin, becoming teachers. She admired female education in France and in America, and noted that American girls were more competent domestically than the English. This happily proved to her that it was possible to combine academic study with domestic efficiency, for it was still, she thought, important to preserve traditional skills: 'let middle-class parents regard household qualifications as sacred, not to be encroached upon or slighted for the sake of any other attainments whatever. This being understood and admitted, it does not appear that there is any limit to what women may desire and attempt to learn'.[10]

In 1865, after a petition signed by, among others, the Garrett girls' cousin Rhoda, the Garretts' old governess Amelia Edgeworth, and Louisa Browning (who was the principal of the school the Garrett girls were to go to), girls were for the first time allowed to take the Cambridge Local Examination[11] on the same terms as boys. Emily Davies' *The Higher Education of Women* followed in 1866, putting a strong case for extending more advanced examinations to women, to give a stimulus and a standard. Her book was welcomed in a slightly patronizing review by the *Pall Mall Gazette*: 'we could feel no objection to be prescribed for, nursed, ruled, to be voted for, or even against, by a woman who writes in this style'.

So a change in the approach to education for girls was beginning, though it had a long way to go. Even after seven years at Cheltenham, Miss Beale was to write in a paper for the Social Science Congress: 'I desire to institute no comparison between the mental abilities of boys and girls, but simply to say what seems to me the right means of training girls so that they may best perform that subordinate part in the world to which, I believe, they have been called'.[12] Maurice himself, alarmed by news of Elizabeth Blackwell's medical ambitions – with her American degree and her desire for recognition in England – made it clear that he would not 'educate ladies for the kind of tasks which belong to OUR professions'.[13] He changed his mind later.

Schools were of course less of a problem for the boys. For some reason the eldest Garrett son, Newson, had only a tutor at home before joining the army, but Edmund was sent to the City of London School, Sam to Rugby and on to Cambridge; George had a year in Switzerland to learn German. The small boarding schools for girls – not all of them like Harriet Martineau's 'Ladies' Seminaries' – were often run by spinster sisters; the Brontës themselves had made an abortive attempt to start one in 1844. These schools, generally in family houses, were usually deliberately domestic in character (though Emily Davies said they tended to be more like nunneries[14]), and to take girls until they ended their education at around sixteen. Elizabeth Gaskell had been to one run by the Miss Byerleys in Warwickshire for five years, leaving just before she was seventeen, and she sent all her daughters in turn to various schools for just a year or two. As her biographer commented, 'While she secured her daughters the best education possible at the time to develop what talents they had – whether for music or painting – in order to promote their own pleasure in life and make intelligent companions of them for their future husbands, she never at any time contemplated careers for them'.[15] There was no thought of education for girls after the age of sixteen.

So Newson tried to follow the conventional best practice. After a brief disastrous attempt to send Louie and her cousin Betsy (Richard's daughter) to what turned out to be a totally unsympathetic school in Hampstead, he chose again, with more care. Louie and Elizabeth were then sent to the 'Academy for the Daughters of Gentlemen' (which had 37 pupils recorded in the census of 1851), run by the Misses Browning at the edge of London, in Blackheath. They were related, not only to Samuel Browning, minister of the independent chapel in Framlingham, but also to the poet as his step-aunts. Newson seemed to be attracted to teachers who were related to writers.

Millicent found Louisa Browning a great improvement on poor Miss Edgeworth, calling her 'a born teacher', and seemed even more pleased with a new teacher who took over, 'a really competent teacher who was extremely good to me and to whom I was devoted'.[16] Miss Browning had an exotic taste in clothes, which never left her; Alice, seeing her many years later, described her affectionately as 'so beaming & didactic & funny, with a great flower on a wire stalk jumping about perpetually in front of her bonnet'.[17]

Five of the daughters – Louie, Elizabeth, Alice, Agnes and Millicent – but for some reason not the youngest, Josephine, all had about two years at the Blackheath school.[18] There was, as Millicent wrote later, 'good teaching', with an emphasis on languages – they were supposed to speak French at all times, were taught Italian and German, and had a thorough dose of English literature. There was no science and scarcely any mathematics. Since Newson eccentrically insisted that they should have a hot bath once a week (in a wooden tub by the kitchen range, screened by a towel horse), the girls were known in the school as 'the bathing Garretts'. (Baths for schoolchildren were something of a family obsession – a tub was actually sent out to Switzerland for George.) It was not a 'finishing school' teaching accomplishments to young ladies – needlework was firmly considered to be a subject for home not school, and music seems to have come into the Garretts' lives less through school than through friends who came to live in Aldeburgh who sang and played, and introduced them to Bach, Mozart and Handel.

In that small school community at Blackheath, Louie's friends were the Smith sisters, whose father had been born near Snape, at Little Glemham – another Suffolk connection that may have helped Newson to choose the school. Staying with the Smiths in their home at Acton, outside London, Louie met their brother James; in 1857, when she was twenty-two, she was to marry him. Millicent, thirteen years younger than Louie, did not join the school until 1861, so a happy feature of her London schoolgirl life was an occasional weekend with Louie and James (and sometimes Elizabeth as well) in Manchester Square. These seem to have been rather highbrow weekends, reading Wordsworth, walking in Kensington Gardens, going to 'some fascinating entertainment' on Saturdays, and off to hear Frederick Denison Maurice preach on Sundays – an inspiring change after the preachers at Aldeburgh or Snape. The journey back to Blackheath on Monday mornings could be tough; first presumably with Agnes, but later on her own, the young Millicent would be put on a bus at Marble Arch and would sometimes see the crowd collecting at Newgate to watch a hanging on her way to London Bridge for a train to Greenwich before walking to the school at Blackheath. In the same tradition, she was to give her own daughter unusual freedom to go about alone.

The Garrett daughters each left school at sixteen. Millicent indeed was slightly under sixteen when she left, her time there cut short by one of the periodical hiccups in the family finances – for a brief time there were, she remembered, such hardships as semi-vegetarian meals of Suffolk dumplings without beef. But even though their stay there was brief, school and their new friends had brought new ideas that would never go away. Louie and Elizabeth were particularly friendly with Jane and Annie Crow from Usworth (to the north of Durham) who were in their turn friends of Emily Davies, daughter of the Reverend Dr John Davies, Rector of Gateshead. It was on long visits to the Crows that Elizabeth and Emily met.

Emily Davies, small, tough, determined, passionate about the need for education for women, and six years older than Elizabeth, was to become a major influence in her life. 'In all that concerned women, she was a revolutionary; in all else, a conservative' – this is how Emily's biographer Barbara Stephen described her, though it could have been written of any of the Garrett sisters. Unlike the Garretts, though, she seems decidedly priggish and short of humour or the ability to enjoy life. Her childhood memories, Janet Howarth has written, 'were of a shared family religious and intellectual life. She played with her sister and three brothers at holding missionary meetings and being a candidate for parliament, and compiled newspapers of strongly Conservative tone, filled with denunciations of Popery and Puseyism'.[19]

Growing up as a rector's daughter Emily was caught in the web of household duties, and she became increasingly sure that what she wanted was to help others escape from that sort of emptiness. 'It was indeed no wonder', she said, 'that people who had not learnt to do anything could not find anything to do'. Education for women was the first essential, and then training for the professions; she would particularly like to find a suitable recruit to undertake training in medicine. Between Elizabeth's two visits to the Crows, Emily had been to Algiers, where she had gone to look after a brother dying from consumption. It had been a crucial journey, for it was in Algiers that she met and was inspired by the feminist painter Barbara Bodichon and her sister Annie Leigh Smith.

So through that tiny Blackheath school Louie met her future husband and, through their schoolfriends Jane and Annie Crow, Louie and Elizabeth came to be in touch with the future leaders of the women's movement. Newson, taking care to choose the best school he could find for his daughters, had exposed them to a broader education than he had intended.

3

Introducing the Derbyshire Garretts

The best of cousins is that you can make much or little of the relationship according to your taste or fancy.

Millicent Garrett, in *What I Remember*

In the large cousinhood of Garretts, the ones closest in sympathy to Newson's tribe were the family of John Fisher Garrett, Rector of Elton, Derbyshire. They were not very close relatives – John Fisher Garrett, born in Suffolk, was first cousin to Newson's father. He had married twice; his first wife died leaving three small children, and his second died leaving four more to live in the 'neat stone residence, erected 1838'[1] near the church. Of the first group, two were boys who made their own way in the world, Roland to New Zealand and Frank to an office in London. The third (whom we met in the last chapter supporting the case for girls taking the Cambridge Local Examination) was Rhoda – as forceful a character as any of Newson's family, a powerful feminist speaker and natural leader who might well have been as famous as any of them. Sadly, she died when she was only 41. The second brood were Amy, Fydell Edmund, Elsie and her twin brother John. Their father died in 1878, and Agnes and Millicent were to play an important part in the lives of this young orphaned family.

Rhoda, 'several times removed according to genealogy, but most closely allied in friendship',[2] became particularly close to Agnes but was a friend to them all. Virtually 'pushed out' (in Millicent's phrase) by the second family, she faced the classic problem of a semi-educated daughter of a poor clergyman. Elizabeth, five years older than Rhoda and trying, as she always did, to organize the family, wrote to Emily Davies:

> I am so anxious just now to get Rose [Rhoda] Garrett away from home. She can do nothing there, and her parents are willing to let her go. As they would not permit anything like a manual employment or a situation in an office or a shop (even if she were fit to take one which she is not) there seems to be nothing but teaching to go to. She therefore wants to get a situation as junior teacher in a school, where she would have some

advantages in return for what she has to give – or failing this, she would accept a nursery governess' situation for the sake of making a start.[3]

Elizabeth added caustically that 'She is very Evangelical in creed, but this is the result of education, and has not done any serious harm'. At this stage Elizabeth failed to see the ability and strength Rhoda had in her, writing of her 'native indolence', which made her 'not likely to shine very much'. With Elizabeth's support, Rhoda was taken on for a short time as a pupil teacher at Blackheath while Millicent and Agnes were there.

The teaching was not turning out too well, and Elizabeth became concerned for Rhoda's next move. 'I am sure I don't know about Rose', she wrote to her mother, 'I have not much hope of her ever being a first or even second class governess'.[4] To get some professional training in another field, Elizabeth suggested Rhoda might learn to be a photographer – it was after all in the 1860s that Julia Margaret Cameron was starting to have her great success, photographing the famous, doing all the messy processing herself, putting on exhibitions, winning medals. When that idea did not catch on for Rhoda, Louie came to the rescue, arranging and financing a stay in Alsace (as Charlotte and Emily Brontë had stayed in Brussels) so that Rhoda could become more employable by learning French and German. 'How horribly Mr and Mrs Fisher Garrett seem to have been behaving to poor Rose', Alice wrote from India in 1863: 'I daresay it is meant less as cruelty to her than as a prudent measure for pushing all expense and responsibility about her off on to Louie and James. I remember that when first they were corresponding about Rose's going to Germany, Mrs Garrett wrote some letters which for well bred greediness were worthy of Becky Sharp herself'.[5] Rhoda duly became a reluctant governess until she joined Agnes in 1871 in the apprenticeship that helped to forge their astonishing and original careers.

Reputations come and go over the years, and in the brief account of the Garrett family written in 1916 by the local historian Vincent Redstone, Elizabeth and Millicent and Fydell Edmund are mentioned, but all the others in that generation are ignored.[6] The same three are the only ones to appear in the *Dictionary of National Biography*. Milner's appreciative article on Fydell Edmund ('Fydell' was a family name; he was always known as 'Edmund') gets three columns; Elizabeth has a rather inadequate entry (also with three columns) written, not by anyone in the medical profession but by Fanny Cecilia Johnson, the head of languages at Bedford College; Millicent gets a little more, from her admirer and biographer Ray Strachey. The *Oxford DNB* is more generous, and includes more members of the family, but while the fame of Elizabeth and Millicent has grown, Edmund's has faded.

Coming from the second half of the Derbyshire family, Edmund was born in 1865, far younger than his Aldeburgh cousins. His mother died when he was seven, his father six years later, so the big influences in his life were Rhoda (until her death in 1882, while he was still at school), Millicent, and above all Agnes. It was a close family relationship, bringing him in touch with women's causes, and bringing them companionship and liveliness. He seems to have had charm, fluency in debate and natural ability to write, whether to express political convictions or to entertain with light verse. At Cambridge he got a third class in classics, but in his last year he became President of the Union. When he graduated he went to see W. T. Stead, the evangelical editor of the *Pall Mall Gazette*, to ask for a job – and was given one when he amused Stead by writing up and illustrating the interview. This was the start of a distinguished career in journalism, first in England and then in South Africa, until his promising life was cut short by consumption when he was only 42, living just one year longer than Rhoda.

Edmund's elder sister Amy, and the young twins, came into the family orbit and were influenced by the family radicalism, but it was above all Edmund's lively talent and his passionate involvement in South African politics that broadened the Garrett sisters' interests and was to be a major influence on Millicent.

4

Waiting

*O! if I was only a boy ... I should like a profession so much – not to spend my
life crocheting, mending my clothes and reading novels – which seems the
employment of English ladies.*

Anny Thackeray, 1855

Anny Thackeray's cry was the cry of the Garretts, of Florence Nightingale, and of so many intelligent and frustrated Victorian women.

In 1851, when they left school, Louie and Elizabeth were taken by their
father to Paris and through the Rhine Gorge, before their memorable
visit to the Great Exhibition on the way back. Then they were home,
restless with undirected ambition. Not having to earn their living they
were not doomed to be governesses, but they could hardly be content
with the standard life of more prosperous Victorian women, simply to
be daughters at home doing a little charity work and waiting for
marriage. As Frances Power Cobbe complained in 1863, a woman could
not leave 'her father's roof for any end, however good and noble, save
only that one sacred vocation of matrimony, for which she may lawfully
leave a blind father and dying mother, and go to India with Ensign
Anybody'.[1]

The Garrett daughters were aware, when struggling with the conventions and frustrations of Victorian middle-class life, that they were
not fighting battles for themselves alone. Of course they had their own
ambitions, but they hoped their achievements would open the way for
many others, that all women would have opportunities for education
and professions and votes, and that there would be a revolutionary
change of attitude. Plenty is written now in a mass of feminist literature
about the campaign for women's rights, or of the importance of the
Social Science Association, a 'convention of the most weighty men and
women in England',[2] but general history books traditionally gave hardly
more than a footnote to the movement that tore through the fabric of
Victorian society. Trevelyan, writing one or two pages on 'the eman-
cipation of women' in his enormously successful *English Social History*
in 1942, did not refer to any Garrett or Fawcett; there is, as one might

expect, a little more in Roy Jenkins' biographies of Asquith (1964) and
of Gladstone (1995), but even he does not mention Millicent Fawcett or
the Garretts by name, although their paths crossed fairly dramatically
with both his heroes.

Richard Garrett's children seem to have been more ready than
Newson's to accept the conventional pattern of Victorian life, so it is
not surprising to learn that Newson's eldest daughter Louie – who was
to introduce her young sisters to the preaching of Frederick Denison
Maurice and the politics of John Stuart Mill – refused an offer of
marriage from the eldest of Richard's four sons, her cousin Richard. It
did not help the troubled relationship between the two families.

Richard had much to offer. Joining the Leiston firm when he was
fourteen, he became a highly successful partner ten years later and
under his leadership the firm was to grow enormously. But with his
'hunting, shooting, prize-fighting, horse-breeding and farming'[3] he does
not sound at all the right husband for Louie. He and his three brothers,
all highly competent, strong-willed and obstinate, failed to work
harmoniously together; two of them (first John, then Henry) moved to
Germany, setting up an agricultural machinery firm at Magdeburg,
leaving Leiston to the partnership of Richard and his youngest
brother Frank. Richard never had a family, but Frank made up for this
with eleven children, including four sons who worked with him at
Leiston.

Louie chose her friends' brother James Smith,[4] rather than Richard,
but even after her marriage in 1857 she remained very much part of the
Garrett family, strongly in sympathy with her sisters' ambitions, a base
for them in London whenever they needed it. Elizabeth was to stay with
her in this haven in London, meeting Louie's friends, thinking about
her own future, and finding support and understanding. Louie and
Elizabeth kept up their school friendships with the Crow sisters, and
shared with them their concern with the problems of women's lives. For
a short time Louie was honorary secretary to the first Women's Suffrage
Committee.

Apart from these breaks in London, when Elizabeth left school she
lived at home for nine years, a time of waiting and thinking, of sorting
out her future. After Louie's marriage she had to take on the duties of
an eldest daughter, helping her mother with the large household. But
this was not to be her life: 'I was a young woman living at home with
nothing to do in what authors call "comfortable circumstances". But I
was wicked enough not to be comfortable. I was full of energy and

Louisa Smith (née Garrett) in 1861

vigour and of the discontent which goes with unemployed activities ... Everything seemed wrong to me'.[5]

It was not that she felt a strong vocational call to medicine or to helping the sick. It would be pleasing to picture her as growing up with a clear dedicated ambition, but it would be far from the truth. She had not the single-mindedness of Jessie White who, in her longing to help Garibaldi, had applied unsuccessfully in 1856 to fourteen London hospitals in the hope of becoming a medical student, or of 'Dr James Barrie' who had joined the army medical service in 1813 and only after death was found to have been a woman. For Elizabeth, it was more a powerful undirected urge to do something serious and worthwhile. She coped by studying endlessly, getting her brother Newson's coach to supervise her Latin and arithmetic, helping the younger children with their lessons, and giving all her brothers and sisters Sunday evening talks on 'things in general' – the Hungry Forties, the Irish famine, the Crimean War, the Indian Mutiny, Garibaldi, Carlyle, Macaulay; the leaders of Italian independence became heroes for ten-year-old

Millicent. It is a relief to read that there were also jollier times – riding, boating, picnics in summer, skating in winter, parties with the many cousins who lived nearby.

Elizabeth's path became clearer after she had met Emily Davies. It was in 1854 that Elizabeth went with Louie to stay with the Crow family just outside Gateshead, near the Davies family home. 'The influence of Emily Davies', Elizabeth's daughter Louisa wrote, 'proved to be to Elizabeth what conversion has been to others'.[6] Long talks about putting the world to rights were followed by long letters, and by a second visit to Gateshead two years later. The younger children did not enjoy Emily's return visits to Aldeburgh; they found her excessively earnest and dry. 'Her manner towards us was not winning', Millicent remembered, 'she always seemed to be letting us know of how little consequence we were'.[7]

During Elizabeth's visits to Louie and James in London she saw much of Emily, and through her met the emerging leaders of the women's movement. Notably, there was Barbara Bodichon, who had published two powerful pamphlets, *A Brief Summary of the Most Important Laws concerning Women* and *Women and Work*, and was then financing the *Englishwoman's Journal*. The journal, started in 1858, had moved in the following year to Langham Place and was edited by Bessie Parkes; it carried a variety of feminist articles, and made a point of printing women's contributions to the Social Science Association meetings. The 'Langham Place Circle' also started a Ladies' Institute with a reading room and ran the offices for the Society for Promoting the Employment of Women. It was a stimulating group, with the poets Adelaide Proctor and Isa Craig, the printer Emily Faithfull and other enthusiasts for what Ray Strachey has called 'The Cause'.[8] The same names crop up time and again, recruiting their friends and relations for support and taking part in a variety of campaigns throughout the second half of the century. All the group were young – Adelaide Proctor, born 1825 (two years before Barbara Bodichon), was the oldest – and they were all moved by the same feelings of restlessness that were disturbing the Garrett sisters. Their journal exposed the miserable conditions of poor working women, and tried to help by encouraging apprentices to trades such as hairdressing, printing, law-copying, dial-painting;[9] they were concerned at the way of life offered to governesses, the lack of decent alternatives. It was just the place and just the group of friends that Elizabeth needed. To make her feel even more at home, the secretary of the Society for Promoting the Employment of Women was her school-friend Jane Crow. And Emily Davies and her mother moved south into a house nearby after the death of the Reverend Dr John Davies in January 1862.

It was in the *Englishwoman's Journal* that Elizabeth first read about Bessie Parkes' relative Dr Elizabeth Blackwell. Born in Bristol but brought up in America, Dr Blackwell had, after considerable difficulty in being accepted, graduated in medicine from Geneva College, New York State, in 1849. The course, including a break, had lasted only about fifteen months (although it awarded an M.D.), but Dr Blackwell had gained more experience afterwards by working as a pupil midwife in La Maternité in Paris; she had then come to England, where she had studied under James Paget at St Bartholomew's Hospital, and had become friendly with Florence Nightingale before returning to New York. In 1859 she was back in London, getting her name on the newly set up Medical Register and giving lectures, arranged by Barbara Bodichon, on 'Medicine as a Profession for Ladies'. The idea that many women would like to be looked after by women was growing. Elizabeth Garrett, disturbed to hear Newson disparage Dr Blackwell and the idea of women doctors, defended her. Newson, prejudiced but interested, was persuaded at least to discuss the problem with his business friend Valentine Smith. Smith, who was a cousin of Barbara Bodichon, responded by sending a letter of introduction to Dr Blackwell for Elizabeth. So Elizabeth, having joined the Society for Promoting Employment of Women, went to the lectures. 'The most important listener', Elizabeth Blackwell noted, 'was the bright, intelligent young lady whose interest in the study of medicine was then aroused – Miss Elizabeth Garrett'.[10] Ominously, this was in 1859, the year after the Medical Act had established a standard of training as well as a medical register for qualified medical practitioners; such qualifications depended on training at (exclusively male) universities and medical schools, and taking examinations that were closed to women in Britain.

Hearing of Dr Blackwell's struggles, and learning how she had lost an eye from purulent ophthalmia caught from a patient (which had ended any ambitions she had towards surgery), Elizabeth might well have been put off the idea of studying medicine. But after the first lecture Barbara Bodichon gave a party, Elizabeth met Dr Blackwell and, to Elizabeth's alarm, Dr Blackwell spoke to her as if she were already a committed student. 'She assumed that I had made up my mind to follow her', she said, 'I remember feeling very much confounded and as if I had been suddenly thrust into work that was too big for me'.[11] Unsure of herself,

Elizabeth felt she was 'thoroughly ordinary', with 'no particular genius for medicine or anything else'. There were to be many more talks with Emily and the Crows before she finally made up her mind.

The opportunity for those talks came almost immediately, as Annie Crow was to be married and Elizabeth, Emily Davies and Jane Crow were to be bridesmaids; they stayed together for some weeks while plans for the wedding mixed with plans for their future lives. And what a future it turned out to be – Emily as founder of Girton College, Cambridge, where Annie (as Mrs Austin) was Mistress from 1870–2, Jane as secretary of the Society for Promoting the Employment of Women, and of course Elizabeth as the first woman doctor to qualify in England. The fact that this group of friends achieved so much was more than chance – it all very much depended on the strong character of Emily as catalyst. As Elizabeth wrote later, 'Miss D. talked her ideas over with me. It seemed to us that the duty of ministering, as a physician does, to the care of women and children would be work not unsuitable to a woman, and also that it was work they ought to be free to take up if they chose'. Put like that it sounded reasonable and simple, but 'Naturally neither of us knew much of the details of medical education, nor did we realise how long and sustained an effort would be needed before our end could be reached'.[12]

Elizabeth's mind was made up, but before she could make any sort of start she had to persuade her family that such work was 'not unsuitable to a woman', and that she was the person to try to do it. It was not the best moment to announce such an idea in Aldeburgh – Newson had once again overstretched the family finances by his grand schemes at the Maltings, and his temper was in a more than usually touchy state. So Elizabeth went on waiting for another year, filling her mind with planning and reading, before approaching her father in June 1860. She had already become involved in the Ladies Sanitary Association, founded in 1858 to help spread the principles of public health among working class women.[13] She studied Dr Blackwell's letter in the *Englishwoman's Journal* outlining a medical course: a year of basic reading, six months in a laboratory, six months as a nurse, a year in a college – perhaps in America as it was not yet possible in England – and a final year to include six months' midwifery, perhaps in Paris as again it could not be in England.

Louie and Emily were thoroughly on Elizabeth's side. They understood the meaning of the Medical Council's change of rules since Dr Blackwell had registered – how qualifications from America or France or Europe would no longer be accepted. Elizabeth Blackwell had after all been able to call herself 'doctor' after little more than a year; Elizabeth Garrett would have to take the far tougher option of opening the way for women to go to a British medical school and take British exams. Emily, dominating as usual on her visits to Alde House, pushed her views on education and her pioneering plans for Elizabeth – 'Miss Davies is a good deal my senior and if I live to be 100 she will still be so and I will feel it as much as she did when I sat at her feet in girlhood', Elizabeth wrote much later.[14] But at the time she responded by getting the local schoolmaster to coach her secretly in the necessary Greek and Latin, and by sending English compositions to Emily for criticism. She read Ruskin, and the newly published *Origin of Species*, and Mill's *On Liberty*; the latter two both appeared in 1859. At last, when Newson's finances seemed back on an even keel, she told him she wished to study medicine. He exploded. 'The whole idea is so *disgusting*. I could not entertain it for a moment'.[15]

His worries were understandable. Florence Nightingale had warned that 'both nurses and medical men, as well as medical students, have died of zymotic diseases prevailing in hospitals',[16] and that in the new Edinburgh Infirmary 'hospital gangrene is never out of the wards if full'.[17] She had attacked the overcrowding, the bad ventilation, the hopeless sanitation, the dangerously absorbent surfaces that became 'saturated with organic matter'.[18] There was no antiseptic surgery. Surgeons' coats were stiff with dried blood, and the filth of an operating theatre was appalling.

It is more surprising to find how soon Elizabeth won Newson's support. Recovering from the shock, he even ended that first discussion with 'at least I cannot agree to it without more thought'. And the more he thought the more he came to realize that Elizabeth, like him, was a fighter, and that as Garretts don't lose fights he must do all he could to help her win.

Getting her mother on her side was a harder matter, with plenty of ups and downs. Ten days later Elizabeth reported to Emily that after a two-hour talk her mother was 'on the whole sufficiently encouraging', and shortly afterwards that she was 'pleased with my parents' tone' in their discussion of her plans with visitors.[19] But at times poor Louisa felt devastated; she would shut herself in her bedroom, make herself ill with crying, then beg Elizabeth to stay at home and be a governess to the younger children. It was not easy to be tough and ignore such unhappiness, particularly when even Newson was overwhelmed and burst out to the family 'I don't think I can go on with it, it will kill your mother'. But Elizabeth could be tough, and ignored the weeping – rather as some mothers let their young babies cry on the excuse that they will get over it and they have to be left to sleep. Agnes had the strength and understanding to write to Elizabeth that she thought Louisa's depression came from a mixture of causes and would pass.[20] She was right. The disapproval soon faded, and through all the difficulties and disagreements Elizabeth and her mother were always able to keep up an affectionate correspondence. Later, hampers of country food and home baking made their welcome way to London, and as time went on Louisa became increasingly proud of her doctor daughter.

Newson took Elizabeth to London, and together they tested the water by calling on the medical consultants of Harley Street. It was not encouraging. 'Why not be a nurse?' asked one – there was a new awareness of nursing, for Florence Nightingale's school was about to open at St Thomas's: 'Because I prefer to earn a thousand rather than twenty pounds a year', she replied. (Mary Wollstonecraft had been well ahead of her time in hoping that 'women might certainly study the art of healing and be physicians as well as nurses'.[21]) For Elizabeth it was of course not really a question of money – she wanted to be in charge herself, not to have so-called 'woman's work', where 'the quick eye, the soft hand, the light step and the ready ear, second the wisdom of the physician'.[22] And class-consciousness came firmly in as well. As Emily wrote, medicine was 'eminently suitable for women of the middle class', while 'the business of a hired nurse cannot be looked upon as a profession for a lady', being 'in every way too nearly allied to that of an upper servant to be in the least appropriate for the daughters and sisters of the mercantile and professional classes'.[23] Or take Elizabeth herself in 1866: 'It is not true that hospital nursing cannot be done well by women of inferior rank and culture, and therefore it cannot be entirely desirable that those of a higher class should spend their time doing it'.[24] All the same, no medical school would accept her as a student, Newson and Elizabeth were told, and she would not be allowed to sit the qualifying examinations.

Newson had to go back to Aldeburgh, but once there he thought it over, did not want her to be discouraged, and less than a week later he wrote to her: 'I have resolved in my own mind after deep and painful consideration not to oppose your wishes and as far as expense is concerned I will do all I can in justice to my other children to assist you in your study'.[25] He was to stick to this decision, backing her through her struggles, encouraging her after her disappointments, and rejoicing at her success.

Elizabeth stayed on in London with Louie, while Emily enthusiastically introduced her to anyone she felt might help. Through Emily's brother the Reverend J. Llewelyn Davies, Elizabeth met Mrs Russell Gurney, who had promised Dr Blackwell that she would promote the cause of medical women; she was to become an important figure in Elizabeth's life. Married to the reforming Recorder of London, Emelia Gurney had inherited much of the energy and enthusiasm of her evangelical grandfather, Wilberforce's friend John Venn. The Gurneys in their turn introduced Elizabeth to William Hawes[26] – a good choice, for William Hawes knew Newson, was a governor of the Middlesex Hospital, and was in favour of women studying medicine, although he was well aware how difficult that would be. He suggested that Elizabeth should first spend six months as a hospital nurse in a surgical ward at the Middlesex, not as an end in itself but to make her familiar with the horrors of life at a hospital. If she could stand that, she could think about the next move. After all, Dr Blackwell had submitted to working as a student nurse in Paris as part of her training.

Once the decision had been made there seemed no need for Elizabeth to wait any longer. On 13 July she wrote to Mrs Richard Garrett (her mother's sister, married to her father's brother):

> For some time I have been gradually making up my mind to an important step, and now that the time for action has come, I do not like to take it without telling my friends what I am about to do. During the last two or three years, I have felt an increasing longing for some definite occupation, which should also bring me, in time, a position and moderate income. I think you will not be surprised that I should feel this longing for it is indeed far more wonderful that a healthy woman should spend a long life in comparative idleness than that she should wish for some suitable work, upon which she could spend the energy that now only causes painful restlessness and weariness. I have decided that the study of medicine offers more attractions to me than any other kind of work, and I have resolved to enter upon it. It is generally admitted that there would be no impropriety in women and children being attended by physicians of their own sex, and it is these branches of the profession which we wish to see opened to women.[27]

At the end of July, only a few weeks after confessing her plans to her parents, Elizabeth left home.

Alice, Agnes, Millicent and Josephine were then aged eighteen, fifteen, thirteen, and seven. Elizabeth had left for good, but she remained constantly in touch with her family, still felt responsible for her young sisters, anxious that none of them should be sucked into the deadening life that she had fought against. She was to try to educate and organize each of them in turn.

Life was of course more straightforward for the boys of the family. The eldest son, the second Newson, was the only failure. Tutored for the army instead of going to school, he seems to have been always a misfit, never mentioned by Millicent in *What I Remember* and only listed in an appendix by Elizabeth's daughter in her life of her mother. He joined the Royal Artillery, where he was to earn Elizabeth's scorn by his 'social pretensions, his contemptuous attitude to the Indians when serving in that country, and his shiftlessness about money'.[28] Later there was a scandal of bankruptcy.

Edmund, the quiet conservative member of the family, joined the Maltings and also became manager of the Bow Brewery. When in 1871 there was a suggestion that Agnes, still uncertain about her future, might join the Maltings herself, it was Edmund's opposition that was to block the idea and turn Agnes to make other plans of her own. He is on record as saying in 1860, when Elizabeth Blackwell's qualifications as a doctor were being discussed, 'if I had been an examiner, I would have refused to examine any woman'.[29] All the same, it is good to find Elizabeth writing to Emily later that year that Edmund's opinion 'had changed a good deal, for he felt that I was the best judge and that I should not do anything but what I believed to be right, so we were very affectionate over it and I felt immensely relieved'.[30]

Sam and George were still children when Elizabeth left. George, born in 1854, would sit sleepily on Elizabeth's lap while she gave her serious Sunday evening talks. Millicent liked a childhood story of him a little later:

> He had begun making a small collection of coins, and was familiar with the terms 'obverse' and 'reverse' as applied to them. On Sunday in church the hymn selected contained the lines:
>
> Oh, my spirit longs and faints
> For the converse of the saints.
>
> He thought this was an example of the extraordinary ideas grown-ups had of enjoying themselves. He had mixed up the word 'converse' with 'obverse' and 'reverse', and thought the hymn indicated an uncontrollable desire to turn the saints upside down or inside out.[31]

He grew up to marry Millicent's friend, the bookbinder Louisa Wilkinson, and to become a partner in the Maltings. Sam, Millicent's favourite brother, became an undergraduate at Cambridge at the time of Millicent's early married life there, on his way to train to be a solicitor. There was indeed no problem about careers for boys.

5

Breaking the Mould

I fancy girls are often just in the frame I was then, wishing to do something above anything in the world.

Elizabeth Garrett to Emily Davies, December 1862

Traditionally, women had cared for the sick for generations, whether at home, in nunneries, as nurses or midwives, or as the providers of folk medicine and herbal knowledge. But during the nineteenth century the effort to put medicine on a more scientific footing, and a growing feeling that the profession should be formalized, led to the 1858 Medical Act which set up a register of qualified doctors. As the only route to qualification lay through the inaccessible universities or medical schools, by excluding the unqualified the Act inevitably excluded women. What women were demanding, therefore, as Sophia Jex-Blake wrote, was re-entry to a profession that they had contributed to since the time of the ancient Greeks.[1]

It was not only the training of doctors that was to be re-organized; nursing was to be regulated too, and here of course women were welcome. In 1860, after the horrors of the Crimea, Florence Nightingale set up her Training School for nurses at St Thomas's Hospital to show that nursing could be a respectable profession and that it needed at least a year of proper teaching. It was in that same year that Elizabeth started her six months at the Middlesex Hospital, with the outrageous aim of turning the new regulations upside down and training, not to be a nurse, but to be a qualified physician on equal terms to a man.

The Garrett mould-breaking was to involve not only Elizabeth. Emily, always ready to recruit disciples, suggested that the next sister, Alice, should stop being her mother's companion, and should try to be a pioneer as the first woman civil servant. Alice, who seems to have been short of the 'extra amount of daring', had no desire for such glory, backing away to avoid putting their mother 'in a great fright'.[2] Elizabeth wrote Emily a revealing letter, analysing her own position while thinking about Alice:

Alice has a good deal of housekeeping to do and wants time for study as much as I do ... I do not think it is quite true that a profession would not separate daughters from their families more than marriage does. In my case I fancy the separation is more distinctly felt now, after one year, than it is with Louie after four years. I think a profession, specially when it is connected with a certain amount of difficulty and social prejudice, brings a woman into an entirely new set of interests and friends, while the life of a married daughter is to a great extent a kind of repetition of the mother's early experiences ... Alice surprised me by her ability to get on with stupid people ... though I am sure she would enjoy better people as keenly as I do.[3]

As a compromise, when she was nineteen Alice, 'a prodigy at mathematics',[4] was given a clerkship in her father's counting house. It was carefully arranged so that she and the other clerks would be, as Elizabeth wrote to Emily, 'sufficiently separated for their mutual comfort'.[5] 'Alice will be in the office 5 or 6 hours a day', the letter goes on, 'chiefly employed in accounts and writing letters for Father. It will be drudgery at first, but it is the only way of entering a business properly, and it is what all the boys begin with. Alice is very quick with figures and will write clearer letters than most boys do, so I have no doubt she will give satisfaction'.

Elizabeth could be over earnest, particularly with Emily; there can have been no intention of promoting Alice in the same way as her brothers, and this reads simply like a rather boring reference. It also reflects a surprisingly persistent attitude to women in offices. It was, for example, not until 1888, five years after work on the *Dictionary of National Biography* had started, that its editor, Leslie Stephen, was persuaded to employ a woman clerk: 'I do not care to see the young lady beforehand', Stephen wrote, 'I fancy that our typewriter will want some grooming. It may be a little rusty and the blacking has to be done. But I suppose our young lady is up to that – Is she to be in the next room?'[6] And it was not until 1953 that women clerks first appeared alongside the men on Dickensian high stools in the merchant bank A. Keyser & Co in the City of London. Women were not allowed on the floor of the London Stock Exchange until 1973.

As it turned out, the question of whether Alice would make the same progress as the boys in Newson's business never arose, for in 1863 she was to become the next daughter to marry, and marriage took her overseas. Her husband was Herbert Cowell, a rather conventional barrister from a Suffolk family, working in India. He had nailed his

conservative colours to the mast when he was only seventeen by a
weighty article in *Blackwood's Magazine* in 1854 arguing for an end to
the coalition government.[7] Newson had to be persuaded not to send
back the tea-set given as a wedding present by his brother Richard, but
showed his own doubts by giving Alice the return fare to India 'because
you are sure to want to come back when you see him'.[8] Alice waited in
Aldeburgh for her brother Edmund's wedding before setting off; her
father, when it came to the point, supported her decision by escorting
her as far as Malta and then handing her over to suitable company for
the rest of her journey.

Elizabeth's daughter Louisa has described the close Garrett sister-
hood: 'Louie supplied spiritual grace, Elizabeth determination, Alice
literary taste, Millicent and Josephine wit, and Agnes, who did not
marry, motherliness. All possessed public spirit and an intense desire to
help other women'.[9]

With Alice away, Agnes became the eldest left at home, and Elizabeth
next found time in the middle of her own struggles to worry about her.
She wrote to Emily, in 1862:

> I think if she gets fretted with home dullness, she may grow very fond of
> staying with people with the hope of getting married to escape from it.
> There is a great deal more good in her than I was inclined to think there
> would be, but her faults and prettiness are enough to make one desire the
> best and most educating influence for her. She may grow into a flirt of a
> vulgar kind, or she may grow into a very unselfish bright woman.[10]

'Unselfish' and 'bright' turned out to be the right adjectives. 'You
should have come to me to hear about Agnes', Millicent told an
interviewer who was writing an article on Agnes in 1890, 'she will never
say much about herself; but she is always doing things for other people'.[11] The only one of Newson's daughters who never married (though
Alice longed for her to 'marry somebody nice and come out to India'),
Agnes was slow to sort out her life. Nothing in the 1860s showed what
strength there was in her, and how she would later launch so successfully on her own.

The next sister was Millicent, but before turning to her, here is the
little that is recorded about the youngest, Josephine. We only know that
she became Mrs Salmon on her marriage when she was twenty (after an
earlier engagement fell through, apparently to her family's relief), and
she had two children. She lived at one time in Suffolk, either in one of

Millicent and Agnes at home, about 1865

her father's Aldeburgh houses or in Bury St Edmunds, but for much of her life she was in Yorkshire (where Millicent often stayed in the summers in her old age). She died in 1925 within a few weeks of Alice. With a less forceful personality than her sisters, she emerges only occasionally in the family story – 'a stunning girl and prettiest of the lot' according to her eldest brother. She went at the age of eighteen to the sites of the Franco-Prussian war with Elizabeth and Sam, she presided at a suffrage meeting in Suffolk in 1883, she turned up at her niece Louisa's hospital in Paris in 1916 – 'a most cheering visitor and made a visit to every bed like a Princess'.[12] She was never well off, and for the last eight years of her life had an annuity left her by Elizabeth. John Wood, the director of the Maltings in its final phase, was her grandson.

Millicent had to leave school shortly before she was sixteen, but as compensation was given her own bedroom and undisturbed use of her old schoolroom for reading and study in the mornings – peace and a room of her own long before Virginia's Woolf's plea that women needed money and a room of their own to give them freedom to think and to write fiction. Millicent's only successful excursion into creative fiction was to be *Janet Doncaster*, and that was not until 1875, but there is much that must be autobiographical there in Millicent's account of Janet's education. Living in a town that was recognizably Aldeburgh, Janet 'never had received any intelligent teaching from her governess: Mangnall's Questions, the multiplication table, the Church Catechism, the names of the kings and queens of England'; but away at school 'it was possible to enjoy learning' so that by the time she came back 'she had learnt to see the world with new eyes; she had learnt to fill her life with new interests. Books of all kinds that came in her way she read greedily'.[13]

Millicent and Agnes used to study together, read aloud, learn poetry. 'You certainly know much more about Plato than I do', their cousin Edmund wrote to Agnes many years later, 'more shame to me whom you sent to college'.[14] They had a lively social life too, 'riding, dancing, skating, walking, and boating on the Alde', and plenty of music; Agnes sang, and Millicent, though not a performer, learnt to find music 'a perennial spring of consolation, hope and endurance'.[15] There were occasional visits to their older sisters in London, where they went to dances and concerts and discovered their love for opera. On Sunday afternoons in Aldeburgh Millicent would retreat to her bedroom to read Shakespeare in order 'not to distress her mother's Sabbatarian con- science'.[16] Agnes and Millicent were educating themselves and, without at that stage having a conscious direction for the future, preparing themselves for their pioneering lives.

The London cultural activities were mixed with doses of politics. A significant moment came in 1865, when Louie and James took Millicent to hear an election speech by John Stuart Mill, a candidate who had the courage to speak in favour of extending the franchise to working men and also to women. 'I was', she wrote, 'a woman suffragist, I may say, from my cradle, but this meeting kindled tenfold my enthusiasm for it'.[17] Mill, who was a powerful influence on many political thinkers, had to face much mocking laughter but was supported by 73 votes in parliament (with 196 against) when he proposed changing the word 'man' to 'person' in the 1867 Reform Bill. This limited success may have produced premature optimism, but Millicent was inspired, and was to become inspiring in her turn. 'Under whatever conditions, and in whatever limits, men are admitted to the suffrage', Mill had written, 'there is not a shadow of justification for not admitting women under the same'.[18]

This was the time too of the American Civil War, and Louie and her friends were passionate supporters of the North. On the day that news of Lincoln's assassination reached London, Millicent happened to be with Louie at a party given by Mr and Mrs Peter Taylor, prominent among radicals and reformers.[19] The blind politician Henry Fawcett, a supporter of Mill over women's suffrage and a fellow guest, was struck by her comments and her voice.

Fawcett's fortune, as a Cambridge academic and an aspiring politician, was small, but he was clearly in need of a wife. He had proposed unsuccessfully to Bessie Parkes, he had briefly been engaged to Eleanor Eden (daughter of the Bishop of Bath and Wells), and in 1865 (shortly after the Taylors' party) he proposed to Elizabeth Garrett. It was not the first proposal she had had, but it stirred her deeply. She refused sadly, confessing to her parents: 'I have not the least doubt about having been right in decidedly refusing though at the same time I know of few lives I should have liked better than being eyes and hands to a Cambridge Professor and an MP ... I wish though that it had been Agnes'. A few days later she added: 'you see marrying him would involve completely giving up my profession ... Mr Fawcett's wife wd also have to give up her time to his pursuits even more than most people's need do. Anything like independent work in a completely different life would be impossible'.[20] She asked Newson and Louisa to keep Fawcett's proposal secret so perhaps, as Elizabeth's biographer Jo Manton thought, Millicent never knew.[21]

The following year Fawcett proposed not to Agnes but to Millicent. Elizabeth, not too pleased, wrote to a friend that 'Mr Fawcett says frankly that Millicent is extremely like me and that that is how he first thought of her'.[22] She tried to put Millicent off, warning her of the problems of blindness and of poverty. Millicent confided in Louie:

I have been rather heavily jumped on by dear old Lizzie and the parents during the last few days. I had a most awful letter from Liz on Sunday morning ... Lizzie also offered to get for me Mme Bodichon's, Miss Crow's and others' opinions of Mr Fawcett ... Judging from Dr Bodichon's appearance, I should say that it was improbable that we should agree in the choice of husbands. Dr Bodichon is more like a he-hag than anyone else I can recall just at present. I have not written to Lizzie, for I am afraid of vexing her which I should be dreadfully sorry to do, for I know that it is out of pure love for me and anxiety for my future that she wrote as she did ... I believe she would think we were throwing ourselves away if we married the Archangel Michael with twenty thousand a year ...'[23]

Certainly nothing there to hint that she knew of the earlier proposal. Louie, who did know, behaved admirably, encouraging and making peace. She had thought marrying Fawcett would have been wrong for Elizabeth, but she thoroughly approved of him for Millicent: 'I believe that dear old Lizzie is as wrong as ever she was right in being afraid', she wrote to Millicent, 'and I am quite sure that no one will be more glad than she will to have it proved so'. Louie was right, for Elizabeth soon managed to build an excellent sisterly relationship with Fawcett. 'I have just been writing to Mr Fawcett [Louie went on] I only asked him to come and see me, for I couldn't talk when Edward [Fawcett's secretary] made a necessary third. By the by, Madam, how do YOU manage? For I suspect that your objection to a discriminating audience is even greater than mine'.

Millicent was happy to give her time to Fawcett's pursuits. He was a radical member of the Liberal Party and a disciple of Mill. What more could she want? Through being his eyes Millicent was to have a political education that absorbed her. Poverty is relative, and Henry Fawcett's income of £800 was sufficient, with care, to give them homes in both London and Cambridge. They were married in April 1867, and Barbara Bodichon offered them her house in Sussex for their honeymoon.

But in February 1867 there had been tragedy in the Garrett family. To the endless distress of all, Louie died from appendicitis. She had been, Elizabeth's daughter Louisa wrote, 'a perfect elder sister ... one of the few people to whom Elizabeth turned for advice. They had been inseparable'.[24] As Louie lay dying, Elizabeth promised her she would care for the four young children as if they were her own.[25] 'I now have a feeling against ever marrying in order to keep my best love and keenest interests for them', she wrote to Alice. She went to see them every few days, gave them holiday outings, kept in touch with the girls when the boys went away to school. She may have rejected Fawcett because life with him would have been totally demanding, but she was always anxious to prove that marriage and motherhood were compatible with a professional career. Marriage and her own children were to come to her later, but she never lost her responsibility and affection for Louie's children. 'They evidently feel it is a momentous change for them, as it is', she wrote to James Skelton Anderson during their engagement. 'It is an immense rest to me to feel that we shall be so much more likely to do well and wisely by them than I should have been alone.'[26]

6

Medical Student

The apple of discord is to be cast into our hospitals.
The Lancet, 6 July 1861

In 1866, the year before Millicent's wedding and Louie's tragic death, Elizabeth's name appeared for the first time in the Medical Register. It was a triumph, after the dedicated lonely student days that had started six years earlier when she had moved to London to experience life working as a nurse in a surgical ward. All her Garrett determination and optimism had been needed in those six years.

In the beginning she had stayed with Louie, keen to learn all that the doctors and nurses at the Middlesex Hospital would teach her. It was the approach that had been advised by Dr Blackwell:

> ... the advantages of seeing practice in a great hospital are so indispensable, that no-one who has the true spirit for this work in her, will hesitate to accept the wearisome details of the nurse's duty, for the sake of the invaluable privilege of studying diseases on a large scale. All pride and assumption of superiority must be laid aside; and while diligently performing the distinct duties of the poor, you accept, observe, and privately make a record of whatever belongs to your proper medical work.[1]

After a week at the hospital Elizabeth wrote to Emily Davies:

> I get to the hospital by 8 a.m. and as I am now familiar with the different cases in the 2 surgical wards in which I am located, I begin at once to prepare for the dressings by spreading the different ointments, preparing lint, lotion, poultices, bandages &c. While I am doing this at a side table, the sister is going round and examining all wounds &c. The simpler cases she leaves entirely to me very often, but the more difficult ones, such as cancer, she dresses herself while I look on. If I can manage to be in the medical wards with the house doctor, and then return to the surgical cases in time for the surgeon's visit I like to do so. The doctors are uncommonly civil to me, from the house-surgeon upwards ... My father was here last night, and seemed in good spirits, and interested in all my details.[2]

Elizabeth in 1865

Aiming for a position that no woman had achieved before, and looking younger than her 24 years, Elizabeth needed a full measure of independence and confidence. She was very concerned about the proper way to behave, not to be 'too frigid and stiff' with the other pupils, but to be careful that friendliness did not bring gossip. As for being taught by the doctors, she told Emily the next month, it did not make any difference whether they were young or old, married or single:

Dr Willis [the senior resident medical officer] takes everything so calmly that I do not feel half as much awkwardness with what he says to me and shows me, as I do with the hesitation and would-be modesty of some of the old physicians ... I went through my first operation yesterday. It was a stiffish one, and I did not feel at all bad, the excitement was very great but happily it took the form of quickening all my vitality instead of depressing it. Experience is modifying my notions about the most suitable style of dress for me to wear at the hospital. I feel confident now that one is helped rather than hindered by being as much like a lady as lies within one's power. When my student life begins, I shall try to get very serviceable, rich, whole coloured dresses that will do without trimmings and not require renewing often.[3]

In the same way, the American pioneer doctor Mary Putnam was advised by her father in 1863 to 'be a lady from the dotting of your i's to the color of your ribbons, and if you must be a doctor and a philosopher, be an attractive and agreeable one'. Concern for the right lady-like image and the right feminine approach to the doctors runs constantly through Elizabeth's letters. It embarrassed her that her Langham Place friend Ellen Drewry, who she suggested might study chemistry with her, looked 'awfully strong-minded' in 'short petticoats and a close round hat and several other dreadfully ugly arrangements'.[4] Of course Elizabeth had a strong mind herself, but as an adjective 'strong-minded' did not give a desirable image. Gladstone's secretary, for example, later wrote approvingly of Millicent that 'she is a very nice attractive ladylike little person and bears no trace of the "strong-minded female" about her'.[5] Perhaps Mary Seacole's definition of strong-mindedness as 'judicious decisiveness' would suit the Garretts.[6]

In October Elizabeth was given a room at the hospital – where, rather surprisingly, one of the nurses offered to cook for her, and where she could do her dissecting 'to spare Louie's nerves'.[7] Night duty turned out to be hard but instructive, and she coped well apart from a loneliness which she did not often allow to show: 'dusting and polishing was always a favourite amusement of mine and I like the manual work after the night's duty. When I sit down to breakfast it feels uncommonly like college life, and if one had but "fellows" with whom one could be friendly it would be very jolly'.[8]

So far so good, and she hopefully studied the prospectus of the Middlesex Hospital Medical College. She managed to squeeze some concessions from the treasurer; she was not allowed to pay fees, as that would recognize her as a student, but she could give a donation to the hospital and stay through the winter, learning as much as possible by watching. That was as far as she could go, for it would not be possible for her to be a normal college student, the treasurer said, as 'a lady's presence at lectures would distract the other students' attention',[9] and all other London colleges would feel the same. She was, though, allowed to arrange for the apothecary to take her as a pupil in Latin, Greek and *materia medica* – which he did, apparently, three or four hours a day for six months.[10] The apothecary, Joshua Plaskitt, was young but fortunately 'safe' and not 'flighty'. She also managed to arrange for Dr Willis (another teacher she considered 'safe') to come to Louie's house as a tutor three nights a week for two hours to teach anatomy and physiology; his lessons were to cost a guinea a week, but her father was happy to pay for anything she thought necessary.

In fact her father was altogether happy and proud, and her mother soon seems to have accepted her daughter's strange ambition. 'Father and Mother are here now and Agnes', Elizabeth wrote to Emily from Louie's house in December, 'they all came yesterday. I enjoy seeing my Mother, she is so well and cheerful, and the half-solicitude she shows about me is rather pleasant after five months' independence'.[11] Before Elizabeth went home briefly to Aldeburgh for Christmas, Plaskitt and Willis both gave her examination papers on the work she had done.

Family ties took Elizabeth to Louie in January for the birth of her god-daughter Dorothea, but she was back at the Middlesex when the baby was a week old, ready for study. She hoped that she would be able to edge her way fully in, gradually and patiently, by persistence mixed with charm – although 'I feel so mean in trying to come over the doctor by all kinds of little feminine dodges but Mrs Gurney seemed to think they did not matter. She said it was often a matter of perplexity to her, to know if feminine arts were lawful in a good cause'.[12] She managed to get accepted for chemistry lectures and demonstrations and into the dissecting room, paying separate fees. Next came admission to the lectures on *materia medica*, and Elizabeth began to think it might be possible to enrol as a regular student in October 1861.

That June she wrote an encouraging letter to the *Englishwoman's Journal*, making her progress sound simple, and saying that no one should be put off by exaggerated ideas of difficulties ahead for women wanting to be doctors; she signed it A.M.S. (A Medical Student):

> It is now nearly two years since I determined to enter upon the study of medicine, and the decision was arrived at more from a sense of the fitness of

the profession for women than from any strong personal bias towards it or any other science. Probably a large majority of women would be more ready for the study than I was. The first year was spent at home in the study of Latin and the rudiments of Greek; and then, to test my nerves and physical fitness, I entered a London hospital as a probationary nurse in a surgical ward. Here the duties were light and almost nominal, but the opportunity of learning, by watching the nurses, was very valuable. It was still more valuable to get a footing in the hospital, and make the acquaintance of the physicians and surgeons. I was soon delighted to find that both personal and social difficulties had been overstated. The work was not too much for any moderately healthy person. Some of the doctors were friendly, none offered opposition, and the students were willing to treat me with respect and courtesy.

She went on to say that the students were courteous in the chemistry lectures too. The only problem, she said, making light of the difficulties, was that it was not possible to be taught dissecting with the students, but she hoped that it might soon become possible to have a separate dissecting room for women.

Perhaps she was too confident. Certainly she was too successful. The examiners who gave her certificates of honour were worried, asking her 'to use every precaution in keeping this a secret from the students'.[13] Then she was tactless enough to be the only one who could answer a question from a visiting physician on a ward round. The majority of the students, already mocked by rival hospitals, had had enough, and circulated a 'Memorial' round the lecturers: 'the promiscuous assemblage of the sexes in the same class is a dangerous innovation likely to lead to results of an unpleasant character ... the presence of young females as passive spectators in the operating theatre is an outrage on our natural instincts and feelings ... the presence of a female student in the Middlesex School has become a byword and a reproach'. Elizabeth decided to write an open letter in her own defence, but the students sent a firm reply; they could not sanction 'the impropriety of males and females mingling in one class while studying subjects which hitherto have been considered of a delicate nature'. Not all the students were against her, and nor were all the staff, but they could not ignore such an outburst.

Trying to behave as if nothing had happened, Elizabeth sat the chemistry examination, then wrote to her parents suggesting they might endow a medical scholarship for women at the Middlesex. The examination went well but the offer of an endowment was a failure. The

School Committee would not consider the idea, and resolved instead 'that it is inadvisable to admit Ladies to any of the lectures delivered in this College'. Elizabeth confessed to Emily that she felt 'horribly crushed'.[14] But a few days later, with a return of her usual determination, she wrote: 'I don't despair, trials are good and I very seldom have any, and it won't stop me from finally doing my work whatever that may be'. A letter assuring her that 'the substance of that Memorial is not an expression of the sentiments of the whole of the students of this School of Medicine' cheered her, but the damage had been done.

The Lancet trivialized the 'apple of discord' shamefully: 'is she to be welcomed? ... Or should we resist the charge of parasols? ... It is not our intention to discuss the question of the advisability of educating women for the medical profession. We have already expressed a negative opinion'.[15] They could not leave the subject alone; the next month there was another jibe: 'in Medicine there is scant scope for intuition and impulse. Hard study, protracted labour, are required to master – (why do we say master? Has the female correlative ever been employed to signify thoroughness of knowledge or power?) – the secrets, often repulsive, of nature. Science seems always to have exacted the service of men'. What would be the point of hospitals and medical schools admitting women, the article continued, since they could not graduate and get a diploma? Anyway, it was not a question of general interest 'but purely exceptional – a matter of restless – shall we say of morbid – agitation of a few, in which no great human principle is involved'.[16]

To her mother, Elizabeth once again showed her determination: 'having a clear and deliberate conviction it is right, it would be mean and despicable in the extreme to give it up at the first breath of difficulty ... It is not true that there is anything disgusting in the study of the human body; if it were so, how could we look upon God as its Maker and Designer?' So she finished the courses, sat her examinations, qualified for her certificates, then went back to Aldeburgh in the summer of 1861 for two months, conforming to the trivialities of family life, but at the same time working and planning, determined to find some way round the barrier to graduation and a diploma.

'We all followed with keen interest my sister Elizabeth's struggle to get her name inscribed on the British Medical Register', Millicent wrote, 'and sympathized with her in her absolute rejection of anything which would-be friends recommended as "just as good"; for her acceptance of this advice would have consigned women to a lower rank in the profession than that open to men'.[17] This principle was held strongly by all

the sisters throughout their lives and ran through all their work, whether it was for professional qualifications, education, or voting rights.

Elizabeth suffered endless refusals before she found a possible way –
the Society of Apothecaries, licensed by an Act of 1815 to examine
medical candidates,[18] had never examined a woman but, unlike the
Royal Colleges, had no law against it. 'You will be almost as surprised
and pleased as I am', she wrote to Emily, 'to hear that the Apothecaries
are willing to examine me if I will go through the five years of
apprenticeship and the usual routine of lectures etc.'[19] Joshua Plaskitt,
the apothecary who had been helpful when she first went to the Middlesex, had agreed to the formality of accepting her as an apprentice.
That left of course the major problem of finding a medical school to
provide the lectures, but she very much hoped to be able to arrange
something for the following autumn.

Meanwhile, guided by John Chapman of the *Westminster Review*,
who had been introduced to her by Bessie Parkes, she organized an
eclectic course for herself – Latin, Greek, history, geography, logic and
mathematics on her own, botany at the Pharmaceutical Society, physics
at the Royal Institution, Huxley's lectures on natural history and physiology at the South Kensington Museum. She was joined at the
Museum by other young women – Chapman took his daughter, two of
Octavia Hill's sisters came, and Ellen Drewry, and Sophia Jex-Blake
who, not yet planning to study medicine, was teaching mathematics at
Queen's College.

Somehow, with all this activity, Elizabeth also found time to join
Louie in her work for the Society for Promoting the Employment of
Women, to go to concerts and art galleries and to have something of a
social life. In fact the social life led to a startling marriage proposal from
her helpful chemistry lecturer V. R. Heisch, with whom she had enjoyed
the harmless activity of discussing religion – 'I suppose I was a goose',
she confessed to her mother, 'to believe in the possibility of friendship'.[20] She had no problem in decisively refusing; according to her son
there were other offers, none of them hard to refuse apart from the
disturbing proposal from Fawcett.[21] Marriage was not to come to her
until she was a fully qualified doctor, and even then it was to someone
able to respect and support her career.

Her overwhelming concern at this time was to get accepted by a
university. Emily Davies, who had spurred Elizabeth to start her medical
struggle, was now in her turn involved by Elizabeth in the fight for
higher education for women. With Emily's help, Elizabeth applied to

matriculate at London University, writing to every member of the University Senate and to the press to say that she was doing so – quiet and retiring in some ways, she was never afraid to pull every string she could find. All the same, her application was refused, the Senate deciding by one vote that they were not able to admit women now any more than they had when Jessie White had applied six years earlier: 'Lizzie is a wonder [Louie wrote to Newson], she is bearing this disappointment beautifully. It is quite a moral lesson to me to be near her. If practice makes perfect, she will grow very accomplished in meeting and overcoming one drawback after another'.[22]

The Lancet, on the other hand, was pleased:

> We confess that we should have found ourselves embarrassed in that fair company, and congratulate the profession on escaping from a predicament which would have promised sore trials to their gallantry ... Patients, these ladies should remember, are of two sexes, male and female. Are the ladies prepared, as we are, to take under their care nine-tenths of the male diseases? Or if they are prepared to do so, how are they to acquire the necessary knowledge? We know of no hospital at present at which the ladies would be admitted to study these diseases in mixed classes with male students.[23]

Newson, refusing to be defeated, sent a memorial to the Senate arguing for change in the new university charter, and followed it up by financing and helping to organize 1,500 circulars to send to prominent men and women. When these efforts failed too (by the Chancellor's casting vote), Elizabeth decided to turn from London to Scotland, trying first Edinburgh then St Andrews.

This was the year when Emily Davies' paper 'Medicine as a Profession for Women' was read for her by Russell Gurney at the great Social Science Association meeting in the Palace of Westminster. 'It is an unquestionable fact', she had written, 'that women of all ranks do earnestly desire the attendance of physicians of their own sex'. Elizabeth went to the meeting, though she hated the mocking and sneers that met such papers, because, she wrote to her mother, although

> I don't feel sufficiently alive to the good likely to result from such a universal pow-wow about everything ... it would look churlish not to go, so I shall get a ticket and diligently attend the week's meetings. It presents an opportunity for doing some knitting, if I were great in that line. I believe the meetings go on incessantly, with relays of fresh subjects and speakers (and audiences too it may be hoped) for nine days.[24]

Sophia Jex-Blake was by this time at Edinburgh studying mathematics, and Elizabeth, having met her at Huxley's lectures, wrote to her
for help. They campaigned together, and were joined by Newson, but
the Edinburgh physicians voted by 18 to 16 to reject Elizabeth. On to St
Andrews where George Day, Regius Professor of Medicine, offered to
tutor her but could make no promise about admission to the faculty.
Also there was no hospital for clinical teaching. Newson offered to pay
for her to train in America, but she would not hear of it:

> Believing as I do that women physicians of the highest order would be a
> great boon to many suffering women and that in order to have them the
> legal recognition must be given here or in England, I think my work is
> tolerably clear and plain viz. to go on acting as a pioneer towards this end,
> even though by doing so I spend the best years of my life in sowing that of
> which other students will reap the benefit. I feel very much that probably
> there is a divine and beautiful fitness in my being the one appointed to do
> the work.[25]

Admirable, but it strikes an excessively high-minded note, which is
never there in the equally pioneering Millicent.

In any case, the British medical establishment was becoming
increasingly suspicious of the qualifications on offer in America for
women, enjoying any available gossip. *The Lancet* warned the following
year that in America 'The conjunction of women-physicians with spirit-
rappers, magnetic operators, and woman's right reformers, is ominous
... it is well to bear in mind that the female physician movement in this
country is of Transatlantic origin'.[26] Elizabeth would have had no
patience with the unorthodox fringe, but such an article only added to
the prejudice she had to face.

After a brief time back in London, to look after Louie at the birth of
her fourth baby, and to take the pre-clinical test at Apothecaries' Hall,
she went back to St Andrews, to her battle to matriculate. The University Secretary innocently accepted her examination fees (£1 each for
chemistry and anatomy), but this was challenged and annulled, in spite
of Elizabeth's appeals, in turn by the Vice-Chancellor and by the Senate
in St Andrews, and by the Lord Advocate in Edinburgh. It was a miserable time, but Dr Day was on her side through these ordeals, and
Emily Davies travelled up to Scotland to give her moral support. The
Spectator had suggested cynically that the Senate's vote might be
favourable because 'the chance to secure all wealthy female medical
students is worth something to a small University'.[27] Newson, now

always ready to take up arms for Elizabeth, consulted his Member of Parliament, Sir Fitzroy Kelly, who had been both solicitor-general and attorney-general, but his verdict too was against her – as the Charter stood, he said, the Senate could not admit a woman. Still unwilling to accept defeat, Elizabeth went to the editor of the *Scotsman*. All she achieved by that was publicity, and not all of it was welcome. Here is the *British Medical Journal*: 'the female doctor question has received a blow instead of a lift at St Andrews University. It is indeed high time that this preposterous attempt on the part of one or two highly strong-minded women to establish a race of feminine doctors should be exploded'.[28]

But staying on at St Andrews, Elizabeth studied anatomy and physiology privately in the evenings with Dr Day, and the Society of Apothecaries agreed that certificates from Dr Day, and her earlier certificates from the Middlesex and from the Pharmaceutical Society could all count towards her qualification. She was on the way at last, even if it had to be in a roundabout way, built from private tuition and private money.

The theoretical part of the course was conquered. The next step was the clinical, and for this she moved to Edinburgh and approached James Simpson, the famous apostle of chloroform, who had accepted Elizabeth Blackwell's sister Emily as a pupil nine years earlier. He sent her to Alexander Keiller to learn gynaecology at the Royal Infirmary and midwifery at the Edinburgh Maternity Hospital. It was a primitive hospital with a terrible death rate from infections, but the teaching was good, she learnt about vaccinating the new-born, and she was moved by the magic of birth:

> About 6.20 I was called with 'Miss Garrett here's a case and it's yours'. I being chief for the first time. Of course I was up and dressed in a twinkling considerably excited with the prospect of a case 'all to myself'. However, as I did not like risking relying on my very immature judgement I sent for the doctor and he called and I had his confirmation of all I had diagnosed ... We went steadily till ten when a very nice boy came into the world. He weighs 8lb and is 22ins. long, so you see he is a good size. I did everything a doctor does usually, and found it very easy.[29]

Perhaps this is the case she wrote about to Alice, who commented to her mother: 'I had a very interesting letter from Lizzie written while at the Maternity Hospital – Fancy the patients biding their time with short clay pipes in their mouths! I am very glad 'Garrett McQueen' flourished and throve'.[30]

But still there was no way in to the anatomy classes in Edinburgh, and there seemed no point in staying there any longer. So Elizabeth went back to Louie, once more tackling the dreary round of applications and refusals. She was not to be put off, even by letters such as the one from Aberdeen which pronounced 'so strong a conviction that the entrance of ladies into dissecting-rooms and anatomical theatres is undesirable in every respect, and highly unbecoming'.[31] Newson now offered to endow a separate 'Female Medical College', but a substitute for the standard colleges was not at all what Elizabeth wanted.[32] One letter of encouragement would be enough.

Luckily one did come, from L. S. Little, a demonstrator at the London Hospital Medical School who offered to take her for a six months' course of dissecting and anatomy, and she was also able to follow a course of descriptive anatomy. At the same time she built up some clinical experience at the grim London Dispensary in Spitalfields. Desperate for more hospital experience, and with all the normal routes still closed, she then once more entered the wards nominally as a nurse, this time at the London Hospital – the same 'unsatisfactory anomalous position'[33] as she had earlier endured at the Middlesex Hospital (and living, as it happened, in Whitechapel only half a mile from the pawn shop where she was born). Here she was taught and encouraged by Nathaniel Heckford, who in 1870 was to give her her first hospital job. She was stimulated by their course in midwifery and vaccination, but she again had to face resentment and opposition from a lecturer in medicine and from many of the students, and her plea to take the examination of the Royal College of Physicians was rejected.

She reported the state of play in a letter to Elizabeth Blackwell, then in New York:

> The *Lancet* sneers. The *Medical Times & Gazette* treats me as a marvellous exception to other women & gives offensive praise. The *Medical Circular* goes into more detail, draws a fancy picture of trials! that I have gone through (till I am almost eager to write and say how much I enjoyed it all, & how infinitely happier it has made me) ...
>
> I am glad they cannot say I am masculine; it is a providence that I am small & un-angular & still good-looking. For some reason I am very careful to dress well habitually, rather more richly in fact than I should care to do if I were not in some sort defending the cause by doing so.[34]

For her last year as a medical student, Elizabeth had private tuition in morbid anatomy with L. S. Little, and in principles and practice of medicine from S. J. Goodfellow, a doctor at the Middlesex. She was also able to enter some of the wards at the Middlesex as an unofficial observer until March 1865, when she had finished her necessary clinical practice and was told she must leave: 'Poor old Lizzy!' Alice wrote, 'I am so sorry she has been disappointed again at the Middlesex – Success *there* would have been twice as nice as anywhere else.'[35]

This was a critical time for Elizabeth, as it was a little earlier, through the Crows and Louie, that she had met Henry Fawcett. The proposal had come in May 1865, three months after the first meeting. Supported by Louie, she made the difficult decision to refuse him. Instead, she concentrated on her final course of lectures, toxicology and forensic medicine, which she managed to arrange with George Harley, a distinguished professor at University College. She also found time to read a paper to Louie's group, 'What is the Basis and what are the Limits of Parental Authority?' – perhaps she was well qualified to offer useful advice as she had faced a major break with her home upbringing, although her career now depended, and continued to depend, on vigorous parental support. And she managed to do some voluntary teaching – there is a description of her demonstrating the dissection of a frog for the Working Women's College, an institution which had opened in 1864 in emulation of Frederick Maurice's Working Men's College.

Elizabeth was ready now for the Society of Apothecaries to examine her. At the last minute, the Society tried to back-track, and it was only Newson's threat of a lawsuit that made them stick to their promise. She presented her certificates, had no problems with her *viva*, and reported to Emily that the examiners said 'it was a mercy they did not put the names in order of merit, as in this case they must have put me first'.[36] 'Success to her must be doubly sweet', Herbert Cowell wrote cautiously to Mrs Garrett, 'I wish I could more heartily *believe* in the cause. It is a great thing to open out a career for English women; but I hope there won't be many feminine medical students'.

Her local Suffolk paper had no such doubts, and was bursting with pride:

> Miss Garrett has done everything that lies open to one of her sex to constitute herself a fit and useful member of the noble profession she has embraced: but if this result affected herself only, she would, we believe, be the last to consider it a triumph. Her true achievement consists in proving it possible for any woman of sufficient nerve, culture, devotion, and intelligence, who desires to enter such a vocation, to do so in England with full professional sanction, and invested with due professional authority.[37]

Emily Davies was less ebullient, but equally confident and misleading: 'the medical profession is now accessible to any competent woman who is able to defray the cost of instruction ... There is no difficulty in the way of apprenticeship, and lectures and hospital practice are attainable'.[38]

Such confidence was premature. Anxious not to repeat their mistake, the Society changed their rules so that in future candidates could come to them only through regular medical schools. Elizabeth had been the only one to get through the net; in 1865 she was able to put up her brass plate, 'Elizabeth Garrett L.S.A.',[39] on a house in Upper Berkeley Street rented and furnished for her by Newson.

In 1865, too, Elizabeth had joined the new Kensington Society, a discussion and campaign group which flourished for three years, led by Charlotte Manning and her step-daughter Adelaide, who were involved in educational reform and in the social problems of India. The group included many familiar names – Barbara Bodichon, Emily Davies, Dorothea Beale, Frances Buss, and John Stuart Mill's step-daughter Helen Taylor. So, encouraged by the Kensington Society, Elizabeth was busy on the suffrage front. This was the year when Mill stood for parliament and when James Smith took Louie and her sisters to hear him plead for a widening of the franchise and for the vote to be given to women on the same terms as men. Mill was elected, and to support his views Barbara Bodichon and her friends hurried to organize a petition for women's votes. They were following a custom of petitions that had grown during the anti-slavery agitation a generation earlier, and in 1856 had collected 24,000 signatures in favour of married women's property rights; now 1,500 signatures were collected for women's suffrage – not including Millicent's, for at nineteen she was too young to sign, but it did include many other members of the Garrett family. Emily Davies and Elizabeth Garrett took the petition to Parliament. Making it even more of a family affair, Elizabeth's new dining room had been the office, so in effect her new house saw the birth of the first British suffrage society. Louie became the secretary of the newly established Suffrage Committee, though most of the work was done by Emily, who was anxious to keep her own name out of it 'to avoid the risk of damaging my work in the education field by its being associated with the agitation for the franchise'.[40] But the two causes were inextricably mixed, and for the last year of Louie's life, Elizabeth and Millicent were involved with her in work for women's rights, united in their passion both for education and for politics.

It was time for Agnes to join them.

7

'Architectural Decorators'

It is only within the last few years that architects and other competent designers have again begun to think the subject of domestic furniture and decoration worthy of their serious attention.

Rhoda and Agnes Garrett,
Suggestions for House Decoration, 1876

Agnes was twenty in 1865, full of the undirected ambitions that Elizabeth remembered only too well and longed to help:

> I think it is possible [Elizabeth wrote to her mother] that you and Father might silently find ways of meeting what is working in Agnes's nature by perhaps giving her work in the Counting House [as had been done for the nineteen-year-old Alice] or in some other way making her responsible for definite and really employing work – not make believe or useless work not that which (as sewing) only occupies her fingers and leaves her mind at liberty.[1]

Nothing came of that, and the next year, when Newson's finances were once more in a state of minor crisis, Elizabeth wrote to him:

> Agnes is very eager to do something … She thinks she could get a situation as a daily governess in some aristocratic family in this neighbourhood [Upper Berkeley Street]. She could then live here and gradually prepare herself for a better kind of work. I think she might get £70 or £80 a year without much difficulty in this way and after a time I might be able to make use of her as assistant to me.[2]

She also suggested that Agnes and Millicent (then eighteen) might be able to work in an insurance office or a bank.

It all sounds a little patronizing, particularly from someone who had said that she herself hoped to make £1000 a year as a doctor. Elizabeth was sympathetic, but not seeing Agnes as a pioneer in her own mould. Agnes did go to live with her, with a vague and unfulfilled promise that she might study for the Apothecaries' examination in her spare time – spare time, that is, from acting as Elizabeth's housekeeper. She would have met Elizabeth's stimulating group of friends, but her work can't have been much more stimulating than her duties as daughter at home in Aldeburgh. Elizabeth, telling her mother of a lecture she had given in her drawing room, praised Agnes for making the room fresh and pretty; but perhaps, as well as being simply menial work, this gives a clue to Agnes' interest in interior design. At any rate Agnes soon went back to Aldeburgh, possibly after an illness (Alice's letters constantly worry about Agnes' illnesses), and was replaced by Elizabeth's school-friend Jane Crow, at that time the secretary to the Society for Promoting the Employment of Women.

Late in 1866 there was even a passing suggestion from her father that Agnes might join her brother and sister in India. Alice was relieved to hear that their mother did not approve:

> It might possibly do her health good but it would be a risk, and although India is a happy enough place to people who have their own homes here, it must be very dull if not worse to those who have not ... I am quite sure if you knew what life here in this 'marriage market' was for girls, and what is thought and said of those who come out unmarried (except of course to their parents) you would never think of it again.[3]

Agnes was not to join the 'fishing fleet'.

Writing in 1869, Alice mocked a remark from Elizabeth's friend Harriet Cook that she was pleased Agnes was doing office work, because she 'thought she would find it so much more amusing than improving her mind'.[4] Agnes' mind was impressively active and full of ideas; the snub from Edmund, objecting to the suggestion that Agnes should find a career in the malting business at Snape, was to push her into a more fulfilling direction. Twenty years later, in her interview for the *Women's Penny Paper*, Agnes loyally brushed out any memory of Edmund's opposition. The version given there was that 'her father, who was in a very large business as a brewer, was most anxious one or two of his daughters should become lady maltsters, and enter his own business. Agnes consented to try it, and for some period devoted her energies busily to brewing, acting chiefly as her father's secretary, and very useful he found her'.[5]

This may well be true, but it is certainly not the whole truth. Edmund had made it clear that there was no future for 'lady maltsters'; for a serious career Agnes would have to strike out for herself. Alice's letters show she found it all puzzling, but she did her best to keep her parents happy: 'You know dear Father I can't look upon her longing for a

separate life & work as any sign of want of love & consideration for you
& the mother or of love for the old home – although I am very sorry
that she could not find that work as I thought long ago it was settled she
should in helping you either at Snape or Woodbridge'.[6]

Agnes' unmarried cousin Rhoda, a determined character and her
friend since their schooldays with Miss Browning, joined her in planning for a better future. Their plans, in proper Garrett style, struck new
ground by extending current ideas for women's opportunities. As Elizabeth had found her place in the movement for medical education, and
Millicent was to fit into and help to lead the movements for higher
education and for the vote, Agnes and Rhoda showed how women
could run their own business as part of the flourishing arts and crafts
movement.

'I don't know what to say to you about Agnes' plans dear mother',
Alice wrote:

> I am afraid that at first at least it will have been a trouble to you – & yet I
> think it must be a wise and right move for her to look forward to & prepare
> for an active & independent life. I do wish we could see all girls brought up
> for some trade or profession as much as a matter of course as their brothers.
> I should hardly think though that the architecture scheme is a very hopeful
> one, unless one has developed a strong taste for it, especially as Agnes would
> begin at 25 where a boy would have begun at 15. I wonder whether she ever
> thought of a farm ...[7]

Architecture, Alice wrote anxiously, was 'an over-crowded profession
already with only room in it for first-class talent, & although the same
might be said about doctors, yet in their case there is an especial field
for women'.[8]

But there were many influences pushing Agnes and Rhoda to their
architecture scheme. In *Culture and Anarchy* (1869) Matthew Arnold
had used Swift's phrase 'sweetness and light' to describe how intoler-
ance and narrow-mindedness should give way to enlightenment; his
ideals were to materialize in art galleries, museums, and a revolution in
design. John Ruskin and William Morris, both preaching doctrines of
beauty and craftsmanship, were current giants in the tradition con-
necting art and social reform – a tradition where Agnes and Rhoda
fitted completely. Ruskin could be brutally critical of women artists, but
he had faith in them as craftsmen.[9] There is no evidence that Agnes and
Rhoda knew either Ruskin or Morris personally, but they were strongly
influenced by Morris and they certainly knew Octavia Hill, who was

Rhoda and Agnes

Ruskin's disciple both in art and in her whole social outlook. She was a friend of F. D. Maurice and Barbara Bodichon, had joined in the petition for married women's property rights, and later turned her life to pioneering housing reform (which was patronized by Ruskin), the National Trust, and the need for open spaces.

Many women were becoming known in the arts, one way or another – Barbara Bodichon herself, for a start, who had been given a solo exhibition in Ernest Gambart's gallery in Pall Mall in 1859. Times had improved since Mendelssohn's sister Fanny had published her songs only under her brother's name in her brother's album – in 1820 her father had written to her that 'Music will perhaps become his [Felix's] profession, while for *you* it can and must be only an ornament'. Morris' wife and various female friends and relations designed and worked for him, his daughter May taking over the embroidery department in 1885. Among the many emerging names were Pre-Raphaelite women painters, such as Anna Mary Howitt; the great traveller Marianne North, who set off to illustrate the flora of Jamaica and Brazil in 1871; Julia Margaret Cameron, famous in photography in the later 1860s; Mary Fraser Tytler (soon to be Mary Watts), who mixed art and philanthropy by practising as painter and potter and running pottery classes at a club for bootblacks in Whitechapel; Gertrude Jekyll, perhaps nearest of all to the Garretts in her artistic interests, described when young as competent in 'carving, modelling, house-painting, carpentry, smith's work, repoussé work, gilding, wood-inlaying, embroidery, gardening, and all manner of herb and flower knowledge'.[10] Laura Herford, who was to paint Elizabeth Garrett's portrait in 1866, had in 1860 become the first woman student at the Royal Academy; more women – including Kate Greenaway, later to become both a patient and friend of Elizabeth Garrett – were among those taken by the National Art Training School (later the Royal College of Art); the Society of Female Artists held its first exhibition in 1857; the Royal School of Art Needlework, providing 'suitable employment for poor gentlewomen', was started in 1872. 'There are', Anny Thackeray wrote in 1861,

> Schools of Art all over the kingdom, where young men and young women are taught the same things by the same masters. It is a fact that the women generally take higher places than the men in the examinations; and when they leave, a person in authority has assured me that he did not know of one single instance where they had failed to make their way.[11]

So the climate was there – as it had been in the world of politics and education and medicine for Millicent and for Elizabeth. Agnes and Rhoda turned out to have great natural taste, and skills almost as wide-ranging as Gertrude Jekyll, but where they stand out as different from most of their contemporaries is their emphasis on the importance of thorough professional training and their ambition to be their own masters. They wanted to do more than practise 'the humble art of house decorators', painting 'the doors, shutters, and other woodwork with various kinds of designs, coats of arms, etc.'[12] after a few courses at an art school. They dismissed the idea of dilettante amateurs (although there were some very distinguished ones around) rather as Elizabeth dismissed the idea of nursing or of some medical qualification for women that was lower than the standard qualification for men. Agnes, with a father who had designed and built the Snape Maltings as well as his own and other houses in Aldeburgh, and with an architect cousin,[13] must have grown up well used to discussions of designs and plans. Familiar, too, through her father's business with the idea of apprenticeships, Agnes decided that she and Rhoda should get themselves apprenticed to an architect. This was a year before the *Art Journal* tentatively suggested that 'if we allow that women may undertake certain branches of work, it must follow that we also grant a system of regular training or apprenticeship for girls'.[14]

In 1871 Agnes and Rhoda found an architect, Daniel Cottier, who was prepared to give them some training in his studio. Cottier had studied under Ford Madox Brown at the Working Men's College in London; then, after making his name in his native Scotland as a stained-glass artist and furniture maker, he had come back to London in 1869 and set up his firm of 'Art Furniture Makers, Glass and Tile Painters'. There are several links to the Garrett family and their friends. His London office was in Langham Place, the road where Barbara Bodichon had run her office ten years earlier; one of the Scottish churches he had worked on had been designed by John James Stevenson, a relation of James Skelton Anderson, who married Elizabeth in February 1871; when Elizabeth was planning alterations to her house before her marriage, she had written to Skelton saying that they 'ought to go to Cottier pretty soon, he is slow and unpunctual like most artistic people even when Scotch'.[15]

Newson did not take easily to the idea of another daughter branching out on her own. But she had her sisters' support, and Henry Fawcett wrote to Newson defending their offer of a home in London for Agnes when she first moved there:

I do not feel that I have in any way influenced Agnes; she is old enough and has ability enough to judge for herself without interference from me. I think it is quite as laudable on her part to desire to make her own living as it was for Lizzie to do the same. Agnes was chiefly influenced in her desire to obtain something to do in London from a very proper motive that she did not like to be the cause of a family disagreement, and from the tone Newson [her eldest brother] and Edmund adopted with regard to her entering the malting business, family discord would be the inevitable result. The only advice I gave Agnes was that she should write to you before anything was settled; this I know she did, as she told you about Cottier ... I further advised her that as Skelton Anderson had great business experience, that in the event of your not coming to London she should consult him in all business matters.[16]

Agnes and Rhoda were with Cottier probably for eighteen months before spending a further eighteen months under John McKean Brydon, another Scot who had worked with Stevenson in Glasgow. In London Brydon shared an office with Basil Champneys, and the cousins finished their apprenticeship there about the time that Champneys became the architect for Newnham College. It is not clear why they left Cottier – possibly from personal difficulties, possibly because they wanted to study under someone who was more an architect than a designer. With Brydon they had to learn 'all the mysteries of drawing to scale, of designing as applied to houses and even the uninteresting *minutiae* of the construction of a drain, or the laying of a gas pipe'.[17] More aesthetically, they were probably involved with Brydon's work building a studio for the artist James Tissot. It was usual at that time for architects to train as apprentices in an architect's office and work without taking official examinations – Thomas Hardy, just beginning to emerge as a writer, had done so, and was at that time working on the new schools for the London School Board. There were no professional women architects in Britain until 1898, and the Royal Institute of British Architects (founded 1837) was closed to women until 1902, but in the 1891 census there were twelve women in London counting themselves as architects besides those, including Agnes and Rhoda, who described themselves as designers.[18]

Agnes and Rhoda learnt all the practical side of their work, from mixing paints to drawing plans for altering staircases or windows, but they did not undertake new building. Agnes remarked slightly wistfully in her 1890 interview that 'had I begun a few years earlier I think I should have gone in for building';[19] 'but', she added, 'I never attempt a thing I do not thoroughly understand'. When they started their apprenticeship she was 26 and Rhoda was 30; setting up and running their own business as 'architectural decorators' was challenge enough.

Before setting up they spent a summer touring round England sketching the interiors and the furniture of grand houses. Rhoda particularly showed a historical interest, and was to become (with Anny Thackeray Ritchie) one of only two women on the first committee of the Society for the Preservation of Ancient Buildings, and a member of the Royal Archaeological Institute.

In 1874 they were ready to launch the firm of R & A Garrett House Decorators, moving into Gower Street the next year. At that time Gower Street was closed to through traffic and its late-eighteenth-century architecture, appreciated by the Garretts, was unfashionable. They furnished and decorated their house with friezes, fireplaces, designs of flowers and birds on ceilings and panels – all probably both for their own pleasure and as showrooms for possible clients. Their little book, *Suggestions for House Decoration*, was commissioned for an 'Art at Home' series and published by Macmillan in 1876, to give guidance in painting, woodwork and furniture for the 'cultivated middle classes'[20] – how elegant results could be achieved without great cost; the fine drawings in it, which they did themselves, actually show the decoration and furniture of their own house.[21] Without William Morris' love for

Fireplace from House Decoration

the medieval and the gothic, and with more feeling for comfort (and more emphasis on economy), they strongly shared his belief in good craftsmanship and unity of design, and his dislike of anything shoddily mass-produced. Their ideal was the so-called 'Queen Anne style', of brick not stucco, with no 'useless and meaningless ornament'. Their general rules are still acceptable: 'never make a thing or a material look like what it is not' – as painting wood to look like marble; 'do not go

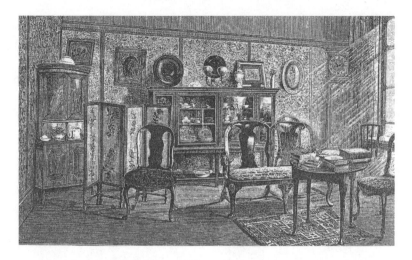

Drawing Room (probably 2 Gower Street) from *House Decoration*

out of your way to hide the construction of your house or of any part of your furniture', but instead 'make it so good that you feel no anxiety to conceal it'; 'always secure a considerable amount of plain neutral colour in your rooms'. They warned of the danger of overloading rooms with ornament, and pleaded that trained designers should be allowed a free hand, that it was specially important to have good chimney pieces, and that all details mattered or the result would not be harmonious. Only the grandest houses had bathrooms by then, but it is a pity that the Garretts did not give any suggestions for kitchens.

The result was elegant 'arts and crafts' furniture in fine materials, wallpapers clearly influenced by Morris (they had Morris paper themselves) and, as Agnes herself said in her interview in 1890, 'rooms restful to the eye'.[22] 'I cannot bear an inharmonious room, or an over-decorated one, and I like all my work to bear the individual impress of my mind. It should, to my idea, resemble a picture, each detail should go to the forming of the whole, and this can only be achieved by its being the work of one mind'.[23]

They had an 'honourable mention' and were specially noticed by the Prince of Wales for their display at the international exhibition in Paris in 1878, but had no ambitions to take on more work than they could run personally. The firm was R & A Garrett with no '& Company', and it is perhaps because they were deliberately working on a small scale that they are generally forgotten and little of their work survives. Even the

Gower Street house (the only house in the row that is in fact stuccoed, though the Garretts were not responsible for that) now has a blue plaque commemorating Millicent, who lived there later, with no mention of Agnes or Rhoda. Yet it has been claimed that in their day they 'came to be seen as influential on a par with Morris and Co in spreading new and artistic ideas of taste in the home from the 1870s'.[24]

Circular Ward in the New Hospital for Women

There were plenty of friends and relations to give them a chance to show what they could do. Sadly though, much house alteration and decoration is only ephemeral, and only a little is still recorded. With Millicent deeply involved in the early stages of planning Newnham College, and with Basil Champneys appointed as architect, it is likely, although there is no definite evidence, that Agnes and Rhoda played some part in the design and certainly in the interiors there. Elizabeth and Skelton moved in 1874 to a new and larger red brick and terracotta house in Upper Berkeley Street, where Agnes and Rhoda advised on the furnishing. Later, after Rhoda's death, Agnes worked with John Brydon on much of the interior design for Elizabeth's Hospital for Women, and for her own project, the Ladies' Residential Chambers.[25] James Beale, who was a director of 'Ladies' Residential Co. Ltd.',

commissioned furniture from Agnes for the house Philip Webb built for
him in Standen, Sussex.[26] At that time, too, Agnes did some work for
her family in Suffolk – decorating houses for Elizabeth, Alice, and her
brother Edmund and for her parents, in Aldeburgh, and for her sister
Josephine in Bury St Edmunds. Her cousin Edmund, then a journalist
in South Africa, talked of a possible commission to decorate a house in
Mayfair for the diamond magnate Alfred Beit, but it came to nothing –
later, as South African problems grew, Edmund wrote that he was '*so
very* glad about the work coming in', but he thought it was lucky that
Agnes was not involved with Beit.[27]

A personal picture of Agnes and Rhoda Garrett themselves and at
their work came from one of their most distinguished clients, the
composer Hubert Parry. It is not clear whether he came to them
through the enthusiasm he and his wife Maud had for women's suffrage, or whether they kindled the enthusiasm. At any rate he was, as he
wrote, their great admirer: 'it is a real pleasure to spend time with such
people, who discuss every point worth talking about with no person-
alities. Their whole conversation and everything about them rings
true'.[28] Dining with them, he recorded 'a tremendous dinner and great
fun',[29] and as for staying with them for a fortnight, 'I was never so spoilt
in my life. They seem to divine all one's wants before one has thought of
them oneself. They are the best company I ever knew, and to live in
their house is a very great element of happiness in itself. The quiet and
soothing colour of the walls and decorations and the admirable taste of
all things acts upon the mind in the most comforting manner'.[30] They
laughed together at plays, and they went to *Tannhäuser*. It was a very
happy fortnight.

Parry employed the Garretts for his new Kensington house, and
noted in his diary how they worked beyond the call of duty:

A carpenter and a carpet man & woman arrived early & got to work to put
things in their places – & shortly after Rhoda – who took off her great coat
& said 'I have come to work' & work she did. First fetching a charwoman to
help our servants & then setting to dust & arrange everything & directing
everybody else what to do; progress was made with quite marvellous
rapidity so that by the time Maud arrived in the afternoon the house in
some parts looked positively comfortable ... meanwhile Agnes arrived & the
house was put more & more into order & then having given further
directions the two devoted Garretts departed to find a cook for us.[31]

Troubles were not quite over, as Rhoda had to come round some weeks later to instruct the builder how to deal with a crisis in the drains.

Rhoda and Agnes, breaking from the family tradition of Aldeburgh houses, rented a cottage in Rustington, Sussex. Ancient, rambling, and thatched, it became a much-loved holiday home and a centre for a lively artistic circle – the composer Ethel Smyth, Arthur Llewelyn Davies (a brother of Emily), J.M. Barrie and William de Morgan's sister Mary [32] were among the neighbours and visitors. Ethel Smyth called it the focus of her English life, admired the Garretts, and said she had never been happier in her life than there – they captivated even her father, she said, 'in spite of their arty clothes'.[33] The Parrys joined the circle too, getting Norman Shaw to build them a country house just near, buying Morris paper, de Morgan tiles, and Garrett furniture and carpets. Having the Garretts in the village, 'is as good as ever so much physic to Maud', Hubert Parry wrote in his journal, 'as she is perfectly devoted to them, and they keep her in wonderfully good spirits'.[34] All the same Maud, a wayward character, could be critical of the Garrett style at times. After seeing the 1888 Arts and Crafts Exhibition she noted in her diary: 'saw Agnes's dowdy room. All her furniture covered with old men's trousers and the walls painted a bilious yellow – of a different shade than the carpet'.[35]

Agnes and Rhoda directed all the design work for the firm and carried out intricate painting themselves – there is a description of them being interviewed 'up on a scaffolding, lying flat on their backs close to a ceiling which they were painting'[36] – and they had a loyal group of workmen. Believing in the importance of professional training, and having been through apprenticeships themselves, they took on female apprentices for not less than three years at a premium of £300 – one of them was their niece Theodora Garrett, daughter of Edmund, the brother who had objected to the idea of Agnes as a colleague in the family malting business.

The cousins shared the work of organizing, designing, painting, whatever was needed. And at the same time they were both deeply involved in the suffrage campaign, starting their careers as public speakers at about the same time as they started to work for Cottier; being self-employed, they could arrange to go off to meetings and rallies. More radical than Millicent, they joined the Central Committee of the National Society for Women's Suffrage, which had split from Millicent's London group because they believed in supporting Josephine Butler in her crusade against the Contagious Diseases Acts.[37] For a year from 1872, Agnes was joint honorary secretary of the Committee.

Rhoda became a particularly powerful and effective speaker, equally ready to talk either on interior design or on the suffrage. She was 'one among a thousand in her wonderful charm and influence', her half-brother Edmund wrote, 'but she was one among a million in the use she made of these'.[38] Ray Strachey, born five years after Rhoda died but well aware of her reputation, wrote that she was 'in every way a brilliant young woman, easily the most eloquent and convincing of all the early speakers, and popular wherever she went'.[39] Ethel Smyth described her as 'more amusing than anyone I have ever met – a wit half-scornful, always surprising, as unlike everyone else's as was her person'.[40] Her 'wit' is mentioned by one friend after another, but it is not something that comes across on paper. Her obituary in the the *Englishwoman's Journal* talked of her 'passionate eloquence and appealing pathos'. In 1876 she had the biggest audience of the meeting at the National Association for the Promotion of Social Science with a paper on interior design – 'woman's sphere and woman's mission is one of the most important problems of the present day, but here, at least, in the decoration and beautifying of the house, no one will dispute their right to work'. Four years earlier she had toured with a lecture that was printed later as 'Electoral Disabilities of Women'.[41] There she set out to show how the suffrage was the basic first step to help the educational, economic and legal position of women. She protested at an educational system that prepared boys for life in the world and girls only for life in the home. But,

> Would they consent to be excluded from a fair share in educational advantages if they could make their voices heard in the Legislature of the country? Would not their claim to be educated as solidly, and in the same branches of knowledge as men, be argued with a far greater chance of success, if they possessed the power of urging its justice before that tribunal where men are able to lay their grievances, and enforce their redress?

(It was, of course, a complicated circular argument – some thought women would not be ready for the vote until they had more education, while others, like Rhoda here, argued that if women had the vote they would see that there were proper opportunities for education.)

Working-class women, Rhoda said, rarely receive proper training and are paid less than men, even if they are doing similar work, such as being a cook or a hairdresser. And life can be even more difficult for 'the more educated middle-class women', who besides having no useful training have to face prejudice against working at all: 'for an educated

woman there is no middle path. Either she must be Queen of England –
the head of the State – or she must be shut out of nearly all of the
advantages of a citizen in a country over which a woman rules'.

The only work on offer for women in any government office, she
added, was in the lower grades of the telegraph offices. They were totally
excluded from the Church, or from the law, parents never provided the
capital to set their daughters up in a trade, and it was not surprising that
they looked on marriage as the only escape. And the Married Women's
Property Act of 1870 had gone only a little way towards improving the
legal position of married women. If all this was to change, women must
have the vote. They should

> Demand the removal of their electoral disabilities ... until this is done they
> can have no efficient weapon with which to fight their battles. We are
> constantly told, in tones of scorn, that the women who desire the suffrage
> are a mere handful of female fanatics. As compared with the entire female
> population we *may* be only a handful, but we are an ever-increasing handful
> of very obstinate people.

One injustice was removed when the Married Women's Property Act
was extended in 1882. But on 22 November of that year Rhoda died
from typhoid and bronchitis, aged 41, and was buried at Rustington.
Agnes went over to see Parry the next day, and he played Bach to
console her. She wrote to Maud:

> I know all she was to me helping me perpetually from sinking into com-
> monplace aims and low ideals. I feel as if I were an ear of wheat that has
> been threshed and robbed of all the living grains. It is this that has made me
> shrink so from going on with our work – as if I should have no freshness no
> originality no delicacy to offer people – in fact that I should be that which
> she hated so – a charlatan. But no one else seems to think so ... I have
> determined to go on at any rate for the present.[42]

Rhoda's young brothers and sisters needed her, Agnes realized, and she
needed to be able to keep Rustington as a family meeting place for
them.[43] With courage and strength, she went on alone.

8

Doctor at Last

From our youth up some of us have known how certain of the wisest and most appreciated of physicians have insisted that the health of women and their children will never be guarded as it ought to be till it is put under the charge of physicians of their own sex.

The Edinburgh Review, April 1859

We left Millicent about to be immersed in politics as the wife of Henry Fawcett, and Elizabeth with her brass plate on the Upper Berkeley Street door ready for her first patients. 'Elizabeth Garrett L.S.A.' was careful wording, avoiding both the assertive word 'doctor' and the inadequate word 'Miss'. But in spite of the brass plate the struggle was by no means over; with no hope of any hospital appointment or a normal position in general practice, Elizabeth hoped she might be able to find an opportunity and fill a need as a consultant physician for women and children.

She was not the only one to see that need, though she was the only one to try to fill it as a fully qualified woman physician. Emily Davies had written that 'women of all ranks do earnestly desire the attendance of physicians of their own sex'; but, for all her ambition, had added 'it would not be necessary for ladies to compete [with] picked men at the head of their profession'.[1] Dr James Edmunds, with his Female Medical Society (founded 1865) started to teach 'midwifery and its cognate subjects' but was doubtful about women 'practising medicine and surgery in general'. Indeed his main arguments seemed to be that there were too many unregulated midwives (Sarah Gamp comes to mind), and that it was better to have qualified specialist midwives than medical men arriving on the scene spreading infections from their last cases.

The Lancet gave Elizabeth a patronizing welcome, in spite of claiming earlier that the medical profession was 'the least adapted to the female nature' and that obstetrics was the most unsuitable branch of all, because it involved emergencies that women could not cope with, and unsuitable lonely visits at night.[2]

We amicably salute this blue-eyed priestess of Aesculapius, and congratulate her upon the favourable termination to a hard-fought struggle. The

industry, the ability, and the determination which she has shown augur well
for that success which we heartily wish for her. She has achieved a position,
entirely exceptional, at a great sacrifice. But we apprehend that it is likely to
remain entirely exceptional. We cannot accept the event as an omen of
coming change.[3]

It did seem as if it would be exceptional, as each step taken by these
pioneers was blocked in a panic lest others should follow. It was after Dr
Blackwell had got her name on the new Medical Register that the Medical
Council resolved that they would not accept foreign diplomas in future;
and it was after Elizabeth Garrett achieved her L.S.A. that the Society of
Apothecaries resolved that candidates must have worked in a recognized
medical school in future – an impassable barrier until examinations and
degrees of the University of London were opened to women in 1878. The
old ladders were pulled up, and new ones had to be found.[4]

Since no established institution would accept Elizabeth, in 1866 she
started her own nearby; besides seeing patients in her own house, she
opened the St Mary's Dispensary for Women and Children – once again
following Dr Blackwell, who had opened her own dispensary in New
York nine years earlier. Elizabeth had the support of her friends Barbara
Bodichon and the Russell Gurneys, and the strong approval of Emily's
brother J. Llewelyn Davies. The threat of a cholera epidemic that year
underlined the need and encouraged philanthropic subscriptions. Elizabeth wrote a disconcertingly hard-headed letter to her St Andrews
friend Harriet Cook: 'Of course the real motive in the case of any one
doing the work I do at St Mary's is the desire to gain knowledge. You
are glad that incidentally the poor people are cured, but that is not the
motive'.[5] But the record of the Dispensary was far better than she
implied. There were eminent consultants,[6] there were 3,000 new cases in
the first year, Elizabeth herself held outpatient clinics three times a
week, visited patients at home, took charge of local midwifery. 'She has
settled in a great centre of population, and aspires to a special practice
amongst women and children' was The Lancet's comment; 'this we
believe to be the only condition under which females can successfully
practise medicine'.[7] To a lesser extent she also saw private patients and
practised surgery which, she wrote to her mother, 'pays capitally, and it
is very interesting, if one could but have some more practice at it would
be the best line to work in'.[8] She did not want to spend too much time
on midwifery, since there were already plenty of midwives attached to
hospitals in the area.

Elizabeth planned to give clinical training in the Dispensary to three women who would follow her by studying for the apothecaries' qualification, but when this route was blocked the three went off to Zurich. Two women were taken on in the first year to learn to dispense medicines, but that was all the training Elizabeth could offer for the time being. She had written to her mother of bigger dreams:

> It might become the nucleus of a hospital with beds. The upper rooms could be used as a school, one room for dissections, another for lectures, others for private study, library etc etc ... I should be the general manager of the school, tutor to the pupils as well as a medical attendant in the dispensary, and I should have as much power as would be wanted to keep things straight. The lecturers would naturally be friendly to me & would be willing to let me share in their work and this wd be the best way of creeping into a position of teacher which should be recognised by the Medical Council ... I hope you and the dear father will understand the scheme & think as well of it as I do.[9]

(All the family tended to use the definite article when referring to either of their parents in letters.)

At a time when other doctors, with varying success, were trying to establish their own specialist hospitals, this was not such a strange idea.[10] Elizabeth's mother showed sufficient sympathy to send hampers of food, and Elizabeth wrote back weekly with her news. But the conversion of the upper rooms to a mini-hospital had to wait until 1872, another six years.

Elizabeth read papers on the administration of medical charities, and on volunteer nursing, to the Social Science Association, although she was rather a hesitant contributor to the meetings. She confided her doubts and hopes to Emily Davies:

> For several reasons I incline to doing it myself, but I shall not like to do it if you think it unwise. My reasons are 1st that it is a pity to let the woman's element in the Assn, expire for want of people who will use the liberty offered them. 2nd that reading papers is the first step towards being allowed to join in discussions: 3rd that the paper would be more attended to if I read it myself: 4th that I have a tolerably strong voice and am neither hideous, young, nor beautiful. If you think these reasons sufficient, I will practise reading aloud.[11]

Trying to spread interest in medicine among upper-class women, Elizabeth gave drawing-room lectures on physiology, with audiences ranging from the high-powered Lady Amberley[12] and Mill's step-daughter Helen Taylor, to 'a whole row of dear old ladies who are by no means up to modern views as expounded by Darwin and Huxley'.[13]

The house in Upper Berkeley Street became a meeting place for an impressive group of friends – Louie and James Smith (until Louie's death in 1867), Emily Davies, Emily's brother J. Llewelyn Davies and his wife, and Barbara Bodichon on her summer visits to London. This was the time of Gladstone's Reform Bill, which proposed extending the vote to every male householder, and of the famous petition supporting Mill's amendment. The suffrage movement was of course to become primarily Millicent's territory, though Elizabeth and other members of the family remained deeply involved.

But now Elizabeth's medical ambitions were the strongest influence in her life. 'I am so glad to hear your practice is doing so well dear old lady', Alice wrote, 'professional success seems to be one of the sweetest of sweet things even to men & you have especial reasons for longing for it'.[14] When Elizabeth heard that she might improve her qualifications by getting an MD in Paris, she left the suffrage committee so that she could spend all her spare time studying for the examination. There was encouragement from Amelia Murray, a lady-in-waiting to the Queen and a founder of the Governesses Benevolent Association, who sent for Elizabeth to come to the Palace and tell her about her plans and how she was getting on. 'My dear, I think you are doing quite right', she said to her, 'and I really believe if I were a woman myself I would do the same', adding, 'I mean of course if I were in that station of life'.

One of the 'Calcutta great men' went to talk to Alice about Elizabeth:

He 'had heard about her, that she was gentle & feminine & a most won-derful woman' & he thought her undertaking & the way in which she had carried it through ought to be compared with the accomplishment of the Suez Canal. I don't know when I have heard such energetic enthusiastic admiration of her – certainly not before in India.[15]

The pioneer in Paris was the New Yorker Mary Putnam. Six years younger than Elizabeth, she also had a father who supported her career although he considered medicine a 'repulsive pursuit'. Like Elizabeth, too, she was to show in time that women doctors could combine their careers with marriage and children. Working in Paris hospitals since 1866, she had managed to persuade the Faculty of Medicine at the Sorbonne to admit her as a medical student in 1868, news that encouraged Elizabeth to apply to take the examinations without

repeating her course or moving to live in Paris. Initial opposition from
the Faculty council was overcome (partly by intervention from the
Empress Eugénie who took a personal interest in women's education),
and Elizabeth coped triumphantly with her first *viva*. Next came the
ordeal of performing two operations publicly, followed again by a *viva*,
then later the written papers, and finally an examination in clinical
medicine midwifery and surgery, and a thesis on migraine. To add to
her problems all this was of course in French, but here the insistence on
French speaking at the Blackheath school paid off. She passed it all with
credit, and in June 1870 (a month before France declared war on Germany) became the first woman Paris MD. As the Paris correspondent of
The Lancet reported: 'the hall was literally crowded with students, and,
on Miss Garrett's crossing the courtyard to leave the school, I observed
with pleasure that almost all the students gallantly bowed to their lady
confrère. All the judges, on complimenting Miss Garrett, more or less
expressed liberal opinions on the subject of lady doctors'.[16]

Elizabeth's parents were there. 'I was very glad to hear all about the
Paris expedition last mail', Alice wrote, 'give my love to our dear old
doctor. I should have liked to have been there to see her get her honours. It seems to have been a rush of a visit, but June is a pleasant &
busy time of year at home & I daresay you were all glad to get back
again'.[17] Mary Putnam became the second woman to gain a Paris MD.[18]
In 1872 she was to become the first woman member of the New York
Academy of Medicine; Elizabeth was not elected to the British Medical
Association until 1873.

Fully qualified and with an MD, Elizabeth had yet to get fully
accepted by the medical establishment. She sided with her professional
colleagues and, for once, against her sisters and most of her friends, over
the question of the Contagious Diseases Acts. Under these acts, meant
mainly to apply to ports and garrison towns, any women suspected of
prostitution could be forced to be examined for venereal disease.
Infected women were to be kept in hospital for up to three months;
those who refused to be examined could be imprisoned for a month –
but there was to be no punishment or inspection for men. Elizabeth, as
she explained in an article in the *Pall Mall Gazette*[19], defended the acts
as a necessary evil, because her medical experience led her to believe that
they would help to reduce venereal disease. She sincerely felt compulsory treatment might help to tackle the problem in its early stage, would
provide care for those whom hospitals often refused to admit, and
would help to protect vulnerable women and children – 'I believe that

among the poor, the number of innocent people who suffer from the worst and most lasting forms is greater than the guilty'. Emily Davies agreed with her, as did Sophia Jex-Blake; Millicent strongly disagreed although, unwilling to allow her suffrage work to be muddied by sexual problems, she avoided any involvement. Elizabeth Blackwell (who had vehement if unrealistic optimism about morality and social purity) and Agnes and Rhoda (who were realists but were appalled at the double standards and the treatment of prostitutes) vigorously supported the repeal campaign. Pioneers who run campaigns are likely to have strong views and to stick to them – it is not surprising that they clashed at times, but it was difficult for them all. Making up for her reticence at the time, in 1927 Millicent wrote, with E. M. Turner, a short life of the leader of the repeal campaign, Josephine Butler. It was a work of hagiography – written to celebrate the centenary of Mrs Butler's birth – for the Association for Moral and Social Hygiene.

Elizabeth had been guided by her beliefs, not by any motive of medical politics, but the result was to irritate many members of the women's movement, while not in any way affecting her status in the medical profession. The thaw though was beginning. The first move – and it turned out to be a crucial one – was in March 1870 when she was offered a post as visiting medical officer to the East London Hospital for Children; as *The Times* commented, it was 'the first hospital in Great Britain which has recognised in this manner the female medical movement'.[20] The hospital had been set up by Nathaniel Heckford and his wife, who had befriended Elizabeth during her training at the London Hospital and who now proposed that she should be appointed.[21] It was at her interview with the East London board that she first met the hospital's vice-chairman and financial adviser James George Skelton Anderson. Having come to the meeting doubtful about appointing a woman, Anderson was properly impressed by Elizabeth, voted for her, introduced himself to her afterwards, and told her he had a sister who hoped to study medicine.

The hospital, poorly equipped and in a sadly poor part of Stepney, had moved Dickens to one of his most pathetic descriptions of lead-poisoning, of out-of-work starving families, and of this one struggling effort to help. 'Insufficient food and unwholesome living are the main causes of disease among these small patients', he wrote, 'so, nourishment, cleanliness, and ventilation are the main remedies'.[22] The medical work was the best that the unpromising conditions allowed, but the chaotic way the place was run roused Elizabeth's autocratic longing for efficiency. Both the Heckfords were thoroughly well-meaning, but unbusinesslike and sentimental; outpatients pushed in uncontrolled crowds, dispensing was unsupervised, vermin abounded – Heckford was said to have refused to kill a black beetle because 'death would probably be as disagreeable to him as it would be to me'; a little mongrel dog ran cheerfully round the patients' beds. Elizabeth worked out a programme of reform and wrote to Anderson about the problems in a despairing and rather hard-headed mood:

> I cannot afford to waste time and strength in merely being kind to the miserable people at the Hospital. Unless they help me on my road some one else must be kind to them. It almost breaks one's heart to realize what their lives are, what they must be whatever one gave up in order to help them, but this is no reason for allowing them to interfere with more important objects. Mr Heckford thinks this sort of thing is mere selfishness. He is wrong ... I almost think I would go on and sell my soul for the cause I care most to help. It is my business to become a great physician, nothing else I could do would help women so much as this, therefore if the hospital helps it is welcome, if it hinders, away with it.[23]

She was in danger, as Anderson told her, of letting success go to her head after her Paris MD – of suffering from 'too much butter'. Defensively, she told him that she had 'an enthusiasm of admiration for those before whom one's self is pigmied. It is only in Lilliput land that I could be stuck up and thank heaven I am not living there yet'.[24] It is a measure of their growing friendship that she could accept such criticism. In time, marriage was to be a softening influence, and traces of arrogance would disappear.

Her success was changing the attitude of the medical press. When she was encouraged by the husbands of her dispensary patients to stand for election to the new London School Board in Marylebone (set up after the 1870 Education Act), her decision was welcomed by *The Lancet*; the editor hoped everyone would support 'an ornament to the calling that she has embraced'.[25] Everyone did, although Elizabeth, panicking, had written to Emily, 'I can't think of anything to say for four speeches! and after Huxley too, who speaks in epigrams!'[26]

It was the first time that women ratepayers had been allowed to vote in any municipal elections or to serve on such an official body. The news reached the Indian papers, and 'the version of it which reached Herbert in the bar library', Alice wrote, 'was that Miss Garrett was a candidate to be M.P. for Marylebone'.[27] Elizabeth polled 47,858 votes, more than any other candidate in London and way ahead of Huxley who came second with 13,494. 'I am much pleased at Miss Garrett's success', Lord John Russell wrote to his son, 'she ought to have a vote for Westminster, but not to sit in Parliament. It would make too much confusion'.[28] Emily, always rather prim and serious, was glad that such a majority did not make Elizabeth try to become chairman when there were senior men about: 'I should be sorry for you to do anything which might give colour to the charge of being "cheeky", which has been brought against you lately. It is too true that your jokes are many and reckless. They do more harm than you know ... I have had a nice note from Mr Anderson. I like him the best of all your friends'.[29]

It is good to find that there were many jokes as well as plenty of serious work. Told off again, Elizabeth cheerfully passed the comments on to Anderson: 'most people like compliments, particularly when they have the charm of perfect sincerity, so I send you one from Miss Davies. The contrast between my share and yours is rather trying, but I do not mind a little north-east wind, and I know it is good to have it as a check upon any tendency to uppishness which 47,000 might induce'.[30]

The news of Elizabeth's triumph reached India – 'the Indian news-papers have been full of it', Alice wrote, 'I have had calls of con-gratulation & been quite a celebrity too with reflected glory'.[31] In this same election Emily was put on the School Board in Greenwich. 'Well done, gallant Greenwich and gallanter Marylebone!', *Punch* com-mented, 'your chivalry will be rewarded'.[32] They were the first women members of the new Boards in London; Edinburgh and Manchester also each elected a woman member. The success launched Elizabeth into a new social scene – 'I am above par just now, so I am eating an unwholesome number of good dinners', she wrote happily to Anderson. It was another 'first', appealing to her urge for efficient administration and 'to do the women's cause great good', though it was not a sig-nificant move in her career. She contributed to the weekly meetings, and produced a statistical report about London educational needs – any-thing she undertook she tackled thoroughly. But her life was already overwhelmingly busy, with the East London Children's Hospital, her own dispensary and night calls. Finding that the School Board took more time than she could spare, she resigned three years later, to be replaced by her sister Alice, now back after nearly ten years in India and very ready to be involved[33] – 'a great card for the meetings, she speaks admirably and in a most attractive way', as Elizabeth wrote to Emily Davies.[34]

Alice's husband, Herbert Cowell, seems to have been less sympathetic to the women's movement, and was soon to show his stuffy hostility to Elizabeth's aims by another excursion into *Blackwood's Magazine*:

> If it would not emasculate the female sex too much, we would suggest that they would have much more chance of attaining medical diplomas if, instead of asserting identical claims with men, to study in the same dissecting and lecture rooms, and an identical right to practise, they would limit themselves to claiming women and children as their appropriate patients ... they should have in view as the ultimate aim of female development, not merely the success of vulgar self-assertion, but improved relations to man and his descendants.[35]

Not a way for a brother-in-law to write even in private, let alone in print.

There was a further major change coming to Elizabeth's life – her fast-growing friendship with Anderson. She met him first at the hospital interview in March, was invited to see him in the summer when he was with his regiment – the London Scottish – on Wimbledon Common, wrote him a ten-page letter from an extraordinary adventurous holiday she had with her brother Sam and young sister Josephine visiting the battlefront of the Franco-Prussian War in September,[36] and in October had made him chairman of her election committee for Marylebone. Naturally she saw a good deal of him in the course of the election, and a month after the poll they became engaged.

'Next to the approaching nuptials of the Princess Louise with the Marquis of Lorne, the announcement that Miss Garrett is about to assume the bonds of matrimony is the great theme of conversation in social circles.'[37] *The Lancet*, enjoying the gossip, went on to wonder whether Elizabeth would continue to practise medicine, and asserted (wrongly) that as a married woman with no separate legal existence she would at any rate have to leave the school board.[38] (It was quite a possibility, though, for two schoolmistresses were made to resign in 1890 when it was discovered that they had got married;[39] married women generally could not legally stay in the profession until the Education Act of 1944, and it was not until 1946 that women were allowed to remain in the Civil Service if they married.) Some in the women's movement felt that Elizabeth was sacrificing her ideals for her personal happiness. They too were totally wrong. The marriage, as it turned out, was a wonderful partnership, and an example of how a woman – admittedly as long as she had enough money to have all

Elizabeth Garrett and James Skelton Anderson - Engagement photograph 1871

domestic needs taken off her hands – could combine her career with a family. Anderson was a successful businessman in a shipping firm, but with his brother a doctor at the Middlesex and his sister struggling for medical training in Edinburgh, there was plenty of medical tradition in his family.

Elizabeth went to Aldeburgh to break the news just before Christmas, and Anderson followed. He charmed her mother with his biblical knowledge, and her young sisters with his stories and party skills, but took longer to win over Newson, who worried that Elizabeth was throwing away her career. On Christmas day Elizabeth wrote to Millicent (already married to Henry Fawcett):

I quite meant to write to you yesterday, but on Friday night my horizon was suddenly changed by Mr Anderson's asking me to marry him. We are engaged. I do hope, my dear, you will not think I have meanly deserted my post. I think it need not prove to be so and I believe that he would regret it as much as I or you would. I am sure that the woman question will never be solved in any complete way so long as marriage is thought to be incompatible with freedom and with an independent career, and I think there is a very good chance that we may be able to do something to discourage this notion.

He came down one train after me yesterday and is already quite at home with every one. I hope you will like him and that Harry will too when you meet. This afternoon we have all been on the ice, he introduced himself to Aldebro' on it (having been hidden in the Corporation pew this morning) and won a favourable verdict by beating them all.

The dear parents are very pleased about it, tho' the father was I fancy a little disappointed that I should marry at all. However they like him, which is a great point.

I am very happy, dear Milly. I think we shall be married at Easter – there is nothing to wait for as our joint income will be a very good one and we are both certainly old enough.[40]

She was 34, two years older than him, and it was to be, for those times, an unusual partnership; each was to go their own way in their career, respecting and admiring the other. The first Married Women's Property Act, which gave women the right to keep their own earnings, had been passed in 1869 (it was not until 1882 that this was extended to inherited property),[41] and between them they did have plenty of money. Elizabeth was not a great spender: 'I should *very* much like to be married in London, entirely without millinery, and almost without cookery', she wrote to Anderson, and to have 'a common purse to which each contributed and from which each could draw'.[42] It was to be a marriage between equals – 'fancy my being "given away"'! she added, 'monstrous and ludicrous notion, 'tho lucky no one ever tried to do it.' She managed to persuade him that they did not need to start their married life in a bigger house than 20 Upper Berkeley Street, though she did agree to employ a third maid and to accept a sealskin jacket and a carriage. The jacket was embarrassingly grander than her usual style: 'if it would suit you to call here, we could go to the Old Masters together', she wrote, 'I feel sure that I should be shy in the sealskin unless with you'.[43]

Alice was as delighted as everyone else. 'I have felt so full of dear Elizabeth's news all this week & should have dearly liked a talk about her with some one who did not regard her solely from the "celebrity" point of view, as naturally most people do here', she wrote to her mother.[44] And the next week she added, to her father, 'I rejoice in the engagement as heartily as is possible without knowing him. A happy marriage seems to me the very best thing now we could wish for, for her & her career & "the cause" & every one & everything concerned'.[45]

The surgeon Sir James Paget (who had been helpful to Elizabeth Blackwell at St Bartholomew's back in 1850) congratulated her on both the Marylebone election and her engagement: 'he asked me what I liked best, being the elect of 50,000 or of one. I said I rather despised the 50,000. He thought nothing could be happier on beginning public life than to have 50,000 and to despise them in comparison with one. I liked his quiet way of assuming that I was really beginning public life, not leaving it'.[46]

They were married on 9 February by James Skelton Anderson's cousin the Reverend James Anderson. 'In all my mass of affairs this week I believe you have never been told the hour', Elizabeth wrote to Millicent, 'It is 8.30. Do come, my dearie, and get Harry up in time too. Breakfast at 9.30.'[47] There were only 30 guests, all of them relations except Emily Davies; Elizabeth (unlike Millicent) was not asked to promise to obey.

Honeymoon plans were minimal – Elizabeth had suggested a week-end in an inn near Dorking: 'it would be a great satisfaction to me not to be suspected of being a bride, and no one would, I think, suspect it, however happy we were, if we were walking and without luggage. We should probably be thought lunatics instead'.[48]

They did better than that, though, for there is a letter, self-consciously signed E. Garrett Anderson, describing an alarming ascent of Snowdon, clutching each other's hands through mist and frozen snow. 'I am very happy dear Father', she wrote, 'this week has shown me more than ever that I have won a prize.'[49]

9

The Fawcetts and Academic Life

A talk of college and of ladies' rights
Tennyson, *The Princess*

Unlike traditional Victorian fathers who were only too anxious to marry off their daughters, Newson was reluctant to accept his future sons-in-law. We have seen him disapproving of Herbert Cowell (cautiously giving Alice her return fare to India), and we have seen his dismay when he thought Elizabeth might throw away her hard-won career. Half-way between these two traumas he had to face Millicent's marriage to Henry Fawcett.

Not long after Millicent had got to know Fawcett, Newson met him at a gathering of the British Association, liked him, and invited him to Alde House in October 1866. 'If you invite Fawcett to stay with you', he was warned, 'he will want to marry Milly'; Newson did not believe it – 'stuff and nonsense' was his reputed response – and the engagement took him by storm.[1] Henry, in spite of his blindness, had already established his career as the first Professor of Political Economy at Cambridge and the Liberal Member of Parliament for Brighton – but Millicent was still only nineteen.

Newson, grunting and groaning, 'for his sole pleasure' insisted on a month of separation. Millicent's mother made matters worse by saying that she was 'tormented by the idea that very likely, now he has had a little quiet time to think of what he has done, Mr Fawcett may heartily regret what has passed'.[2] A tactful letter from Henry himself to Mrs Garrett helped to cut the waiting time, and Louie wrote what turned out to be her final gesture of support: 'I do think Milly is admirably fitted to be happy as the wife of a man who is intensely interested in public work – to enjoy the society which this state of things will bring her into – and to make her husband very happy and proud too'.[3] The marriage, in Aldeburgh church the following April only two months after Louie's death, was a slightly muted occasion, but there were flags on Aldeburgh houses and Millicent was a proper bride in white satin and orange blossom. And in spite of his blindness Henry cared a great deal about how Millicent looked. Ray Strachey has left an enthusiastic description:

Millicent's wedding to Henry Fawcett, 1867

She was very small, and looked all the smaller beside her huge husband; but she was, and appeared to be, in radiant health. She had a lovely complexion, and masses of shining brown hair, and a certain calmness of expression which corresponded to the serenity of her mind. Her voice, which was very clear, was all that Harry could judge; but he was always asking his friends how Milly was looking, and begging them for descriptions of her face. He took, too, the greatest interest in her clothes; and though Milly herself was not by nature fond of fine raiment, there is no doubt that she dressed to please her blind husband.[4]

'You ask me what we in India think of the marriage', Alice wrote to her father:

I think we are all rejoicing in it as heartily as one can rejoice in an unknown brother-in-law. The dear little sister seems so thoroughly happy & contented ... Trottie [Millicent] overslept herself & then came down in a hurry with a rough head & very sleepy eyes to bid me goodbye the morning we left London together & I have a distinct picture in my mind of the little slight girlish figure in her short dress which I am trying in vain to alter into somebody matronly and dignified & altogether older looking.[5]

A recent essay on Henry Fawcett described him as 'insufferably cheerful'.[6] But the cheerfulness attracted Millicent, and some of it seems to have rubbed off on her. Through all her endless struggles and frustrations, her patience and optimism helped her to keep a determined good temper, insisting that she got great enjoyment out of life. 'Milly, Milly, where are you?' her blind husband would call, 'are you enjoying yourself?' And when Henry died she managed to recover by throwing herself back into her work. There was obvious pleasure in music or in travel but also, running through all the accounts of her long political life, there was an enviable ability to get pleasure from observing people and their behaviour, whatever their views. But her life was by no means trouble free. Ray Strachey in her biography, and Millicent herself in her memoir *What I Remember*, both make one suspect that they protest too much in endlessly emphasizing how happy she was.

While her sisters fought for their professional education, Millicent was thrown into hers by her marriage to a radical politician. This was her apprenticeship. Elizabeth was a qualified doctor before she married at the age of 34, and was supported and encouraged in her chosen life by her ship-owning husband. Already famous, she kept her own name and became known as Elizabeth Garrett Anderson. Millicent, marrying two months before her twentieth birthday, still 'looked like a schoolgirl rather than a married woman', as John Bright's sister remembered many years later, and dropped the name 'Garrett', becoming known simply as Millicent Fawcett. For seventeen years Millicent was to work happily and closely with Henry, but at 37 she was widowed, with more than half of her life left to struggle with pioneering ideas on her own.

By 1867 Henry Fawcett was prominent among the small group of Members of Parliament, led by John Stuart Mill, who campaigned for votes for women. Millicent, wrote Henry's friend Leslie Stephen, 'was in entire sympathy with his principles, shared his intellectual and political labours, and was a main source of most of the happiness and success of his later life'.[7] More than that, because of Henry's blindness Millicent became his reader and constant companion – Louis Braille had died in 1852, but official books and papers were not available to Henry Fawcett as they were to David Blunkett, the blind politician in Tony Blair's cabinet 130 years later. So she was totally involved in his work, whether it meant going down a Cornish copper mine so that she could describe it to him, or discussing any of his political interests – the 1867 Reform Bill, the abolition of religious tests at universities, the extension of the factory acts, the poverty of agricultural labourers, the preservation of common land,[8] Indian finance and the rights of native Indians. Alice, in a supportive letter from India, wrote that she was appalled to learn from Henry's campaigns that English farm labourers were only getting 12 shillings a week, and she hoped their strikes would succeed.[9] Henry opposed the 1878 Afghan War and Irish Home Rule; as Postmaster General under Gladstone in 1880 he looked after his postal workers well, encouraged the employment of women, and started parcel post, postal orders, cheap telegrams and savings stamps.

Millicent's life was transformed. She had met Henry through her enthusiasm for Mill and all he stood for, and her occasional forays into London life had brought her to the edge of radical political causes. But now, to her intense pleasure, she was immersed in those causes, and found her beliefs welcome among her husband's friends as she was herself welcomed into his family. There were even occasional dinners with Mill, where she might meet Herbert Spencer and a battery of intellectuals. (As early as 1850 Spencer had written, in *Social Statistics*, that 'equity knows no difference of sex', and 'the rights of women are equal with those of men'.[10]) She read newspapers and parliamentary blue books so that she could interpret them for her husband, and she went to the Ladies' Gallery of the House of Commons for important debates – proudly hearing Mill refer to Elizabeth's success in her effort to open the medical profession to women. Not that the 'Oriental seclusion' of being behind the grille in the Ladies' Gallery was much pleasure: 'the interstices of the heavy brass work were not large enough to allow the victims who sat behind it to focus it so that both eyes looked through the same hole. It was like using a gigantic pair of spectacles which did not fit, and made the ladies' Gallery a grand place for getting headaches'.[11]

It was in July 1867, less than two months after her wedding, that Millicent became a member of the new committee of 'The London National Society for Women's Suffrage'. 'I sometimes tell my children', John Bright's sister wrote to her many years later, 'how when you first came to our Woman's Suffrage Committees, those held in Mrs Taylor's at Aubrey House . . . you listened to opinions and suggestions as they fell from different members, and would then throw in your own counsel, which always seemed the right thing for us to accept'.[12]

At the first public meeting for women's suffrage, Clementia Taylor

Millicent reading to Henry, about 1868–9

and Millicent were the only two women speakers among a distinguished list of men including Henry Fawcett, John Stuart Mill and Charles Kingsley; a fellow Member of Parliament complained that 'two ladies, wives of Members of this House' had disgraced themselves by speaking in public.

There was excitement and challenge too in the other side to her new life. As Professor of Political Economy, Henry had to spend at least eighteen weeks of the year in Cambridge. Cambridge in the 1860s was still full of rigid hierarchies and conventions. Millicent could look at it all with detached amusement but, guided by her husband, she could also make friends and get enormous pleasure from being at the edge of the university, from meeting a wide variety of people and, under the guidance of Sedley Taylor, from hearing wonderful music. Like every generation at Cambridge, she believed she was seeing the last eccentrics. Throughout her life she had pleasure in observing people and treasuring odd remarks or unexpected behaviour. Her memoir is full of good Cambridge stories, written with wit and affection – Dr Kennedy, sure his *Latin Grammar* was the best possible and that everyone must have read it; Dr Sidgwick, who 'stammered with great skill'; Dr Moulton, Master of Christ's College, whose little son excused himself when young Hester Peile beat him to a Latin prize by saying 'well, papa, you see Hester has such a clever father'; then there was Dr Geldart, Master of Henry's college Trinity Hall, who had been left great wealth by a stranger he had been kind to when travelling on a stage coach:

> The younger fellows of Trinity Hall used to say that they were spending their lives convoying old ladies across Regent Circus, or performing other deeds of desperate daring on behalf of strangers, but no one had ever left them a fortune. The Master of Trinity Hall was a devoted fisherman, and he became in time a great judge of wine and food. When he ventured into the sphere of theology he was commonly believed to have said that to him the strongest evidence of design in the work of creation was that when salmon went out turbot came in.[13]

And she could appreciate the eccentricities of Mrs Geldart, who belonged 'almost to the eighteenth century', and not hold it against her that she was strongly opposed to women's suffrage.[14]

She had much pleasure at that time, too, in being able to see a good deal of her undergraduate brother Sam, the next to her in age and always her best friend among her brothers. So Millicent enjoyed Cambridge, and Henry's sister reported to Elizabeth that she was 'filling her place at Cambridge most satisfactorily, managing the house well, doing all that Harry wants done, & at the same time keeping up her own interest in things independently of him'.[15]

She had arrived in Cambridge at the right time, for the movement for higher education for women there was just starting. Spurred by Emily Davies, in 1865 the Cambridge Syndicate had, for the first time, opened their Local Examination (for sixteen to seventeen-year-olds) to girls, after an experimental examination held privately two years earlier.[16] Henry was among those who had supported the move, and he was also among a small group of professors who were opening their lectures to women – a group that grew to include three-quarters of all the university professors by 1875.[17] Cambridge was by no means alone in this. A

'Ladies' Educational Association', started in Edinburgh in 1867 to put various existing lectures on a more organized basis, had attracted 600 women in its first two years,[18] while the North of England Council for Promoting the Higher Education of Women was busy running lectures in 23 centres by 1870.[19] There were similar opportunities in London, where Lady Amberley was going to 'the same courses as those at University College' on 'Eng. Lit.' and on Experimental Physics.[20] There were Huxley's lectures that Elizabeth had been to at the South Kensington Museum. In 1860, Huxley had written to Sir Charles Lyell: 'I am far from wishing to place any obstacle in the way of the intellectual advancement and development of women. On the contrary, I don't see how we are to make any permanent advancement while one-half of the race is sunk, as nine-tenths of women are, in mere ignorant parsonese superstitions'.[21]

The Royal Institution, from its foundation in 1800, had organized courses for the general public, including women; Humphry Davy's chemistry lectures were so popular and fashionable that Albermarle Street would become blocked with elegant carriages. Other places could be less welcoming, even when women showed their enthusiasm – Caroline Fox noted in her diary in 5 June 1838 that 'Wheatstone [the physicist] has been giving lectures, and in fact is in the middle of a course. No ladies are admitted, unluckily; the Bishop of London forbade it, seeing how they congregated to Lyell's, which prohibition so offended that gentleman [Lyell] that he resigned his professorship'.

The enthusiasm, which had been flourishing in blue stocking circles for some time, grew throughout the century. Caroline Slemmer, visiting Cambridge from America and shortly to become Mrs Richard Jebb, wrote home that 'society is very pleasant' and that she was 'planning to attend Prof Sedgwick's lectures on Zoology, and Prof Fawcett's on Moral Philosophy, and if I can, I want to gain admittance to Vernon Harcourt's course on International Law. Then, every Friday we are to go to Mr Harcourt's German readings.'[22] At that time Alice was also educating herself, studying German with a friend in India. Millicent was working on Dante with her friend Emma Miller in the mornings and going to two courses of lectures; Elizabeth commented that Henry's sister Maria was 'quite astonished with the ability she showed in discussing their subjects afterwards. Of course Maria is easily astonished but I have no doubt Milly will develop quite unusual brain power if she can keep herself from being absorbed and distracted by the interruptions of life'.[23]

'It is no uncommon thing in Cambridge', Millicent wrote in 1868, 'for a professor to have a course of lectures largely and regularly attended by ladies'. This was in her first published work, an article in *Macmillan's Magazine*[24] in April 1868, called 'The Education of Women of the Middle and Upper Classes'. If the title seems disconcerting today, remember that it was only in 1870 that an Education Act set up School Boards to provide elementary schools for all where needed; higher education for the working classes was still hardly discussed. The article brought Millicent £7, the first money she had earned, and she sent it to the fund for Mill's election expenses. In the article she deplored the lack of structured education and mental training offered to girls, particularly in any kind of mathematics. Even Christ's Hospital, she wrote, originally meant for both boys and girls, now gave a full education to about 1,200 boys while their girls' school simply trained about 40 girls to be domestic servants[25]: 'we should therefore wish to see equal educational advantages given to both sexes; to open all the professions to women; and, if they prove worthy of them, to allow them to share with men all those distinctions, intellectual, literary, and political, which are such valuable incentives to mental and moral progress'.

Millicent was of course by no means alone in these views, but she was highly articulate and well placed. Her time as a leader was to come later; now she could fit into the group of reforming academics, and contribute powerfully to a growing movement. And as if to confound those who claimed that intellectual activity was incompatible with motherhood, in the same month that this article appeared in *Macmillan's*, she gave birth to her daughter Philippa.

Henry encouraged Millicent to write, and her next publication, 'The Medical and General Education of Women', appeared in the *Fortnightly Review* of November 1868. Here again she pleaded for good education to be open to all, blind to race, creed or gender, and she praised American schools for giving boys and girls 'exactly similar training and the same advantages' and for training female teachers to a high standard. 'The object of all education ought to be to produce good and cultured men and women', she wrote, and it was 'vastly important for national welfare that mothers of children should be persons of large, liberal and cultured minds'. The article was strongly written, moving Alice to write home that 'Milly's fame as a "terrible little Radical" has spread to the Cambridge men here'.[26] In the same article Millicent argued that it would be better to try to insert women gradually into the existing system at Cambridge than to found a new institution in the hope that the whole new unit would become accepted.

For it was in 1866 that Emily Davies had started to campaign for a college for women. A committee was formed to promote the idea; Alice became the local secretary in Calcutta. Three years later the institution that was to become Girton College opened with five students in Benslow House, Hitchin, half-way between Cambridge and London. The students were all required to study for a full tripos course. Like Elizabeth Garrett, Emily Davies was firmly opposed to any idea of a soft option for girls, however much they might have suffered from lack of earlier education; indeed Elizabeth, still Emily's disciple, was among the first subscribers to Emily's college and at her suggestion her husband Skelton joined her on the committee in 1871 – though he soon resigned, disagreeing with the provision of religious instruction and services.[27] In her speech to the Social Science Congress in 1868, Emily asserted that 'the College is intended to be a dependency, a living branch of Cambridge. It will aim at no higher position than, say, that of Trinity College'. As *The Times* commented, 'such a degree of humility will not be considered excessive'.[28] *The Times* editorial concluded: 'that education will always be the best for girls which is the most domestic, and English homes will always be the schools in which English wives and mothers can best be trained'.

The group of campaigners that included the Fawcetts would have disagreed profoundly with that conclusion, but they were not yet proposing a new college. They had a more pragmatic approach than Emily Davies, believing in building gradually on the existing foundations of 'pick-n-mix' open lectures, and establishing new courses designed for girls who had not had the same educational background as the men and were not ready to tackle a tripos. It was not such an odd idea, because in those relaxed days not all the men tackled it either: 'in the early 1900s a fifth of the undergraduates did not actually complete degrees, a third still aimed for an ordinary BA degree, study for which could be spread over many years, leaving just under half studying for an honours degree, which normally had to be completed in a minimum of nine consecutive terms of study'.[29]

Henry Sidgwick (unlike Henry Fawcett) believed too that it would be wrong for a new women's college to adopt the old-fashioned classical curriculum; rather, he thought this could be an opportunity to branch out into the subjects he and his friends wanted introduced to Cambridge generally – into modern languages, science, and social science. They found a disciple in Anne Jemima Clough, sister of the poet Arthur Hugh Clough, who had run her own small school in Ambleside (where the seven-year-old Mary Arnold[30] went as a pupil), had organized lectures in the North of England and 'worked for education because she believed in education, not because it was a part of the Women's Movement'.[31] To Emily's fury Miss Clough, who was to become the first Principal of Newnham College, was prepared to accept the approach of different treatment and special examinations for girls. There was a meeting to consider the proposed plan of lectures for women – no mention yet of anything more formal, whatever long-term ambitions anyone may have had – and the Fawcetts were asked to lend their drawing room for the discussion. As Millicent wrote later:

> Professor Henry Sidgwick, the real founder of Newnham, asked me and my husband to lend our drawing-room for the first meeting ever held in Cambridge in its support. So far as I can remember, this must have been in 1870. We were then occupying a furnished house which possessed a drawing-room of suitable size for such an occasion. I therefore recognise that the birth of Newnham under my roof was more or less accidental; nevertheless, such is human folly, I go on being proud and pleased about it. I know that Philippa was a little baby girl at the time, but was old enough to be brought in at the tea-drinking stage at the end of the proceedings and to toddle about in her white frock and blue sash among the guests.[32]

It did indeed turn out to be 'the birth of Newnham'. Four years after the first British suffrage society had met in Elizabeth's dining room, the first meeting for Newnham was held in Millicent's drawing room.

A few days before this meeting Millicent had written to Mill's step-daughter Helen Taylor that: 'all the promoters of this scheme feel that it will probably be the means of ultimately admitting women to the University. They do not urge this publicly in favour of their scheme, because it would frighten so many excellent people who are now willing to help us'.[33] It was a different approach from Emily's, less blatant and challenging, but the goal was the same. Millicent was involved in organizing the lectures, raising money, recruiting, encouraging and entertaining students, and was to be on the Newnham College council from 1881 to 1909.

In 1871 Miss Clough was persuaded to move to Cambridge to run the house that Henry Sidgwick had rented for the new group of five students – a scheme that Emily resented, calling it 'the serpent which is gnawing at our vitals'.[34] The idea had been rumbling on for some time. As early as May 1868 Alice had written cheerfully from India:

The hostel at Cambridge idea is a capital one. I wonder whether residence may be kept in the same way at Oxford? If so I should like to go home I think and start a house there. Herbert could go on circuit & I could take care of my young ladies – Really though if only one could get the under-graduates it would be a splendid life. I wonder if I could get the promise of Louie's little girls & Ethel [her brother Newson's] if we should start in it some 12 years hence – or whether they must all go to Cambridge.[35]

As well as disagreeing about the tripos, Emily did not 'care to have a set of lawless young Radicals [presumably Sidgwick and Fawcett] thinking it clever to disbelieve, and setting aside Christian teachers as narrow old fogies'[36] – there was never to be a chapel at Newnham. In a public lecture in November 1871 Millicent, for her part, seemed to welcome Emily's plans, saying that 'nothing can be more desirable than that the Hitchin college should ultimately prove completely successful'. But she then went on to point out how hard it would be for such a college to raise all the money it needed, compared with the economical and financially sound scheme developed from the Cambridge Lectures.[37]

So Emily and the Sidgwicks went their separate ways, though they came together in the 1880 campaign for official recognition. The vote in February 1881 gave a majority of ten to one in favour of admitting women to the Honours examinations. 'You will have heard of the triumph of the Ladies at Cambridge', Charles Darwin wrote to his son George, 'the majority was so enormous that many men on both sides did not think it worth voting. The minority was received with jeers'.[38] Yet seven years later Charles Darwin's wife Emma could still write: 'the fact is that I do not care about the higher education of women, though I ought to do so'.[39] When the proposal to give degrees to women was debated in 1896 there was fierce opposition – including, surprisingly, from Alfred Marshall, Fawcett's successor as Professor of Political Economy and the husband of Mary Paley, herself a distinguished economist and one of the first Newnham students. Degrees for women were not to come in Cambridge until much later – titular degrees in 1921 and full degrees not until 1948.

Clough, Sidgwick, Peile, Kennedy – all these names are familiar to Cambridge students from the fine group of buildings by Basil Champneys that eventually rose on the south-west edge of Cambridge to form Newnham College. The Fawcett Building, pleasant but less distinguished, was to follow in 1938, named for Philippa because of her triumph in the mathematical tripos, and for her parents.[40] Women's colleges came to Oxford nearly ten years after the foundation of Newnham and Girton – starting with Lady Margaret Hall in 1878 and Somerville in 1879.[41] America had already thought of women's education; starting in 1837 with Mount Holyoke (Massachusetts), there was the co-educational Quaker college Swarthmore (Pennsylvania) in 1864, the women's college Vassar (in the state of New York) in 1861, Smith (Massachusetts) in 1871, Radcliffe (near Harvard) in 1879, and Bryn Mawr (Pennsylvania) in 1885. In 1878 University College London became the first university in England to admit women on the same terms as men.

Elizabeth's medical expertise was recruited by Barbara Bodichon for the education debate when the neurologist Dr Henry Maudsley wrote an alarming article in the *Fortnightly Review*, saying:

> It will have to be considered whether women can scorn delights, and live laborious days of intellectual exercise and production, without injury to their functions as the conceivers, mothers, and nurses of children. For it would be an ill thing, if it should so happen, that we got the advantages of a quantity of female intellectual work at the price of a puny, enfeebled, and sickly race.

He admitted, though, that 'a system of education that is framed to fit [women] to be nothing more than the superintendents of a household and the ornaments of a drawing-room, is one that does not do justice to their nature, and cannot be seriously defended'. But, he hastened to add, 'it by no means follows, however, that it would be right to model an improved system exactly upon that which has commended itself as the best for men'.[42]

Not intimidated by Maudsley's seniority and distinction, Elizabeth replied indignantly that no one was trying, as he claimed, 'to change women into men', but 'the single aim of those anxious to promote a higher and more serious education for women is to make the best they can of the materials at their disposal'. There was no reason, she asserted, why the physiological differences between girls and boys should affect their ability to study, and anyway girls would be well past puberty before they tackled the proposed higher education courses. They needed such courses for their own sakes and for the sake of their children:

> It is not easy for those whose lives are full to overflowing of the interests which accumulate as life matures, to realise how insupportably dull the life

of a young woman just out of the schoolroom is apt to be, nor the powerful influence for evil this dullness has upon her health and morals. There is no tonic in the pharmacopoeia to be compared with happiness, and happiness worth calling such is not known where the days drag along filled with make-believe occupations and dreary, sham amusements.[43]

Looking after Philippa, working for women's education, acting as secretary for her blind husband (until 1871 when a paid secretary was appointed), Millicent could not complain that she had to 'spend a long life in comparative idleness'.[44] There was of course plenty of domestic help, though on visits to her family in Aldeburgh, or her husband's family in Salisbury, Millicent would take the baby with her without a nurse. There were to be no more children though, and perhaps Philippa resented this, for when they got a dog she remarked that 'now, if people ask me if I have a brother I shall say yes'.

But Millicent still had spare intellectual energy and, encouraged by Henry and by their friend Alexander Macmillan, in 1870 she published her first book, *Political Economy for Beginners*. It was immensely successful, but not everyone praised it – some Cambridge economics dons were scornful of the 'howling croppers in it in regard to mere matters of fact'.[45] Designed 'to make Political Economy a more popular study in boys' and girls' schools', it is a tough little book to read, full of John Stuart Mill's philosophy and strongly influenced by Henry. 'It ought to be a success', Alice wrote loyally, 'it has the field to itself I fancy as a school book'.[46] Millicent gave lectures on political economy at Queen's College, Harley Street, for at least two terms in 1879.

The Fawcetts' belief in liberalism and free trade sometimes led them into dangerously deep waters where compassion could be drowned. In *Political Economy for Beginners*, for example, Millicent argued that 'charitable donations often interfere mischievously with the operation of competition'. The distress caused in Lancashire by shortage of cotton during the American Civil War should not, she thought, have been relieved by charity, which 'permanently pauperised' a large part of the population; the unemployed workers should have been left to find themselves jobs in linen or woollen manufacture in other towns.[47] Perhaps this objection to state interference owed something to the influence of their friend Herbert Spencer. It was an early form of Norman Tebbitt's 'get on your bike', an extension of Henry's point in the *British Quarterly* in the previous year, that 'the loans obtained from the Government encouraged these operatives to remain in their own county in a state of semi-starvation'.[48] It contrasts starkly with Mrs Gaskell's 'I only hope that those who have made such large fortunes during these last two years by manufactures will give of their abundance to the work-people in their distress – however improvident these latter may have been'.[49]

Millicent's writings may not have been her greatest achievements, but she wrote clearly, vigorously and, as her letters and her memoir show, often wittily, although her didactic writing could be heavier. There were two more books on economics – *Essays and Lectures* (1872), written jointly with her husband; and *Tales in Political Economy* (1874), an effort to get the messages across through moral stories. Then came the novel *Janet Doncaster*; it reads as a fairly undistinguished tract on drunkenness, but it had some success, and Elizabeth wrote that it would make Millicent so rich that 'we shall see you and Harry careering in the park every day on steeds of your own buying and feeding'. Millicent was clear-minded enough to realize that the book was selling because of her name not because of its merits – she wrote a second novel, published under another name, which failed and cannot even be traced. She seems to have been the only one in the family to write anything not directly connected with their work.

Opinions of Women on Women's Suffrage,[50] a collection of quotations from prominent women in favour of the right to vote (published in 1879), listed Millicent in the unusual guise of a representative of the world of literature – the author of *Political Economy for Beginners*. The prominent women included Elizabeth and five other doctors, as well as Emily Davies, Frances Buss, Henrietta Barnett, Florence Nightingale (who thought the book important but was cynical about how much it would help), and the recently deceased Harriet Martineau and Mary Somerville.

Millicent loved writing, far more than she ever liked public speaking. Her 1991 biographer David Rubinstein lists her as author of around seventeen pamphlets and 280 articles. She enjoyed history, and over the years wrote three full-length biographies[51] and two books of essays on famous women. There was something of a novelist's approach here, for she had an ability – perhaps too romantic an ability – to imagine the life she was describing. Her memoir and her account of her travels in Palestine are more worth reading. But her most passionate writing was about the struggle for women's suffrage, not only in influential articles but also in two histories of the movement.[52] She was following the mission Emily had suggested long ago in Aldeburgh.

The Fawcetts and Political Life

The law which allows every male fool, not absolutely idiotic or insane, to vote for members of Parliament, and forbids the very cleverest and best educated woman, is clearly no specimen of the perfection of human reason.

Punch, 2 April 1870

Millicent's London life, although she said she had to be 'a dragon over every unnecessary expenditure', seems to have been comfortable Victorian middle-class. She and Henry moved in 1874 from a small house fifteen minutes' walk from the House of Commons to a nearby house in Vauxhall with a garden of three-quarters of an acre. A letter explained the need for a 'promising young girl' to be kitchen maid: 'We keep no man or boy, therefore the little maid would have to do a good deal of rough work, clean boots, scrub steps, fill coal scuttles etc. Sound health is accordingly indispensable. After doing this sort of thing daily her work would be to help the housemaid in the morning & the cook in the afternoon'.[1] Millicent was expecting to have her time free for her own affairs.

One of the minor problems of running two homes was where to keep books. Cambridge was so well stocked with libraries that Millicent decided it was their London bookshelves 'which needed nourishing and cherishing' and that books that had to be housed but were never read could be banished to Cambridge. Dr Sidgwick, learning how the curious collection came to be there, commented 'I d-did rather wonder what your p-principle of selection had been'.[2] When Edward Fitzgerald, horrified to hear that fourteen-year-old Philippa was reading Thackeray and George Eliot, tried to wean her on to his selection from George Crabbe, the kind present was added to the Cambridge books.

There was, Henry wrote, 'perfect intellectual sympathy' between the Fawcetts – 'Happy Warriors', as David Rubinstein has called them. If Millicent owed her political education to Henry, she in her turn noticeably encouraged his ideas on women's suffrage; Alice, in her Raj community that read the English newspapers, wrote from India to her mother that 'Mr Fawcett is generally treated to mild chaff upon the "lover-like ardour" with which he took up the question'.[3] Millicent

branched out into political activity after her wedding, and was immediately busy writing articles and, at a time when women hardly ever
spoke in public, took part in meetings round the country and helped to
mobilize friends in parliament. Her first platform appearance was at the
Social Science Association Congress in 1868, when she read a paper on
'Economy and Trade' written by her blind husband. 'The impression of
her early speaking, recorded again and again by her hearers', Ray
Strachey wrote, 'was always the same: clear, logical, self-possessed, and
pre-eminently "ladylike", as the phrase of the period ran. She looked
charming and "modest", she was beautifully dressed, her voice could be
heard distinctly, she made reasonable remarks in a natural manner, and
she sometimes made excellent jokes'.[4]

Not every hearer was as enthusiastic as Ray Strachey liked to think.
Lady Amberley's caustic diary recorded a Women's Suffrage meeting in
Hanover Square Rooms in 1870 where 'Miss Taylor made a long and
much studied speech; it was good but too like acting. Mrs Grote's was
short but natural – Mrs Fawcett's uninteresting & Mrs Pet. Taylor
(chairman) was inaudible fr. Sore throat. It went off very well and was a
great success'.[5]

In 1870, to the alarm of some of her husband's Election Committee,
and to the horror of the local paper which thought 'female political
orators we must regard as altogether intolerable', Millicent made a
speech on the 'Electoral Disabilities of Women' in his Brighton con-
stituency. There had, though, been 'female political orators' a century
earlier when ladies had not only supported a boycott against slave-
produced sugar, but had taken part in debates against the slave trade.[6]
And after the 1833 Act that ended all slavery in the British Empire, many
British women remained involved in a campaign to end slavery everywhere. Millicent was carrying the tradition a bit further by speaking on
an election platform, and she did it nervously but with great success.
Her speech was so effective that it was circulated as a pamphlet; two
years later Rhoda attacked the same theme in her own impassioned
way.[7] Some of the family worried, though. Alice, in India with her
rather conservative husband, wrote to her mother: 'I share your regrets
over Milly's lectures. It is a sensational way of getting one's say said, that
no doubt the Brighton people will appreciate but I very much doubt it
having any really good results'.[8] And she added with elder sister caution
that 'opinion in anyone so young as Milly must be more like purposes
than facts I think'. Didn't she know that her husband set out his opinions in *Blackwood's* at the age of seventeen?

Millicent listed thirteen arguments sometimes used against giving women the vote, refuted them all with elegant logic, and ended with a quotation from Herbert Spencer that summed up her philosophy: 'equity knows no difference of sex. The law of equal freedom necessarily applies to the whole race – female as well as male. The same reasoning which establishes that law for men may be used with equal cogency on behalf of women'.[9] She repeated the speech to a large audience in Dublin and was, as Alice reported to their mother, fulsomely praised by the *Irish Times*: 'Mrs Fawcett's extensive reading, her speculative power, her close reasoning, her evident aptitude for social and political discussions, do not appear to have robbed her of one natural grace, nor interfered with an exquisite feminine culture except to enhance it'.[10] She was busy on the lecture circuit the following year, and Elizabeth contributed with a meeting at Aberdeen because, she said, 'giving women the franchise would be a very great step towards the uplifting of the whole sex'.

There are many accounts of Millicent in action. Alice commented on a rather personal report in a Calcutta paper in 1872:

> The article was very vulgar and impertinent although the description of her was intended to be very complimentary. She was described as very young pretty & ladylike, with glossy hair, dove-like eyes & a complexion like a peach, dressed in lavender silk dress & gloves, a cashmere burnouse bordered with gold (which I recognised as our wedding present) & a bonnet that was a mere puff of feathers & tulle.[11]

Bismarck's famous phrase, 'politics is the art of the possible', dates from 1867. It is a philosophy that guided Millicent in her campaigns – whether for the gradual introduction of women into the universities in order not to 'frighten so many excellent people', or for the gradual extension of the franchise – even though her ultimate aims were ambitious. So (for once, differing from Henry) she was prepared to start by asking for the vote only for unmarried women ratepayers; others could be hitched on later. 'Society', she wrote, 'is one of those things which cannot be made – it must grow'.[12]

After the appointment of a secretary for Henry in 1871, Millicent had more time for her own activities. *Essays and Lectures* consisted of eight of Millicent's lectures and six of Henry's. It included her account (influenced by Mill) of the various forms of proportional representation.[13] Then there were two lectures about women's need for votes. In 'Why Women Require the Franchise' she explained how the power to

vote could help to right the injustices of education and of the legal
status of married women. Some progress for the women's cause had
been made with Richard Pankhurst's amendment to the Municipal
Corporations Bill of 1869; it had included women in the proposal to give
all ratepayers the vote in local elections, and made them eligible to vote
for the new school boards and boards of poor law guardians – or even,
like Elizabeth and Emily, to be elected as members of the school boards.
So, Millicent argued, if women could take part in municipal elections
and serve on school boards, why should they not take part in parliamentary elections? It might, she admitted, take many years, possibly the
rest of her life to achieve, but 'we will endure to the end, and never rest
satisfied with less than victory'.[14] In the second lecture, 'Electoral Disabilities of Women', she effectively demolished all the standard objections to giving the vote to women, mocking an MP's claim that
enfranchising women householders would 'disturb the whole foundation of society, obliterate the distinction of sex and the functions of the
sexes that have existed in every civilized community'. She added that
'the feeling of repugnance towards the exercise of political power by
women is not consistent; for no one feels this repugnance towards the
exercise of political power by Queen Victoria'.[15] And as Ray Strachey
has pointed out, there was a welcome new equality in the 1875 Salvation
Army declaration that 'the Army refuses to make any difference between
men and women as to rank, authority and duties, but opens the highest
positions to women as well as to men';[16] it had after all been founded by
William and Catherine Booth, famously a husband and wife team.

Millicent had worryingly stern Spencerian objections to the idea that
education could be made free for all children: 'If education is as
necessary as food and clothing (and if it is not there is no justification
for compulsion) why ought parents who bring children into the world
without being able to educate them, escape the odium of pauperism?'[17]
She argued that making it free by raising the rates would be hard on
those who had been provident and on those who could scarcely afford
the tax, while more taxation of the rich would hit profits and in the end
damage the labourer. When there was already disastrous dependence on
the Poor Law, 'free education would be an immense extension to all
classes of the poor of the system of out-door relief'. There would be no
incentive to economize or to limit families, for 'with a Poor Law which
gives a right of maintenance to every one, extended by an educational
system which provides free education for every one, pauperism and
intemperance will continue to flourish'.

'Intemperance' was one of Millicent's great concerns. Her stern views came partly from her fear that help for the poor might only leave them more money for drunkenness, the evil that had been the theme of *Janet Doncaster*. With all her belief in education, she could still write that:

> A general system of free education ought to be resisted because it would weaken the sense of parental obligation ... a parent ought to be punished if he makes other people pay for the education of his children, in order that he may have something more to spend in his own enjoyment. If, however, he is too poor to pay the school fees then there is just as much reason why he should be treated as a pauper as if he were unable to feed and clothe his children.[18]

Millicent was still sticking to this approach in 1889 when she opposed free school meals, and in the 1920s this same belief in private thrift and personal responsibility led her to attack proposals for mothers' pensions and family allowances – it was, she had written, a 'socialist nightmare of abolishing the ordinary responsibilities of marriage and substituting for them State salaries for mothers'.[19]

Henry agreed that 'it is no use helping those who show no desire to help themselves', and that 'the poor laws often give a most disastrous encouragement to improvidence'. Going beyond Spencer, he even thought that private charity was demoralizing, and that 'if a more healthy tone of public opinion prevailed, Society, instead of rewarding, would most severely condemn a man who brings children into the world without the means of adequately maintaining them'.[20] But though he was stern in his attitude to adults he was, in his concern for the needs and education of children, anxious that there should be compulsory attendance at the new board schools – though he too did not believe that education should be free.

Similarly Millicent, like Henry, parted from the accepted Liberal view in 1874 over a new Factory Bill. They objected to the proposals to reduce the legal limit of working hours for women, arguing that all adult workers should have equal standing, and that if women had shorter hours than men they would have less status and fewer opportunities. The Fawcetts spoke as one, but this line may have stemmed from Millicent, since Henry seems to have come to it only after his marriage. It was, Ray Strachey has written, the point of view of the official Women's Movement, though she herself thought it might have been better to try to extend the restrictions to men rather than to remove them from women.[21] Millicent argued in *The Times* that the proposals arose from 'the old Trade Union spirit to drive women out of certain trades where their competition is inconvenient. It is true that this cloven foot is dexterously hidden under the drapery of philanthropy and chivalry, but it peeps out from time to time in a manner that cannot be mistaken'.[22]

Women, she prophesied, would then be deprived of 'honest labour' and 'driven to the dismal alternative of starvation or prostitution'. The editors, while agreeing that 'philanthropy has its limits, and if injudiciously employed is apt to defeat its own ends' added that 'political economy is not the sole science of human welfare' and that the complicated problem of interference and control needed more study.[23] Anyway, the Fawcetts' maverick views got nowhere, and the act was passed in 1878, limiting factory work for women to 56 hours a week.

Elizabeth echoed these worries about trade unions putting up barriers against women:

> The medical schools are perfectly free to refuse to admit women; and as they live by being in favour with country medical men who are sending their sons up to London for a medical education, and who are not more free than their fellow creatures from the Trades Unionism which operates so powerfully against women in other directions, it is not likely the schools will doubt in which direction their interest lies.[24]

Individualism and belief in free trade did not stop the Fawcetts supporting trade unions when they thought it right to do so. In 1870 both Henry and Millicent spoke in support of a shoemaker friend, George Odger, who was standing as a trade union candidate against the official Liberal at a by-election. Henry's mother, a staunchly orthodox Liberal, was upset. 'At that time', Millicent wrote,

> It was an unheard-of thing for women to speak on election platforms, and that I had done this on behalf of a candidate who was in opposition to the Liberal Party was to her an almost unforgivable sin. I couldn't promise I would never do it again, but I did promise never to speak in Salisbury [the Fawcett family home town] unless she invited me to do so, and this promise, of course, I kept, and in course of time she did invite me and I accepted the invitation.[25]

In 1874 Millicent allowed her name to be used in support of both the National Union of Working Women and the Women's Protective and Provident League. Presiding over a meeting of the League in 1881, she deserted the ideal of a free market, boldly saying that if political economists thought that 'trades unions had absolutely no effect in raising the rate of wages', they should 'turn from their books and look at facts'.[26] Generally, though, her views were dominated by her belief in individualism, whether for free trade or for career opportunities for women. As she put it in a letter in 1877:

> I think the principal argument is like the argument for Free Trade – train the faculties by a sound and healthy education, and then allow these faculties free scope in whatever direction nature and natural gifts may indicate as the fittest ... The value of the opportunity of free development to the individual is so inestimable that a few mistakes and a few instances of misdirected energy are, in comparison, of no importance.[27]

Gaining in confidence, Millicent criticised Fitzjames Stephen, the brother of Henry's friend and biographer Leslie Stephen, for his outrageous views on women in his book *Liberty, Equality and Fraternity*. He had argued that husbands were like ships' captains, giving orders that their wives had to obey, so that in return they would be protected – 'the protection of losing all control over their own property' she countered, 'no legal right to the guardianship of their own children even after the death of their husbands'. As for the courtesies that Stephen insisted women gained in exchange, she dismissed the idea with scorn: 'it is quite an appalling thought to a woman in whom the English virtue of resistance to arbitrary authority is strongly developed, that, although she is ignorant of the fact, she is daily receiving concessions and having a thousand things done for her on condition of a submission which she never intends to give'.[28] Not that Leslie's own views were particularly liberal, but his deep friendship with Henry had started at Trinity Hall, where they were both Fellows, and it survived Henry's increasing radicalism. The Stephens were altogether a very mixed up family – 'where women and their capabilities were concerned [Leslie] really was a philistine', Noel Annan wrote,[29] and it was Fitzjames' daughter Katharine who in 1911 was to become Principal of Newnham College.

Social and domestic matters occupied Millicent's time as well as politics. In 1880 Henry joined the government as Postmaster General with an income of £2,500 a year, a great improvement on the £800 he had at the time of his marriage. There were minor complications: 'My cook is going to be married', Millicent wrote, 'her young man ... is a postman, so I expect he thinks all his fortunes here and hereafter depend on his marrying the P.M.G.'s cook'.[30]

The new position brought new interests but it did not alter the

PUNCH, OR THE LONDON CHARIVARI.—April 15, 1882.

PARCELS POST OFFICE

REPLY POSTCARD

THE MAN FOR THE POST.

Henry Fawcett as Postmaster General

Fawcett way of living; unlike the Andersons they did not have their own carriage, though Millicent was conventionally presented at Court. Dinner at Marlborough House with the Prince and Princess of Wales amused her, with the guests processing in order of importance 'the greatest swells in order of swelldom & the small fry to bring up the rear ... I presented a most elegant appearance & looked quite the Postmistress'.[31] Dining with the Prince of Wales on a less formal occasion in Scotland, she had pleasure in telling him how right it was that women should become doctors as well as nurses.[32] She had less pleasure from relations with Gladstone (with whom Henry, too, often had 'occasion to differ'[33]). In a rather convoluted speech in 1871, Gladstone had implied that he supported some degree of woman's suffrage, but that was as far as he ever went; in 1884, when the majority of Liberals had promised to support a move to give parliamentary suffrage to women on the same terms as men and Millicent's hopes were high, Gladstone let her down completely – he threatened that if an amendment for woman's suffrage was added to his Reform Bill he would withdraw his support for the whole thing, for 'the cargo which the vessel carries is, in our opinion, a cargo as large as she can carry safely'. Not surprisingly, Millicent came to distrust him. Her notes for a speech ran: 'Mr G. said W.S. [Women's Suffrage] would overweight the ship. The simile is unfortunate. The tradition of British seamanship in peril or disaster is "Save the women first". Mr G.'s instinctive thought that rises unbidden to his lips is "Throw them overboard" '.[34]

Gladstone's action not only destroyed any hope of women's suffrage in 1884 but also, by giving the vote to all male householders and £10 lodgers – in effect extending it to between 63 and 66 per cent of adult men and adding about six million voters – it satisfied male democratic ambitions for the time being and made a further Reform Bill unlikely. As a member of the government, Henry could not vote against Gladstone's Bill, but he abstained, fully aware that he was putting his career at risk. Gladstone, anxious that 'the minds of men' should not be 'disturbed by the resignation of a Cabinet Minister', asked him to stay.

Henry increased the number of female clerks in the Post Office, and improved their working conditions by appointing women supervisors and a woman medical officer, Edith Shove, one of the first two medical students to qualify at the University of London. In 1882, after the Married Women's Property Act, he ensured that women could make contracts in their own name, and so helped them to continue acting as post-mistresses in village shops after marriage. He was shocked at a comment from a supervisor that the girls' health improved with promotion and a rise in salary because then 'they were able to dine more frequently'. 'This answer', Ray Strachey wrote, 'and the facts which underlay it, weighed greatly on Henry Fawcett's mind, and both he and his wife used frequently to quote it in their efforts to improve the position of women'.[35] W. T. Stead, the new editor of the *Pall Mall Gazette*, asked Millicent to write an article on the work of women in the Post Office. She did write for him, not about the Post Office but on the suffrage question, and went on writing occasionally for him until his death on the *Titanic*. One day, she wrote, it would seem 'almost incredible' that the idea of votes for women had seemed 'dangerous and revolutionary'. Why should anyone be afraid?

> A first experiment has been made in giving women the municipal and School Board suffrages. The fears at first expressed have proved altogether imaginary; society has not been turned upside down; the possession of a vote has not made women essentially different from what they were before; we still like needlework; we prefer pretty gowns to ugly ones; we are interested in domestic management and economy, and are not altogether indifferent to our friends and relations; and we ask, therefore, that a second experiment should be made without fear.[36]

At the end of 1882, when the Fawcetts' life and work both seemed flourishing, personal tragedy struck. This was when Rhoda, Millicent's 'extra sister', died suddenly. Millicent went immediately to be with Agnes in her misery, but had to rush back for Henry who had fallen ill with diphtheria and typhoid. He was seriously ill, but seemed to recover well; Elizabeth was one of the doctors who cared for him for the two months before he was fit to go back to work.

Two years later, the year of disappointment over Gladstone and his Reform Bill, Henry suddenly collapsed again, this time with heart trouble and pneumonia. He died, aged 51, after only a few days' illness. Millicent was only 37, as Agnes had been when Rhoda died. Now it was Agnes' turn to come to Millicent, and the two sisters became close companions for the rest of their lives. Millicent had, Hubert Parry wrote, 'a lot of tenderness and sentiment hidden behind the strong and determined front she shows to the world'. He called Henry 'the finest and truest man in the whole range of political life',[37] and he dedicated his funeral ode 'The Glories of our Blood and State', to the memory of Rhoda Garrett and Henry Fawcett.

Millicent found comfort in memorials – the inscription in St George's Chapel, Westminster Abbey, the statues at Salisbury and Vauxhall, the drinking fountain on the Thames Embankment, the window at Trumpington church near Cambridge, the tablet in the church at Aldeburgh, the biography undertaken by Leslie Stephen. On a small scale, it was in the tradition of Queen Victoria on the death of Albert. Unlike the Queen, though, Millicent did not retreat too long into widowhood.

Dr Garrett Anderson

You are not merely women who desire to help other women. You are members of a noble profession. Seek in all things to promote its highest aims and add to its honour.

Elizabeth Garrett Anderson,
speech to the London School of Medicine for Women, 1877

While Millicent was still coping with a barrage of opposition, the medical press had started to report Elizabeth almost with awe; for her, the sniggering and sniping were over.

With an MD, a much loved husband, and no financial worries, Elizabeth could have relaxed, feeling her point had been made, her ambition achieved. She was, her daughter wrote, mellowed and softened but, happy to prove that women could combine marriage and a profession, she was still dedicated to her work. She had, as it turned out, over 30 years' work ahead of her, battling for medical education, organizing new buildings, practising as a clinician, and at the same time raising a family and supporting the movement for the suffrage.

In January 1882 the *Englishwoman's Review* listed 26 'registered medical women'. Seventeen years after Elizabeth had qualified, this was not a great number, and she was still the only one with an English qualification. Introduced by Elizabeth's old friend and supporter Russell Gurney, an act had been passed in 1876 enabling all medical boards to examine women; the King's and Queen's College of Physicians in Dublin was the first board to respond, and they soon had a steady stream of candidates.[1] Apart from Elizabeth herself, and Elizabeth Blackwell with her American training, all those 'registered medical women' had passed their final examination in Ireland even if they had been largely taught in London. Medical qualification for women was still not straightforward.

Elizabeth's clinical work was divided between her private patients and the Dispensary for Women and Children that she had started in 1866. Josephine Butler, the campaigner against the Contagious Diseases Acts, wrote after consulting her: 'I gained more from her than from any other doctor, for she not only repeated what all the others had said, but entered much more into my mental state and way of life than they could do, because I was able to *tell* her so much more than I ever could or would tell to any *man*'.[2] This special ability to treat and understand women remained important. Some time later, when a man wrote to ask 'if gout were in her line of practice' she answered firmly, 'Gout is very much in my line; gentlemen are not'.[3] But some gentlemen certainly were, notably Henry Fawcett who was looked after devotedly by her in his last illnesses.

Elizabeth's connections had also always brought her the occasional 'grand patient – with a carriage and powdered footman', and calls to attend births at high-class houses. In contrast, there had been 40,000 attendances at a penny a time in the first five years of the Dispensary. The Dispensary patients, at first coming with a variety of complaints, were now generally women with gynaecological problems, and there were more than she could deal with even though she now had an assistant (with a degree from Zurich). In 1872 she began to include in-patients, the first move towards a hospital for women with women medical staff. Here the patients had to contribute a small amount towards the cost of their maintenance during their stay, and at the same time the Dispensary charge was raised to sixpence for the first visit and twopence a time afterwards – like Millicent, she thought some payment was necessary to make the service valued and to encourage a sense of responsibility; like her, too, she believed that all parents should pay a small fee for schools. So the New Hospital for Women, which was to become in time the Elizabeth Garrett Anderson Hospital, opened with ten beds above the dispensary.[4] Since no one with only a foreign qua-lification could be on the medical register Elizabeth was the sole member of staff who could do major surgery, which for her was always a major strain, 'a tremendous tax upon one's nerve'.[5]

Another tax upon her nerve at this time was Sophia Jex-Blake. We met her last studying mathematics in Edinburgh and being helpful to Elizabeth in her efforts to get an Edinburgh degree. Elizabeth, in her outspoken way, had been discouraging when she first heard that Sophia wanted to turn to medicine, telling her she was 'not specially suited'.[6] Sophia might have been often criticized for lack of tact, but Elizabeth herself was not always blameless. 'There was', Elizabeth's star pupil Mary Scharlieb admitted, 'a certain brusqueness in her manner that sometimes proved distasteful, especially to people who did not know her well enough to appreciate the underlying unselfishness & the devotion to duty that marked her whole career.'[7]

But now Sophia and six others had matriculated at Edinburgh,[8] and it was Elizabeth's turn to be helpful. She persuaded her friend Lady Amberley to give a three-year scholarship for the Edinburgh course, and she paid for a third of a further scholarship herself. This promising start turned to disaster when one of the seven was refused a university scholarship because of her sex. Riots followed, and Sophia (who was the daughter of a lawyer[9] and should have known better) accused a member of the university staff, Professor Christison's class assistant, of being one of the leaders. She landed herself in a libel action which the plaintiff won, but although he was awarded only a farthing damages, she was left with a bill of nearly £1,000 in costs.[10] A committee of prominent Edinburgh supporters of women's suffrage, together with various Garrett friends and relations, paid the bill for her. The following year Sophia and her colleagues petitioned the University Senate for the right to study and be examined but, in spite of an initial judgment in their favour, an Appeal Court turned them down. To make matters worse, when they were allowed to take the examination, Sophia failed; when in 1873 she failed for a second time she claimed that she had been unfairly marked. Since Huxley himself had seen her papers, he wrote to *The Times*, saying that:

> As Miss Jex Blake may possibly think that my decision was influenced by prejudice against her cause, allow me to add that such prejudice as I labour under lies in the opposite direction ... and those who are best acquainted with the acquirements of an average medical practitioner will find it hardest to believe that the attempt to reach that standard is like to prove exhausting to an ordinarily intelligent and well-educated young woman.[11]

Elizabeth, appalled at all the rows, told Sophia that her 'want of judgement' and 'want of temper' had done great harm.[12]

Nothing could show the difference between the two medical pioneers more clearly than their reactions to the Edinburgh defeat. Elizabeth, as she wrote to *The Times*, thought that for the time being women should be content with foreign degrees (which colleagues would in fact often accept) even though that meant they could not yet be on the Medical Register: "'Nothing succeeds like success", and if we could point to a considerable number of medical women quietly making for themselves the reputation of being trustworthy and valuable members of the profession, the various forms which present opposition now takes would insensibly disappear'.[13]

This Fabian approach did not fit with Sophia's nature. She wrote to

The Times in reply, 'protesting as strongly as lies in my power against this idea of sending abroad every Englishwoman who wishes to study medicine'.[14] In any case, there seems to have been something of 'let them eat cake' in Elizabeth's suggestion; study in Paris or Switzerland, needing money and foreign languages, could only be for a privileged few.

This was just the week when Elizabeth's first child, Louisa, was born. Even Elizabeth, even with a wet nurse and a nanny, could not do everything. She decided she must resign from the School Board, and from her honorary appointment at the East London Hospital for Children – her first hospital post and the place where she had first met

Elizabeth and her daughter Louisa, 1876

Skelton. Her sister Alice (who stuck to her sisters' views on the need for parents to pay a small fee) was prepared to replace her on the School Board, but Elizabeth always regretted leaving the hospital before there was another woman ready to take over.

Young Louisa flourished, but Elizabeth's second daughter Margaret, born the following year, lived only just long enough to learn to walk. She died from tuberculosis caught, it is now thought, from cows' milk long before this hazard was understood. Doctors were aware of various other dangers from contamination and infections in cows' milk, and would recommend that milk should be from a known source, best of all always from the same cow – Alice used her own cow in India for her baby son Philip; sadly, a tubercular cow seems to have been chosen for Margaret. Believing, as her contemporaries did, that tuberculosis was hereditary (the tuberculosis bacillus was not discovered until 1882), Elizabeth in her grief was left with the distressing thought that Louisa and Alan (born 1877) might also be vulnerable. For Elizabeth, as it had been for her sisters, the treatment for grief was work. 'I feel it is a great blessing not to be one of those poor mothers who have nothing to do but to think of what they have lost', she wrote to Skelton's father.[15] There was plenty to do.

Sophia Jex-Blake, after her stormy departure from Edinburgh, was determined to set up a medical school for women in London. This did not fit at all into Elizabeth's vision. She felt it was impetuous and ill-conceived, and that if there were a separate diploma for women 'they would at once be marked as a special class of practitioners, subordinate and inferior to the ordinary doctor'[16] – rather as she had felt, in support of Emily Davies, about the courses for women students planned by Anne Jemima Clough and the Sidgwicks in Cambridge. She disliked, but could hardly refuse, Sophia's invitation to join the Council, even though it came in a bad-tempered letter (in answer to one from Elizabeth which has not survived):

> If I kept a record of all the people who bring me cock-and-bull stories about you [Sophia wrote], and assure me that you are 'greatly injuring the cause', I might fill as many pages with quotations as you have patience to read ... I never said it 'did not signify' whether you joined the Council (though I did say that I believed the School was already tolerably certain of success). I think it is of very great importance, both for your credit and ours, that there should, as you say, be no appearance of split in the camp, and I should greatly prefer that your name should appear on the Council.[17]

Sophia lacked charm, but she could not be ignored. Elizabeth joined the Council at its start in 1874, remaining on it for the rest of her life. The next year she was appointed one of the lecturers in medicine in the new London School of Medicine for Women.

The School could not offer clinical teaching, and although Elizabeth's New Hospital for Women did as much as it could, it was in no position to fill the need; the only patients there were women and children, and not yet even many of them. At that stage, no other hospital would help. Three years later, after Russell Gurney's 1876 Enabling Act, the climate changed. The London School of Medicine for Women became officially recognized as a medical school, and the Royal Free Hospital was persuaded (for quite a hefty fee) to open its wards to female students; since there had never been medical students in that hospital there was no problem of mixed teaching. The hero of the agreement was the politician and social reformer James Stansfeld, Honorary Treasurer of the School, who used his influence on the governors of the Royal Free. Elizabeth, occupied with the birth of her son Alan (9 March 1877), took no part in the negotiations, but was more than happy to hear about it. The arrangement worked well, and Sophia's London School finally merged officially with the Hospital in 1898 to form the Royal Free Hospital School of Medicine for Women. At last there would be house jobs for medically qualified women.

Only those on the Medical Register were to be on the Executive Committee of the School, so this included Elizabeth Garrett and Elizabeth Blackwell (who had herself opened a medical school for women in New York in 1868), but could not include Sophia. Sophia acted as secretary and organizer in the early days, but when the project grew to include clinical students it seemed that the time had come for an officially elected secretary. By then Sophia was a registered doctor (having, in spite of her earlier objections, passed her examinations in Berne in 1877 before being one of the first four to take a Dublin degree), but to her deep disappointment she was not elected, and she gradually disappeared from the scene. She went back to Edinburgh, occasionally turning up for committee meetings – notably to record the only vote against the appointment of Elizabeth as Dean in 1883. In 1897, objecting to the plan to rebuild the School, Sophia resigned as trustee.

So in time Elizabeth accepted and took over Sophia's ambitious scheme for teaching women medical students. She had to use her tact and campaigning skills to overcome the refusal of the Medical Faculty to admit the School's students to the London University examinations.

William Jenner, Queen Victoria's physician and later President of the College of Physicians, said 'he would rather follow his daughter to the grave than see her subjected to such questions as could not be omitted from a proper examination for a surgical degree'.[18] But the day for such prejudice was over. The charter admitting women to London University degrees passed in 1878; it was agreed that women should have the same examination papers as men – and in time Jenner's daughter became an ardent feminist.

That summer Jenner added to his earlier insulting remarks by saying that if the British Medical Association admitted women to membership he would resign. Elizabeth, 'in a ghastly funk at having to speak before this unsympathetic audience',[19] bravely but unsuccessfully challenged this attitude at the Association's meeting. 'I wish your wise counsel beloved were within reach', she wrote to Skelton, 'I should like to know what you would advise'.[20] She tried hard:

> It would be Utopian to say that mutual knowledge would always make people friendly, but it is true that enthusiastic dislikes are maintained with greater difficulty between those who are personally acquainted with each other. Medical men do not dislike each other half as much as they dislike medical women, and there is therefore the more need that they should be brought under the mollifying influence of social intercourse.[21]

She herself had been elected five years earlier without too many members realizing what was happening, and had managed to give a paper on obstetrics to the 1875 meeting – much to the approval of her old teacher Dr Keiller, and to the horror of the President, the Professor Christison who had been so much opposed to Sophia Jex-Blake and the whole idea of women doctors in Edinburgh. But the Association were determined not to let any other women join her. She was to remain the only one until 1892, but became, to her great pleasure, President of the East Anglian Branch in 1896. As her daughter wrote later, 'when the President entertained the Branch at Aldeburgh, Mrs Newson Garrett welcomed the doctors in radiant forgetfulness of the opposition she had shown to her daughter's choice of a profession thirty years before. Mr Garrett's death a few years earlier robbed him of a pleasure which no one deserved more than he'.[22]

The Royal College of Surgeons admitted women in 1895, but the physicians were less welcoming. In that same year fourteen senior physicians wrote a memorandum. They considered that 'the admission of women to the medical profession is most undesirable: and whilst

fully admitting the ability of women to comply with the mere examination tests, we are none the less convinced that they are by nature
unfitted for the pursuit and practice of the medical profession'.

It was to be another 30 years before the first woman fellow was
elected to the Royal College of Physicians. And the general acceptance of
women as general practitioners was appallingly slow – I can even
remember that in my own family it was difficult to reconcile my father
to the idea when our family doctor joined the army in 1939 and his
practice was taken over by his extremely competent wife.

In 1874 the proposal that Elizabeth should become a Fellow of the
Obstetrical Society had been defeated because, the *Scotsman* suggested
sarcastically, the members decided 'no woman could ever be allowed to
join in discussion concerning the treatment and relief of those sufferings
which women alone have to endure'. James Stansfeld thought that
'those practitioners who have devoted themselves to the special treatment of the diseases of women and to the practice of midwifery, more
than others, tremble for their monopoly'.[23] There seems to have been a
division between those who argued that women doctors were only
suited to look after women and those who tried to prevent them doing
so, either from self-interest or from a concern that women should not
go out on their own on night visits. But the Royal Free helped to break
down the opposition by giving women the opportunity to qualify in
midwifery as in all other departments of medicine and surgery.

Of the 26 registered medical women in 1882, six had been wholly, and
fourteen partially, educated at the London School of Medicine for
Women and the Royal Free Hospital before having to get their official
qualification in Dublin. It was another year before students qualified
under the new system, but the first two women medical graduates of
London University took their degrees in 1883 – Mary Scharlieb, who had
a gold medal and a scholarship; and Edith Shove, shortly to be
appointed by Henry as medical officer in the Post Office, at the same
rate of pay and conditions as a man would have in the same grade. 'I am
to have the honour of presenting them to Lord Granville as I am now
Dean of the Medical School for Women', Elizabeth wrote to her father;
'I think in memory of our efforts 21 years ago you should come up for
it'. 'Perhaps the dear mother would come too', she added hopefully.[24]
Newson (but not the mother) did come to see these first two, and there
were soon to be more. In the 40 years following the founding of the
London School 1,000 women were put on the Medical Register, 600 of
them graduates of the Royal Free. Elizabeth served as Dean for twenty

years. An appreciation of her work as Dean, in the magazine of the School in 1903, noted her 'incapacity to tolerate the second-rate'. She became president of the School until her death.

Eighteen eighty-three was a year of professional triumph for Elizabeth, but it came in the middle of upheaval and distress in her family life. Shortly after the deaths of Rhoda and of Henry Fawcett, eleven-year-old Louisa had a serious kidney infection. When Louisa recovered she still seemed weak, and Elizabeth made the radical decision to take a six-month break in 1885, going with Skelton and their two children on one of his Orient Line ships to Australia, leaving the Hospital in the charge of three colleagues, including the previous Dean.[25] It was good for the family and, as it happened, good for the cause of women doctors, showing that motherhood could remain a central part of a woman doctor's life. Louisa got well, and Elizabeth came back with renewed energy for the Hospital and the School. Besides her pastoral and administrative work as Dean, she was teaching at the School, hard at work for the next five years as a physician and surgeon at the New Hospital for Women, and busy with her private practice as well as with building projects. She remained on the Hospital's managing committee until 1904.

The Hospital was growing, and could no longer be squashed into the rooms above the old Dispensary. Not yet ready to undertake the cost and hazard of a new building, the committee took fourteen-year leases on two houses in Marylebone Road, later adding a third. Then as now, one of the main tasks of the head of an institution was to raise money, and Elizabeth was very good at it. She made £600 for the Hospital at a charity concert given by Clara Schumann, and also ran an appeal to raise the money asked by the Royal Free for taking on the women students from the School. By the 1880s she reckoned to raise about £2,000 annually for the Hospital by gifts and subscriptions. It is astonishing, all through the women's rights story – whether for medicine, for higher education or the suffrage – how much always depended on the generosity of benefactors.

A great organizer, hard-working, lively, persistent, patient – but what was Elizabeth like as a doctor? She had, after all, not come to medicine as a vocation but because it offered a possible career for a woman. Certainly, as a lecturer and a teacher, Elizabeth got nothing but praise. As a physician she was kind and efficient; Jo Manton's verdict is that 'it was as a general practitioner that she excelled, with all the qualities of character which that calling demands – courage, sense of duty, good judgement and warm humanity'. As a surgeon, opinions are mixed; although she was enthusiastic for the new antiseptic techniques just introduced by Joseph Lister, there was still a terrible death rate from surgery, and it is hard to know whether Mr Meredith, surgeon consultant at the Hospital, was justified in resigning in 1888 because 'he found the record of Mrs Anderson's operations at which he had been present shewed too high a percentage of failure'.[26] Perhaps others at the time did no better – Meredith himself was cited as the surgeon at an inquest on one death criticized by the patient's family.[27] And Elizabeth was prepared to tackle difficult cases (which might have a higher failure rate), such as an ovariotomy which she performed successfully although it was considered so dangerous that several London teaching hospitals would not attempt it. She may have had failures, but she certainly had triumphs; more and more patients came to her for gynaecological or other problems, and she was able to report interesting cases to the College of Surgeons.

More patients need more beds, and anyway leases run out. By 1888 the problem had become urgent, and after failing to find a large house suitable for conversion the committee decided to buy a site in Euston Road, raise yet more funds and build. The campaign opened in fine style with a meeting chaired by the Lord Mayor at the Mansion House. A letter was read from the great heroine of nursing and medical administration:

> What woman of us has not known many, many poor women who would rather go through any suffering than undergo the necessary examination before men students at a general hospital? To the Women's Hospital, women by preference would go ... We want to press the whole of women's faculties, the scientific, the executive, as well as the sympathetic and the more contemplative into the service of the sick, which is the highest service of the noblest love. Good speed to the Women's hospital is the earnest prayer of – Florence Nightingale.[28]

And she enclosed £50.

Money poured in. Elizabeth ran drawing room meetings, appeals, a great bazaar, and became, as Mary Scharlieb wrote, 'a persistent, shameless and highly successful beggar'. Elizabeth told the building committee: 'I wrote to some friends in the country asking them to contribute liberally; they sent £100, but I returned it immediately with a note saying "If old friends and rich people like you send me £100, what can I expect from the general public? I quite thought you would send me £1,000." '[29] Which they promptly did. And they were not the only ones of the Andersons' worthy wealthy friends to be persuaded to be generous – there were several major contributions towards the £20,000 building costs, including £1,000 from Henry Tate (of sugar and Art Gallery fame), as well as £1,000 each from Elizabeth and Skelton themselves. As Elizabeth explained in a letter to Millicent on behalf of a fund-raising dance, 'the elephant in Euston Road takes a lot of fodder'.[30]

Plans were drawn up by John Brydon, the man who had taught Agnes and Rhoda, and the foundation stone was laid with much publicity by the Princess of Wales. The design followed the 'Queen Anne sweetness and light' architectural philosophy. There was plenty of red facing-brick, terracotta decoration, white paint, gables, narrow twisting corridors, and deliberate un-institutional homeliness for, as Brydon wrote, 'there is no reason why the architect should not seek to impart a certain artistic distinction to the building even of a hospital'.[31] The plans gave plenty of fresh air and light, to conform to the sanitary standards of Florence Nightingale and Douglas Galton, the army engineer (cousin of Francis Galton) who was an expert on hospital planning. It is no great surprise to find that the contract for interior decoration was given to Agnes.

Agnes did not give the lowest estimate, but perhaps it was her design and her connection with Brydon as well as nepotism that got her the job. The work was done to time and to budget, complete with decorative Italian casts in the large wards, bookcases and an elegant fireplace (given by Agnes) in the meeting room, gas wall lights for each bed and a mosaic floor in the operating theatre. Nothing but the best. The *Christian World* got carried away with enthusiasm:

> The blue-tiled dado-ed corridor, the large airy wards with windows that catch the sunshine from morning until evening, the cosy beds with their tasteful coverlets, each occupant of which has an oak cupboard and bookshelf, the polished parquet floors, the delicate art colourings of the walls – painted to the taste and under the personal supervision of Miss Garrett – the cheerful open fires, the bright blossoming plants.[32]

The building included a 'medical institute', where women doctors could meet and have a library. Elizabeth refused to let her name be given to the New Hospital, so it did not become the Elizabeth Garrett Anderson Hospital until after her death.

The need for women doctors to look after maternity cases led

Elizabeth in 1896 to buy a house for a doctor and students. In the tradition of family connections, the house was to be looked after by Charles Essam who had worked for Agnes as a decorator, and his new wife Martha who had worked for Agnes and was the daughter of the Gower Street cook – Edmund sent £5 from South Africa as a contribution to their wedding present. Sadly, Charles shortly died leaving Martha pregnant, and Martha left when she was unsympathetically asked to board out two-year-old Ruby Agnes; it is good to learn, though, that in her will Agnes left £100 to Martha and an annuity of £100 to her mother.[33]

It was in 1896, too, only six years after the New Hospital building opened in Euston Road, that Elizabeth decided the time had come for the growing School to be rebuilt. Once again she would become deeply involved in money-raising, once again John Brydon would be the architect, but this time neither Agnes nor any other interior designer seems to have been involved, though Agnes designed the bookshelves that were given to the School by the Association of Registered Medical Women. The £1,000 donation that got this appeal started came from Charlotte Payne-Townshend, the Irish heiress who was to become Mrs Bernard Shaw. And much more was needed, as Elizabeth wrote to *The Times*: 'the New Hospital has no endowment and this year it is behindhand with the funds needed to pay Christmas bills ... The School has for many years been carried on in small hired houses, and it is now proposed to pull these down and build good laboratories, library and lecture-rooms'.[34]

Elizabeth, like Agnes, had inherited Newson's pleasure in the planning and detail of buildings. She even gave up her post as lecturer in medicine so that she could manage the administration and watch over the builders. In July 1898, as planned, the new School was opened by the Prince and Princess of Wales in a grand ceremony complete with military band and flags lent by Skelton's Orient Line. Elizabeth Blackwell, now aged 77 and Professor of Gynaecology at the School, sent an irreverent account back to America:

The Royal party were arriving to occupy their gilded chairs: the fat prince looking good-natured but silly, the ladylike princess in a grey gauzy dress with a large boa of mauve-coloured ostrich feathers and a hat trimmed to match. Mrs Anderson, looking like a fat college don in her robe and trencher (which is most unbecoming to her) read a long address, to which the prince replied with fluent, amiable commonplaces, patting the lady medicals on the back. Then a procession of little tots presented small bags of money (occasionally dropping one which the prince picked up). Rev. Mr Paget made appropriate prayer and finally all were invited to tea.[35]

The official merger with the Royal Free Hospital came only a month later, with two resident posts at the hospital opened to women. Another four years and the Royal Free Hospital School of Medicine for Women was to become a college of London University.

It was all working out amazingly well – 'to be strenuous and to have to be so brings much happiness', as Elizabeth wrote in a birthday letter to Millicent.[36] Twenty-five years after Elizabeth had passed her examination at the Society of Apothecaries she had her own hospital and was the respected Dean of a flourishing medical school, both in fine new buildings. In 1913, as a final gesture, she promised £1,000 a year for three years for the planned extension to the school.

The Elizabeth Garrett Anderson Hospital survived, with various alterations and extensions, to the beginning of the twenty-first century, moving from Euston Road to Huntley Street only in 2000. But all is changing, as the old building is left to decay while the huge new University College Hospital in Euston Road swallows it up, together with the Middlesex where Elizabeth started her training: 'once the main hospital building is complete, a new purpose-built women's hospital, the EGA Wing, housing women's services will be built by 2008. With shared access to all the facilities of the main hospital, the new EGA Wing will be a new centre of excellence for women's healthcare'.[37]

It will be splendid, and it will be everything the pioneers could have hoped for in the way of equality with the medical establishment, but it will not have domestic charm. As Elizabeth herself has been reduced to initials, the personality will disappear.

Family Ties

People must shape their own lives according to their own ideas & I don't think God could have meant us all to think alike or to mould our lives just into the same shape.

Letter from Alice Cowell to her mother, 27 March 1872

No other family involved in the women's movement had such varied activities as the Garretts. The powerful Pankhurst tribe were as concerned about the position of women, but they decided to concentrate on one overwhelming issue. Emmeline, who had been brought up with beliefs in all liberal causes as well as equal suffrage, was determined that her mission would be to work with her daughters for the vote – as little girls, Christabel and Sylvia had cried to be taken to suffrage meetings. Emmeline herself wrote, 'no member of the W.S.P.U. [the Women's Social and Political Union] divides her attention between suffrage and other social reforms'.[1]

The Garrett sisters were just as determined but less narrowly focused. And their careers evolved naturally and amicably into their chosen spheres of work for the women's movement – without any of the rivalry that had spurred Newson and his brother Richard. The whole campaign was, as Millicent analysed in her memoir, many-sided; there were questions of education, morality, and professional and industrial liberty, as well as political status. The sisters might not always agree with each other over details or methods, but they had the same basic goals, supported each other's ambitions and remained on the best of terms. Agnes, combining her decorating work with enthusiasm for women's suffrage tended, like Rhoda, to join the more radical groups. Even Josephine, the youngest and the least prominent of the sisters, presided at a meeting in Suffolk and spoke in favour of votes for women. Sometimes Elizabeth was so protective of her particular cause that she was anxious not to show how close their goals were. In 1867 she wrote to Millicent: 'I shall be very glad to subscribe £1 1s a year to the Franchise Society, but I would rather not have my name advertised on the General Committee. I think it is wiser as a medical woman to keep somewhat in the background as regards other movements ... I particularly do not wish my name to appear in public advertisements'.[2]

But their beliefs always overlapped. As Elizabeth explained, a little later when she was feeling more secure and able to speak for the suffrage cause,

> It has a great bearing upon the larger question in which I am greatly interested, and in which all the intelligent people in this country are as greatly interested as I am; and that is the general upraising of the whole position of women, particularly the educated classes. And it is because it seems to me that giving women the franchise would be a very great step towards the uplifting of the whole sex, that I take special interest in it.[3]

At a meeting in Langham Place in 1872 she moved a resolution that 'men legislated on matters which they presumed to be for the interests of women, but which they knew little or nothing about, and the very existence of women was often forgotten in the framing of acts of parliament'.[4]

Enthusiasm for the suffrage and for education never left Elizabeth. Somehow, on top of all her cares for the Hospital, the School and her family, she had time for other aspects of women's education and women's rights. To help her students to become well educated she became a governor of both North London Collegiate School and Bedford College, and she encouraged new schools for girls. Her interests naturally carried on into higher education, though as a friend of Emily Davies she was always, in spite of Millicent, in the Girton rather than the Newnham camp; she had spoken at the first appeal meeting for the building of Girton College (assuring worried listeners that studying would actually be good for young women), was a member of the house committee, and contributed financially throughout her life. Elizabeth would later also have a spell in a different camp from Millicent over the question of militancy in the struggle for the suffrage, but these differences never made a rift between them.

For all the sisters the concern was at first mainly for 'the educated classes', or for unemployed and un-enfranchised middle-class women. The poor, they thought, deserved sympathy and needed guidance, but politics lay outside their uneducated lives, and the suffrage should be left for their betters. This would not have seemed so odd in the nineteenth century – it was not until the Labour manifesto of 1900 that adult suffrage first appeared as a party policy. 'I do not believe there is much general demand for universal suffrage', Millicent wrote nine years later;

'any change in the direction of adult manhood suffrage would make our task infinitely more difficult of attainment'.[5] Whatever she may have believed, this was politic; women outnumbered men, so the idea that everyone might have a vote could make many shy away from the cause of women's suffrage.

Working women could not be ignored for ever though, and gradually some began to be politically involved. Millicent met factory women from Lancashire bringing a petition in 1901, and she was moved by a meeting at the Queen's Hall in 1911 that one delegate described as 'entirely composed of really poor working women ... so poor and so loaded with babies and so gloriously enthusiastic';[6] Millicent spoke to them of 'a grand freemasonry between different classes of women'. The radical attitude of Mrs Pankhurst and the social upheaval of the First World War were to push forward a change, but the rights and needs of working-class women were not to come more fully into the picture until the next generation took over, with reformers like Sam Garrett's daughter Margery Spring Rice, author of *Working-Class Wives.*

The religious views of Elizabeth, Agnes and Millicent all developed on similar lines, breaking from their mother's strict evangelicalism, coming (as their eldest sister Louie had) under the influence of Frederick Denison Maurice and the Christian Socialists before moving away from any fixed religion. In her student days Elizabeth would even make notes of Maurice's sermons and turn them into English exercises for Emily to criticize. Walking in Scotland with Sophia Jex-Blake in 1862, Elizabeth had climbed Craig More on a Sunday morning; 'when they were fairly at the peak they indulged in a shout of triumph and then sat down and read the Collect for the day'.[7] But later she had a husband whose belief, which that generation of Garretts came to share, was simply that 'the substance of true religion is morality'.[8] Elizabeth was sorry – more for the sake of Girton than from distress at his views – when his principles led him to resign from the Girton committee:

> To help women is not the passion of your life as it is of mine and Miss Davies. But as in all probability Hitchin (whatever its memorandum may be or its family prayers) will be a hotbed for ultra-Liberalism and as the slight amount of Churchism will probably dispose the young women favourably towards Dissent I think even as a Liberal you ought not to allow such a question to remove you from the list of its supporters.[9]

She gave her own views in her campaign for the School Board election in 1870: 'I am in favour of the reading of Bible in school ... I am not in favour of allowing the Scripture lesson to be made a means of conveying to the scholars the special doctrines of the Church of England, or of any one of the dissenting bodies'. Millicent married an agnostic who worked hard for the removal of religious tests at the universities – 'the three best men I have known were not Christians', she once said, naming them as her husband, John Stuart Mill and Henry Sidgwick.[10] Alice tried to reconcile their mother to this approach, when Mrs Garrett had been upset at Millicent lecturing on a Sunday:

> Believing that all good gifts are from God, can you think that Harry's and Millicent's lives are not guided & illumined by His spirit. Just see how useful & devoted to the lightening of other people's burdens they both are & how almost heroic he is in his patient cheerful endurance of the great affliction of his blindness. Can it be of importance that their formula of acknowledging Him is not the same as yours?[11]

A regular church-goer, Alice had set out her own views of missionaries and religion in an earlier letter from India to her mother, with firm Garrett independence:

> It is a wonderful thing to think of missionaries amongst such a people as this doing their very utmost to instil doctrines & theories most of which have been fought about for centuries by Christians themselves – as if they could be any use! And yet I suppose most of the S.P.G. [Society for the Propagation of the Gospel] men conscientiously & persistently insist upon the 'real presence' doctrine & the Church missionaries upon their pet theories of conversion & election & regeneration & so forth. If we believe that He *is* the light that lighteth every man & that it is He who is being worshipped however ignorantly in every form of faith & worship that exists, I don't see what good we shall be doing by trying to impose our own forms & theories upon other people.[12]

Her cousin Edmund echoed this independence in his obituary of T. H. Huxley –'Cape Town church folk were a bit scandalized – such dear old dryasdusts', he wrote to Stead.[13]

But in old age, when tradition took hold, Millicent and Agnes both turned with some pleasure to the services and sermons of the Temple Church. Agnes seems to have had less of the family relentless logic in her and, particularly after Rhoda's death, to have dabbled trendily in theosophy, Christian Science, and other fringe ideas. 'Agnes came to tea and talked of spiritualism', Lady Maud Parry wrote in her diary in 1887, referring to a description of Agnes and her friends as the 'hysterical

Budhists'. There was some healthy scepticism in Agnes, though, for a later diary entry reads: 'Agnes's talk seems to have shocked some of the party. She said that one of the ladies whom Mohatma the Indian had constantly visited had had since an immaculate conception'.[14] In a series of devastating articles in the *Westminster Gazette* seven years later, Edmund mercilessly debunked the theosophists[15] – though the cult survived to plague the Lutyens family in the early twentieth century and even exists still. Fond as he was of Agnes, Edmund was perplexed by her continued vague fascination with mysticism.[16]

The tragedies of family deaths brought the sisters close together. Elizabeth had been summoned by Millicent's telegram when Henry suddenly became ill, and was there when he died. Millicent, left alone, gave up her houses in London and Cambridge and, together with Philippa, moved to Gower Street, to share the home where Agnes had been living and working alone since Rhoda died. Millicent and Agnes stayed together there into old age; Millicent died in 1929 and Agnes, the last surviving sister, in 1935. Comfortable in each other's company, they had a close but undemonstrative relationship – one day in the 1920s Agnes arrived home looking rather shaken, and after sitting silent for a while, confessed that she had been knocked over by a cab; it was only then that Millicent in her turn confessed that she had been knocked down by a cab the previous week. Neither said any more, but they each confided in Philippa.

In the 1880s the district became something of a Garrett colony. Elizabeth's New Hospital for Women and the London School of Medicine for Women were a short walk away. Their brother Sam, now a solicitor, lived near and looked after their business affairs – he was, as Ray Strachey, Millicent's friend and first biographer, wrote 'the closest and the dearest of her men friends'.[17] Rhoda's half brothers and sisters, cared for by Agnes and Rhoda since the death of John Fisher Garrett in 1878, were under Agnes' special care and were welcomed into this close community. As undergraduate President of the Cambridge Union, Edmund had shown family loyalty by (unsuccessfully) proposing the motion that 'this House is in favour of the extension of the Parliamentary franchise to women'. Now, just down from Cambridge, he was one of the many friends and relations living nearby while he was starting his career as a journalist under W. T. Stead at the *Pall Mall Gazette*. Alfred Milner was to describe him as 'the new Stead, with all his virtues and none of his faults'; he combined charm and wit with a good dose of Garrett morality, determination and sense of justice. In 1892 Edmund's sister Amy, two years older than him, married Edmund's Cambridge friend John Badley, the founder of Bedales School; John Fisher Garrett's young twins John and Elsie, born in 1869, were still at school, but spent their holidays at Gower Street.

It is good to see that this immensely hard-working family with their impressive ambition and dedication always managed to find room for other pleasures of life, or for holidays and travel. Millicent read novels and poetry; at Cambridge she had been able to widen her intellectual interests, and had arranged chamber concerts in her drawing room. Music was a lasting pleasure to all the sisters, taking Millicent to concerts in London, 'over and over again' to Wagner operas at Covent Garden or Bayreuth, and bringing to both her and Agnes friendship with the composers Hubert Parry and Ethel Smyth.

They all had pleasure from friendships outside their family circle. Rhoda and Agnes were among the first members of the all-women Somerville Club in 1879; together with Millicent they joined the Albermarle Club (for men and women) in the 1880s.[18] And they liked food; Maud Parry recorded a dinner with Agnes and Millicent in 1887: 'such a spread. First there was a mayonnaise of crab, then fillets of beef with peas, steamed potatoes and tomato salad. Then came grouse – we had creams and macaroni. Certainly the Garretts know how to live'.[19]

As for Elizabeth, she thoroughly enjoyed giving parties – 'if I give a party it is a good one', she said to one of her students when she was Dean and planning a celebration at the School. She was very social in the early days of her married life – 'I certainly do very much like meeting my fellow creatures' – but in her approach to parties later there is a political edge to her enjoyment: 'to know a good many people and to be able to enjoy their society and to find the best that is in them, is not only an enormous help if you have any public work which you want to promote, but it is a real help to your own mental development'.[20]

In her Cambridge days Millicent would go to the town gymnasium when it was open for women – gymnastics were becoming a fashionable healthy activity. She enjoyed walking and riding with Henry, and perhaps most of all skating. When there was a frost, the Fawcetts would drop everything and take their household and friends off to skate in the Fens until the thaw. This was a Cambridge tradition that lasted well into the twentieth century – 'Gentlemen, skating. The laboratory is closed' appeared on the door of the Physiological Laboratory when Joseph Barcroft was the professor there between the two world wars. Skating seems to have been something of an Aldeburgh tradition too – Skelton

Anderson had endeared himself to his new relatives and to the town with his admirable figure skating on his first appearance there at Christmas. And in London, Parry was delighted to be elected to the London Skating Club in 1879, and spent many hours on the rink in Regent's Park.[21]

Henry Fawcett's other enthusiasm was fishing, and as Millicent made no pretence at liking that, the Fawcetts sometimes holidayed separately – Millicent travelling to Switzerland with Sam and Josephine, or to Italy with Elizabeth. As conscientious tourists, before going to Italy they read up Ruskin and *Romola*, saw all the right sights, and managed to meet both Garibaldi and the Pope. Millicent found Pio Nono to be simply 'a kind, stout, commonplace old gentleman'. Garibaldi was another matter – it was one of her 'most cherished memories to have stood in that noble presence, to have heard his voice, to have pressed his hand',[22] though Elizabeth wrote sadly to Skelton that 'we tried to get him to say something in support of the women's cause but he did not fully understand our questions and answered somewhat at cross purposes'.[23] Millicent travelled tirelessly, sometimes with family, sometimes with friends. Her last and longest journey was a visit with Agnes to Ceylon in 1929 (when they were aged 82 and 84), seeing the sights and promoting the suffrage cause: 'Our time was all too short. We did not realise before we arrived how much there was to interest us in Ceylon. Ignorance, you see, sheer ignorance.'[24]

Elizabeth fully shared Millicent's love of travel, though she hated leaving her family. Setting out for Italy with Millicent she wrote to Skelton: 'I wish you were with me. I shall never elope in real earnest. I don't like leaving you and the bairns tho' I do most thoroughly enjoy the sense of holiday – shutting up books, turning one's mind away from medicine and seeing the out-of-London world'.[25] As her daughter wrote:

> A jaunt abroad always filled her with delight ... They did not leave the beaten track nor wish to do so. Baedeker in hand, the sights were ticked off until exhaustion called a halt. Foreign speech and foreign ways provided endless interest; tea was brewed and consumed in the hotel bedroom from a tumbler – a great economy and such fun! In some ways she had a simple mind.[26]

When younger, Elizabeth could go well off the beaten holiday track, as she had shown in her strange journey with Sam and Josephine to the scene of the Franco-Prussian War.[27] A passionate supporter of the

French, she set out for Sedan, where 82,000 French troops had been captured. Family loyalties were divided: 'The father hopes we are both as Prussian as respectable people ought to be', Alice wrote, 'I don't know – I might have been if the fate of war had been otherwise, but I think sorrow & sympathy for the agony of France is almost uppermost now'.[28] And she wondered innocently whether Elizabeth, Sam and Judy would have seen any signs and traces of the war.[29] In a not very reassuring letter to her father Elizabeth wrote:

> It was very late when we reached Arlon. However we found quarters. The only drawback to the inn was a terrible smell of drains in our room, it was horrible. Having the fear of gastric fever before our eyes, we slept with our heads wrapped in Shetland shawls with three folds over our mouths to keep out the stench. We have no luggage and very little money with us as we are afraid of robbers.[30]

The letter to Skelton (shortly to become her fiancé) was even more alarming. She saw the field hospitals in Bouillon and helped to dress the wounded:

> The soldiers were beautifully patient while their wounds were dressed ... At a quiet country station in the bright moonlight, rows of stretchers on the ground were being carefully lifted one by one into carriages ... the Prussian officer allowed us to sit in one of the ambulance waggons going back to Sedan with stores for the hospital ... At last by moonlight entering the gates of Sedan at 11.30 p.m. we had unwillingly to turn out of our waggon and begin our search for rooms. Every hotel was full and we began to be in despair. Found a church open with one lamp alight, peeped in saw a bier with a dead man on it and thought we would not lodge there ... Saw an officer – thought he looked good and rushed at him with our anxieties – learning that we had tried all the hotels he asked us home with him, saying that J. and I could have his room. This morning we found our good Samaritan had passed the night on a chair. On the return journey by train at a small station we waited 3-4 hours spending the time distributing chocolate and tobacco, water and apples to the wounded. My sister is particularly good at this sort of work as she is pretty enough to be a reviving attendant ... Not being able to get to Metz we are now coming homewards. I am still not sure that to have our best called out is not, even at the price of suffering, a blessing.[31]

Elizabeth's daughter adds a coda to this story about the kind Prussian officer, one that puts Elizabeth in a more human and less efficient light:

After the night at Sedan in his room the three young people had counted their money – a small store unfortunately owing to fear of 'robbers' – and had scraped together enough to buy him a diamond ring as a memento. It was a handsome stone set in a collar of gold – no doubt diamonds were cheap in Sedan at the time. Even so, to buy a diamond at all was a new experience to them, and their eagerness to present this splendid thank-offering can be imagined. Picture their distress as each expected the other to remember in what street the officer lodged, and to what regiment he belonged, and what was his name. But as none of them could answer any of the questions they were never able to thank their kind host and I now wear the diamond.[32]

Soon after Elizabeth got home, she was consulted by two sick American women who had fled from Paris. Realizing that they were coming down with smallpox and that no state hospital or lodgings would take them, Elizabeth kept them in her own house until they recovered.[33] She was an ardent supporter of vaccination, and must, as Alice anxiously asked, have been vaccinated herself, before going to Paris in 1870.

Elizabeth was to have many other holidays abroad, either with Skelton or, because he was often so busy that he could take only a day or two off, with other members of the family – the bonus for us is that separation produced letters. In 1884, shortly before Henry Fawcett's sudden fatal illness, she was in Germany with Millicent and Philippa for an energetic dose of walking and culture. Two or three years later there was the great visit to Australia with Skelton and her two children. It was a wonderful restful time, broken by a difficult encounter with her difficult brother Newson. Having failed at various jobs in England, he was having no greater success in New South Wales; he had just been declared bankrupt and he came to ask for a loan which she sternly refused. Not even family feeling could overcome her rejection of all he stood for.[34] She still had affection for his wife and children though, and we find her taking his daughter Ruby as well as her own children for a holiday in Switzerland in 1892, and Ethel, another daughter, working as a volunteer nurse for three months in Elizabeth's hospital in 1894. Alice's daughter Christina Cowell, together with Millicent, joined Elizabeth and her children in Switzerland in 1893. The following year it was the turn of Alice and two nephews.

There is one great gap in their travels – none of the Garrett sisters ever visited America. Elizabeth had been moved by the story of

Elizabeth Blackwell, but had spurned her father's offer of training in America herself. Millicent had constant invitations from American suffragists: 'do you not ever intend coming to this country?' the veteran campaigner Susan B. Anthony wrote to her in May 1903. Emmeline Pankhurst, on the other hand, went to America three times between 1909 and the beginning of the Great War, and reckoned she was doing great work for suffrage propaganda. Rubinstein's suggestion that Millicent may have been put off by sea-sickness is unconvincing, since she faced the journey to Ceylon and went twice to South Africa, first (taking Philippa with her) to the South African concentration camps, and later to visit Philippa when she was living out there. It seems that for the Garretts, travel was generally more connected with the family than with work. Millicent's only journeys abroad simply for work were for the South African Commission, and to champion the needs of women at the Peace Conference in Versailles in 1919.

But holiday houses in England tied the extended family together even more than trips abroad. Agnes and Rhoda's cottage at Rustington became a centre for family as well as for friends. Imaginatively, there was a railway carriage in the garden as a playhouse for Rhoda's young siblings and for Philippa Fawcett, decorated by the children with frescoes of the Flood and called 'the Ark'. (This was 40 years before Joyce Lankester wrote a story where Milly Molly Mandy and her friends find an old railway carriage and play in it.) 'I have very many memories of old Rustington days', Edmund wrote to Agnes, 'the old cottage; you; Rhoda; my boyish tiresomeness and worshippings; the corner in the churchyard; the seat just the other side of the kitchen garden wall; the picnic breakwater; the moonlight walks; a hundred old pages'.

Elizabeth's family extended to include Louie's children and a large supply of Anderson nephews and nieces. As well as taking them on holiday, she would have batches of them to stay in London, taking them sight-seeing, giving them parties. Naomi Mitchison, in a lecture in the 1920s, wrote that 'those who were children thirty or forty years ago still remember their aunt Elizabeth as a terrifying but irresistibly fascinating witch'.[35] When they were older they were sent off to do their own exploring with a sovereign each – a generous allowance in the late nineteenth century – and told to be back to change for dinner. She would then take them to the theatre – 'Shakespeare from choice, provided that Falstaff were not in it', according to her daughter.[36]

Elizabeth's Scottish husband gave Elizabeth a lasting love of the Scottish countryside. She bought a holiday home at Newtonmore, in the

Highlands, where her daughter's friend Evelyn Sharp, visiting in 1910, wrote of her as 'a fascinating combination of the autocrat and the gracious woman of the world'. Millicent and Agnes were fellow guests and,

> There was a strong family likeness in all the Garretts; and their fine sterling qualities, added to much that was personally attractive, made me feel proud to be a member of the house party that included three of the sisters of the older generation. Miss Agnes Garrett used to accompany Mrs Fawcett everywhere, and when they joined us at Newtonmore, the conversation became noticeably more racy, ... Nothing seemed to daunt these doughty women, ... I saw them tuck up their skirts – there was plenty to tuck up in those days – and don indescribable boots, before starting out to brave inclement weather and face really difficult rambles in the mountains.[37]

Loving the sea, Elizabeth sometimes joined the Rustington party, but her seaside home was in Aldeburgh. Her father, enjoying his status as patriarch, kept the family together with great parties at Christmas and other holiday times – sometimes with as many as 40 of the clan. He also built a series of houses in Aldeburgh, handing them round his children. He liked using odd bits of architectural salvage – Sam's house was called Gower House because it included two truckloads of granite paving stones which Newson had bought when he saw them being torn up one day as he visited Agnes in Gower Street. Elizabeth was always happy in Aldeburgh, and she seems less formidable when living there – she gardened, had a children's cottage, a pony, rabbits and a swing. Sometimes, able to get away for only a few days, Skelton would go there for a brief golfing holiday while she took the family abroad. It is to Skelton with his Scottish background that Aldeburgh owes its flourishing golf course. And it was the Garrett Andersons, moving from their influential positions in London back to Elizabeth's Suffolk roots, who inherited the Aldeburgh mantle of Newson and Louisa.

13

India and Empire

How can they tell me there is no need for medical women in India? Tell them how deeply their Queen sympathizes with them and how glad she is that they should have medical women to help them in their time of need.

Queen Victoria, 1883

The unquestioning pride in Empire, the feeling that nothing could be better for Africans or Indians than a dose of British culture, was very much part of the Victorian scene. British men went out to India from a mixture of motives – to have responsibilities and status far beyond anything they could hope for at home, to run the administration, to serve in the army, to hope to make money. British girls went out on the 'fishing fleet' in the hope of staying there and catching a husband. It could lead to a well-cushioned life, it could lead to early death from disease, it often brought the heartache of separation from small children who were sent back home to school.

Many of the Garretts became involved in Indian life. First, disastrously, Millicent's eldest brother Newson Dunnell had gone there as an officer in the Royal Artillery. With none of the family sympathy or sense of service, he disgraced himself in his sisters' eyes. As George Orwell was to write 'with cheap horses, free shooting, and hordes of black servants, it was so easy to play at being a gentleman'.[1] Newson's letters home are full of self-pity – pleas for money, excuses for debts, exam failures, and hopes for promotion that somehow never happened. When he got a reasonable appointment in the arsenal at Calcutta he hoped it might lead to something in the Ordinance at home, so that he would not have to send his children back without him, but of course it didn't. In his defence, Alice loyally wrote that he was 'so bright and cheery himself, so different from those wet-blanket letters of his'.[2] Life, she explained, really was expensive in India, and 'he spends money freely about little things, but seems to me to be a capital manager and Kate [his wife] is very careful and economical'.[3] Periodically Newson thought of leaving the army; perhaps sheep farming might be a good idea, or emigration to New Zealand, or maybe 'a nice place in the

Brewery would suit'; possibly he might speculate in diamonds or hides or tea. But, as Alice wrote, 'the wild schemes subside just as quickly as they arise'.[4]

There was genuine need for pity when his baby son suddenly died. He was happy with his wife Kate, but she found life in India difficult and went home for a while in 1866, staying till after her next son was born and after the hottest weather – she was there and able to sign the petition for women's votes that Elizabeth and her friends were organizing for John Stuart Mill. Newson, who for once seemed to be settling down in his profession, went home in the spring of 1867 for a few months before bringing her back in November, but with the perpetual Indian exile problem of leaving his children in England with grandparents – a problem Alice hoped to avoid by moving back to England when her daughter was five. In 1868, envious at hearing that Edmund was running the Bow Brewery, he told his father that he really could not manage to support a family on army pay and that he would like to join Edmund in the business. But he was already heading for trouble, with cheques bouncing and his father appalled at his 'indifference in money matters'.

The following year Newson proposed taking two years' leave on full pay, promising to return – but not intending to do so for longer than six months and qualifying for half-pay after that. So, he suggested to his father, since Edmund was at the brewery, and 'it would not have been fair to Edmund to have gone in over him, and I could not of course have served under him ... you should give me the management of the Snape business'. After the two years and the six months he could 'permanently take up residence at Snape as managing partner in the malting business'.[5] A later letter has him fearing that living at Snape would be virtually being 'buried alive'. Alice gave the idea rather half-hearted support, thinking it worth a try; his parents cautiously thought they might accept it, but wondered whether he had become used to too extravagant a lifestyle, whether he might find it socially difficult to be 'in trade'[6] and, worst of all, whether such a partnership might lead to quarrels. The whole idea of staying in England without telling the army his plans was morally doubtful; Alice reported that 'Newson said that if it was known, he might lose his staff pay for the 2 years furlough, so we have been very careful to hold our peace about it'.[7]

Alice's husband, Herbert Cowell, was a lawyer practising in India who lectured and wrote books on the Indian courts and on the British administration of law to the Hindus. His major Indian book '904 pages, double columns & small print' was a '"Digest or Resumé" arranged alphabetically of all the cases that have been decided in the Courts of the three Presidencies ... about 12600 cases collected from about 40 big volumes of reports'.[8] This formidable work apparently sold fast, becoming a text-book for law students. Alice acted as 'a sort of sub-editor', copying, making an index, and correcting proofs.

Herbert came from a Suffolk family full of Indian connections – his cousin Edward was an oriental scholar, a professor in Calcutta and later Cambridge's first Professor of Sanskrit.[9] Newson Dunnell had been appalled at the prospect of this marriage: 'I hope nothing will come of it for two reasons', he wrote snobbishly to his parents, 'firstly he is not at all the man I should like, he is very selfish and altogether not a very good sort of chap. And secondly he is coming out here with not a first rate position, this is a country where that sort of thing is looked upon in a very different light to England.'[10] Alice, he thought, would be out of the social scene and have no friends. Luckily he was wrong. Herbert Cowell was an able lawyer whose position soon improved, and they became every bit as much part of the social scene as Alice could take. The worst that could be said of Herbert, judging by his letters, was that he was a bit ponderous and boring and had a tiresome tendency to fevers. He kept on polite terms with Newson and Kate but, with a belief in the British mission to do good in India, he had little sympathy for their prejudices, thinking their dislike of the country had been 'dinned into them by their Dumdum friends'.

However different they were, Alice enjoyed having a brother near at hand. She wrote excellent letters from India, with something of Millicent's amused observation of people and customs. As Elizabeth had realized years earlier, although Alice had pleasure in the company of 'better people', she had an 'ability to get on with stupid people'. Like her brother, Alice wrote of the strains of Indian life – the heat, the dust, the expense, the fevers, the exhaustion – but while Newson seems to have been almost totally self-absorbed, Alice seemed determined to make the best of her exiled life. She enjoyed the strange sights and made light of the disasters – the host whose illiterate bearer accidentally served a caustic disinfectant after dinner, the party of guests who arrived for lunch when she had forgotten all about them, the servant she had to save from alarming magic treatment when he fainted. At the same time she was full of thoughts and comments about all the happenings in her family in England, enjoying their successes, worrying over their problems. She was away for nearly ten years, from 1863 to 1872 – the years

Alice Cowell (née Garrett)

when Elizabeth became a doctor, Millicent married and became involved in politics, Agnes and Rhoda set up their business, the young brothers and sisters she had left grew up. The letters to her seem to have been lost, though she talks of weekly letters from her mother, fewer (but treasured) from her father, and plenty from her siblings.

British life in India in those days was strangely isolated and, perhaps under the influence of her conservative husband rather than her progressive sisters, she was anxious to keep her small daughter 'away from crowds of children of all shades – native servants from whom she would pick up nasty ways and words'. Her social scene was certainly that of the Raj, with a house full of servants and little other contact with Indians apart from occasional grand assemblies or charitable work. It was a situation that she accepted, though not without doubts: 'there is an immense amount of class prejudice here and of careful exclusion of the natives from English society, which perhaps would be better done away with. But then on the other hand it is no good trying to treat them as equals yet, for they are not equals in any one way'.[11] She enjoyed studying German with a friend, though it probably did not occur to her to study Hindi. She did not, she wrote to her mother in November 1867, go to all the lengths that Newson does about natives, but she did think

> The idea of an English woman marrying one horrible and revolting almost beyond what words can express ... People here are prejudiced it is quite true, but even allowing for that surely the opinion of the mass of people who do know something of the natives is worth weighing against that of people who know nothing whatever of them. Agnes told Newson that she would accept what I said about it, and ... I think people are right to shew them all kindness and hospitality if they wish to go into English society & conform to the manners of it, but I think generations ought to pass for them to increase in purity and manliness before any Englishwoman ought to marry even the best of them. Trottie [Millicent] would say that is because I am in a 'slough of conservatism' but I am sure there is a great deal of truth in it ... We are getting the echoes here now [reported by Newson on his return] of all your great radical discussions at Aldeburgh.[12]

She badly wanted to go home and hear the discussions herself, for she was often homesick. There are wistful letters picturing family birthday gatherings, or Christmas celebrations with her father making mulled claret, his 'one achievement in the cooking department'. She admired the way that Elizabeth, in her struggle to become a doctor, managed to 'bear suspense and disappointment' – she even thought that, although Elizabeth would not want to let her father down, success might bring a hostile reaction, while the way she was 'putting some purpose and earnestness' into women's work was itself worthwhile. Later she wrote that she had seen the *Morning Star* 'with a long account of the opening of Lizzie's dispensary'. And in May 1867 she sent home with pride a cutting from the *Spectator*:

> We have heard the opinion of one of the most eminent of our living physicians that one of the new lady physicians is doing in the most admirable manner a work which medical men would never even have had the chance of doing. Mothers bring their children to her in hundreds to consult her on really important points, on which they freely admit that they would never have thought of taking advice at all had she not been accessible to them. And we should not be surprised to find that even in law, as certainly in literature and art, special fields of exertion quite consistent with feminine instincts will spring up, if they are only looked for.

Alice had been doubtful about the 1866 Reform Bill: 'Agnes and Millie pitch into me so now for being "un-Liberal" that I am half frightened', she wrote to her father, 'but I should think a reform bill is one of the things that would be exacted when the country was ready for it as the old reform bill was, so if it is rejected now it is nothing to make a moan about'.[13] 'Shall we all have great political fights when we come home?', she wondered the following year,

> I rather fancy not but I can't feel quite sure because I don't quite know enough about radical views and opinions ... I don't give Mr Fawcett credit for working any great wonders in that you declare yourself a radical – for though you used to wear the respectable blue badge – I think in reality you always were a radical in politics and everything else to the very back bone.[14]

'I very much wish we knew Harry', she added later, 'I am not at all so afraid of being shocked at his "awful radicalism" as you seem to fancy'.[15] Her interest and sympathy grew. Her brother Newson still considered her a Tory,[16] though she described herself more ambiguously as 'the wife of a Tory'.[17] 'I wonder whether universal suffrage will come in our time', she wrote in June 1867. No one in India seemed to care: 'I suppose the truth is that very few imaginations are equal to the leap of 7000 miles, for really indifference to the reform bill here is not more wonderful than the placidity with which people in London got the telegram of mutiny at Meerut and went off to the Derby without giving it another thought'.

Alice enjoyed reading about the debates, and her imagination leaped cheerfully:

> One hon. member (Mr Onslow I think) says women ought to aim at that ideal of perfection which was in the Creator's mind when he made her (I suppose he thinks he knows exactly what that was) & does the House suppose that He intended her to figure at election polls or parliamentary debates. But nobody has a shadow of an argument against it.

Her views edged tentatively ever further to the left until, disillusioned with most politicians, she was 'often tempted to envy the advanced radicals – the only political party in the whole country it seems to me now, with a creed & leaders in whom they believe'.[18]

By 1868, homesickness, combined with Herbert's health problems, sent Alice's family, too, home for a visit and for the sadness of leaving their daughter behind when they returned. At that time they had only one living child, and had suffered one still-born son. She had a difficult pregnancy again in 1870 – 'I wish I could have our dear old M.D. to look after me' – but Philip, the future senior wrangler and astronomer, was born safely in August, 'quite strong and healthy'. Herbert's election in 1869 to a three-year appointment as Tagore professor kept them in India longer than they had hoped. Letters home became full of anxious self-justification – it must be better, Alice struggled to convince herself, for the child to be in healthy Aldeburgh with her loving grandparents and lots of cousins 'mustering on the beach like an infant school' – but she missed her dreadfully and was not to see her again for four years. Without her daughter, Alice, until she was pregnant, had time on her hands and was busy with good works – looking after the clothing for 60 girls at an orphan school, and being treasurer of an institution for hospital nurses,[19] as well as doing office work and editing for Herbert.

Indian papers helped her to keep well in touch with her sisters' progress:

> Elizabeth and Millicent both had paragraphs in the last 'Overland mail' & that about Elizabeth (of her being made physician to the children's hospital) found its way into the Calcutta daily papers. It is a very pleasant piece of news I think. The English College of Physicians & the Medical Schools can't hold out much longer when degrees as good as their own are to be had as freely by women as by men, & when the only women qualified get large public & private practices. It is very stupid of them to wait to be driven I think – but what nonsense gets talked on both sides. Do you remember that Edinburgh man last year who 'couldn't look with comfort upon a woman who had just left a dissecting room' – as if his comfort was of supreme importance.[20]

Education, of one sort or another, was a constant concern. It was back in 1867 that she had become the local secretary in Calcutta for Emily Davies' plan for a college for women in Cambridge.

Returning home late in 1872 was wonderful for Alice, but of course it deprives us of any further letters and comments. Apart from her three years on the London School Board, she disappears into London and Aldeburgh life, united with all her family and proud to support her sisters' causes. She was to have two more daughters, one of whom went to Girton, and another son.

As for Newson, he did not settle at Snape but disappeared into a brewery in Portsmouth, a brickfield in Surrey, and endless business failures and money problems, surfacing unwelcome and unexpectedly when Elizabeth visited Australia in 1885, the year he was declared bankrupt. His father's will, dividing assets between the children, passed Newson's share to the care of trustees though, as Alice wrote to Sam, 'personal things to be divided as mementoes' should be distributed between all of them, as 'it would vex Mother to suggest that Newson should not share them like the rest of us'.[21]

While Alice's letters from India give plenty of comments on Garrett life, other members of the Garrett family for their part showed great interest in India. Curiously, the members of the family who made a real difference to the life of the Indians – Millicent and Henry Fawcett and Elizabeth Garrett Anderson – studied the problems but never went there. Elizabeth was very aware of the special need for women doctors in India, to treat women who would refuse to be seen, let alone examined, by a man. Her pupil and colleague Mary Scharlieb, who became a distinguished gynaecologist, had worked as a medical assistant in Madras before enrolling at the London School of Medicine for Women, so she was well equipped for the important duty that fell on her of explaining the Indian problems to the Queen. Queen Victoria had a complicated view of women doctors. Disapproving of women practising medicine in Britain – she had been annoyed to hear that Princess Louise had called admiringly on Elizabeth back in 1869 – she felt differently about matters in India when she learnt that women in *purdah* could not see a male doctor. In 1882 a Maharanee who had been looked after by a medical missionary had sent a message to Queen Victoria about the sufferings of Indian women, a message reinforced by Mary Scharlieb the following year before she went back to work in Madras.

There was practical help as well as sympathy when Lady Dufferin, the Viceroy's wife, started a fund at the Queen's request to bring women doctors to India. As Florence Nightingale wrote: 'you want efficient doctors for India most of all, whose native women are now our sisters, our charge. There are at least 40 millions who will only have women doctors, and who have none'.[22] 'Efficient doctors' was the important point, doctors thoroughly trained at the London School, not just medical missionaries with a smattering of knowledge, like Elizabeth's young cousin Rose Grimwood (daughter of the Betsy Garrett who had gone to school briefly with Louie so long ago) who disappointed Elizabeth by going off to India after working for only a year at Bethnal Green Mission Hospital.[23]

It was not only Queen Victoria who was won over to the need for women doctors by the problems of Indian women. Elizabeth, organizing a fund-raising bazaar for her new hospital, had great success by centring it round an Indian temple, with Hindu ladies selling Benares brass, embroideries and lacquer trays.[24] As an article in *The Queen* pointed out, 'there can be no doubt that the imperative demand for medical women in India has had a great moral effect in disarming opposition to the education of women as physicians and surgeons'.[25] Many women went out to help, some as medical missionaries like Rose Grimwood, others as qualified doctors like Edith Pechey (one of Sophia Jex-Blake's pioneering colleagues in Edinburgh), who went to Bombay, or Lillias Hamilton (once a pupil of Miss Beale at Cheltenham) who set up a practice in Calcutta and then became medical adviser to the Emir of Afghanistan. Later, the work done by women doctors in the First World War led to the decision by Lady Dufferin's fund that one of the large military hospitals in Bombay should be handed over to women doctors.[26]

Millicent's daughter Philippa, in India in 1899 on a world tour with Anne Jemima Clough's niece Blanche Athena, was there simply as an observer. Everywhere they went they were welcomed by relations or friends, or friends of friends. They were thorough sightseers, but in true Garrett and Clough style their sightseeing included endless schools (rather more than either of them wanted at times), hospitals, prisons, famine relief works, and women's appalling living quarters – 'not the sort of place one would put a nice dog to live in in England', was one of Philippa's comments. Scornful of the patronizing attitude of the missionaries who were there to convert Indians to Christianity, Philippa admired the work of medical missionaries. In Japan on her way back, she was delighted to meet a hotel owner who greeted her with 'Fawcett, I have heard of Englishman Professor Fawcett, he write book – political economy, I have read'.

But it was in India rather than Japan that Henry Fawcett had made his mark. Though he never visited India and had no appointment in the India Office, he was concerned to see that the government was properly aware of the rights and needs of the Indians – so much so that he became known as 'the member for India'. Alice was rather sceptical about his efforts, feeling that because he had never been there he did not really understand the situation, however good his intentions. He deplored the extravagance of the administration and the way the Indian population were expected to pay for various expensive schemes – buildings, royal visits, grand schemes that outstripped any reasonable local taxation. Ignoring his usual belief in free trade, he defended the right of Indians to levy a tariff against the import of cotton from Britain.

Millicent, as Henry's pupil, inherited his interest in Indian affairs,

and tirelessly widened the scope of her causes to include Indian problems. In 1889 she and Philippa gave £400 for two Henry Fawcett prizes
for Indian female medical students, money that had originally been
raised in India for Henry's election expenses (elections then tended to
cost the candidate around £1000).[27] She campaigned, but with only
passing success, against the custom of child marriages. Shortly before
the outbreak of the First World War she tried to attack child prostitution by taking up the case of an eleven-year-old girl bought by a
planter in Burma. Above all, she was concerned with the perpetual
problem of the miserable lack of education for women and girls in
India. Using all her political connections, she took her campaign for
both education and the suffrage to Edwin Montagu when he became
Secretary of State for India in 1917[28] and, still active in 1922, she led a
deputation to Lord Lytton, when he became Governor of Bengal, for
political and educational reform for Bengali women.[29]

Women's suffrage came gradually to India after 1919. Ten years later,
on her last great journey, when Millicent went with Agnes on the Orient
line to Ceylon, she told the local newspaper that she had come 'as I
heard that the women's suffrage movement is making some advance in
Ceylon'. It was her first visit to the sub-continent, and that was where
she addressed her final suffrage meeting.

14

South Africa and Empire

... bubbling with questions and problems ...
Edmund Garrett, 24 October 1889

A strong connection also grew up between the Garretts and South Africa. The first to go there was Rhoda's journalist half-brother Edmund, whose letters home brought the family in touch with South African life and problems. He kept Millicent well informed and steamed up about the rights of the British in the Transvaal, making her very ready to welcome the challenge when she was asked to go out herself to investigate the welfare of internees suffering in the British concentration camps of the Boer War. Philippa, back from her travels round the world, went with her, and was so impressed by the need for education among the internees that she became involved in pioneering work for education there for three years after the war.

Other members of the extended family eventually emigrated to South Africa. Edmund's sister Elsie went out to join her daughter Rosemary late in life, long after Edmund had left, living to be 90 and producing, at the age of 81, a distinguished book of illustrations of South African flora.[1] The book had arisen from an exhibition of Elsie's paintings, including many of wild flowers, fifteen years earlier, and Elsie had enthusiastically started to work on more plates, but publication had been delayed by the war. She also produced four pages of plates for a little handbook, *Common Succulents*, which was published when she was 86.[2]

It was illness that led to Edmund's time in South Africa. In 1889, when he began to suffer from tuberculosis, his employer W. T. Stead helpfully sent him out as correspondent for the *Pall Mall Gazette*. Edmund took to it enthusiastically – 'South Africa is simply bubbling with questions and problems coming up for settlement', he wrote, 'it is the workshop of our Empire just now'.[3] And he went on to outline some of his ideas: 'interview Rhodes about diamond fields – get copy from description of fields – of illicit diamond trade, &c &c – Work up City interest before I go out ... Gold mining, treat in same way ...

(Fydell) Edmund Garrett, 1895

Question of [English miners] outnumbering Boers – excluded from government – what's to happen ... England from Boer point of view'.

He stayed for two years, reprinted his articles as a book, and two years later, after a cheerful and hard-working spell as Assistant Editor to E. T. Cook at the *Pall Mall Gazette* in London, was once more sent abroad for his health, this time to Egypt. Egypt gave him plenty of interesting places and people, but it did not give him health. For that he took his sister Amy's advice and went for a while to the sanatorium at Nordrach in Germany. There, he wrote to Agnes, he was making 'as fair a start as man could make'; and there, a few months later, Amy came for her marriage to Edmund's Cambridge friend John Badley. His *Pall Mall* colleague Edward Cook visited Edmund at Nordrach too, bringing the news that the *Pall Mall* had changed its proprietor and its politics, and that Cook was now editor of the new Liberal *Westminster Gazette*.

Back in England, Edmund spent two years writing articles for the *Westminster*, translating Ibsen's *Brand*, and helping the Badleys in the early days of Bedales School. Many of his *Westminster* articles showed his continued interest in South African affairs, so in 1895, when a new editor was needed for the *Cape Times*, Edmund seemed the obvious candidate. He returned to South Africa, determined to make his views felt: 'I will be free here, as I have been free all my journalistic life, to praise or censure just as it seems to me right according to such faculties as God has given me'.[4] Like Stead himself, Edmund believed deeply both in social reform and in the importance of the British Empire – a typical Garrett mixture of radicalism and traditionalism.

Edmund's great bundle of long weekly letters to Agnes[5] from South Africa were full of his politics (which he said she could pass on to journalists of *The Times* and the *Pall Mall Gazette* as long as no authority was named), his frustrations, his hopes, and his health. Trying, as he said, to write himself quiet, he poured out reams about his relationship with Rhodes, the politics of South African journalism, the scope of his own influence, his views on the history and disastrous impulsiveness of the Jameson Raid,[6] which might mark the beginning 'of a race war in South Africa, perhaps Europe too, such as none can see the end of'.[7]

These letters to Agnes were eventually offered to the British Museum by Philippa Fawcett, but the museum accepted only those from 1896–98; earlier and later ones were unfortunately destroyed. The way his letters insist on the pleasure and excitement of his work whatever the disappointments and hazards – 'isn't life interesting? Isn't the world made lively for me?' – sounds very much like Millicent. Elsie's grandson, the actor Nigel Hawthorne, born in South Africa long after his great uncle Edmund had died, was proud of his memory: 'in a climate of jingoism, his was a refreshingly liberal presence, ambitious, courageous and humane'.[8] His interest ranged widely over politics, social conditions, education, literature. Starting a circulating library, he was delighted to find 'a Tommy who writes poetry' – Edgar Wallace, not yet a famous novelist.[9]

Agnes went out to visit him in 1895, seeing his friends and his life, and Edmund often hoped she would come again.[10] Another link with home was Dr Jane Waterston, who had been one of the first fourteen students at the London School of Medicine for Women. She was now South Africa's first woman doctor, a prominent medical missionary, and she nobly added to her heavy workload in Cape Town by caring for Edmund in his constant illnesses and exhaustion. A defender of the rights of the black races and wonderfully kind to Edmund, she was never afraid to speak her mind. Critical of the Boers, and critical too of

Elizabeth – 'Mrs Anderson is very clever and does many a kind deed but there is a hardness about her that revolts me and certainly a godlessness that is painful to see'[11] – Dr Waterston became a friend and ally of Millicent over the report on the camps. Agnes sent her various arty presents which seem to have both pleased and embarrassed her – 'it's never safe to give the Physician anything that one thinks pretty of a pronounced type', Edmund wrote.[12] She and Agnes kept up a correspondence.

Critical of the 'the caste feeling of the Dutch about colour', Edmund himself had a rather paternalistic sympathy for the black population. He started a column in the *Cape Times* to give the views of the blacks – 'the *black* side of things' by a 'confessed negrophilist' – and was concerned that they should have better education, better housing, better holidays. He campaigned against the miserably low wages and the all too common physical violence. He believed in free trade and 'cheap food'. The imperial mission, in his mind, was to help the blacks to catch up with European culture, so if the English had 'not wit enough or patience enough' to understand the problems of the blacks 'we have no business here and ought to get out as soon as possible'. Yet he did not manage to accept the idea of marriage between black and white: 'it is a very cheap humanity for us to hold out our arms to the "man and brother" six thousand miles away. It is another matter for the colonist-cousin who is within daily touch'. 'Educate by all means', he wrote, 'but do it to equalise, not to assimilate'.[13] In his belief that the best thing was to spread the benefits of British civilization as far as possible, he welcomed movement northwards as part of 'Englishing the Transvaal':

> When the British Empire has served its turn and gone to pieces, it will be remembered that in its day it made some of the dark places of the earth less dark, that wherever it came it made the strong more orderly and the weak less afraid.[14]
>
> Say not that we are superior and they inferior (a thing by no means true in every respect), but simply that we are *different*, and that the difference involves, as a matter of practical comfort and convenience for both colours, a certain amount of keeping to ourselves.[15]

He was one of the few to emphasize the obvious fact that 'most of the people in South Africa, most of the people in the two new Colonies for which we were Constitution-making, are natives'. He wrote to Agnes of his hopes for 'colonial representation at Westminster', but thought it would only happen 'too far ahead for us to see'.[16]

Edmund became an influential figure in South African life. In 1898 the High Commissioner Alfred Milner even suggested he should be appointed Imperial Secretary, an idea opposed by Joseph Chamberlain, the Colonial Secretary, who thought him a 'conceited self-confident partisan chatterer'. Edmund was more than happy to be elected instead to the Cape parliament.

But in his immersion in South African politics Edmund did not forget his English family. There is a voice from the past in one sad reference to a visit from an ailing James Smith, widower of Louie Garrett, who 'looked and was extraordinarily better though of course under the shade of morphine'.[17] James had continued to support the various Garrett enterprises, joining Skelton as a trustee of the New Hospital for Women; he died soon after the beginning of the new century. And Edmund was always well in touch with Gower Street concerns. 'What about those Degrees?' he wrote, 'tell Milly I wish I was home to help fight that and also that she was here to help me with the Cape women'.[18] When a Dutch member of the parliament introduced a Bill to increase fines for soliciting, Edmund added other offences to it, writing cheerfully to Millicent:

> Your Act on the Statute Book of Cape Colony is, or should be, a useful bit of work. I merely adapted to Cape conditions the English Act which you sent, and read your Times extract to the House to drive it through ... I told, of the two professional obstruction pedants, each that the other was going to play the pedant on it and showed each the paragraph I had ready ridiculing that other as patron of the pimps; and in short, in two days we put it through Committee stage, Report and third Reading in the Assembly, and all stages in Council, and in three days it was law. A most disgraceful precedent![19]

Illness ended Edmund's South African career in 1899 – 'no blow was harder or has left more permanent ill-effects than the break-down of your health', Milner wrote; but it did not end Edmund's concern for South Africa's future. He was still writing, in his last days, of the problem of voting rights for blacks. His article, 'The Unheard Helot', showed how any threshold of qualification would exclude almost all blacks, while manhood suffrage would swamp the whites.[20] He worried, in a way that is still relevant in many parts of the world, about whether democracy could ever be successfully introduced by force – 'our insolence takes the form of imposing equality', he wrote to Stead when he was back in the Nordrach sanatorium. He managed, even there, to write occasional South African articles for the *Daily News* and for the *Contemporary Review*. His view, (suggested in 'Natives and the New Constitutions'[21]) was that an Advisory Council should be set up to look after their affairs. And he was deeply disappointed that the war had 'shattered my special federation scheme, on mixed Colonial Republic lines which I have cherished for ten years'.[22]

One strand in the complicated conflicts of interests that led up to the Boer War – a strand understood all along by Edmund, and that had direct relevance for Millicent and Agnes – was the complaint from the increasing number of Uitlanders (British immigrants) in the Transvaal that they were not given a vote in the government of the country. Indeed Millicent emphasized this as a basic cause of the war:

> They and their industries were heavily taxed; a very large proportion of the whole revenue of the State was derived from them, but they were denied the vote and therefore had no share in controlling the expenditure or the policy of the State in which they lived. They not unnaturally raised the cry, 'No taxation without representation,' and in other respects almost inevitably took up and repeated the arguments and protests which for many years we had urged on behalf of the unenfranchised women of Great Britain.[23]

Firmly patriotic, she supported what she saw as a struggle for British freedom. The greedy rush for control of the gold mines, the way the blacks were sidelined in the quarrels for domination between Boers and British – all this she managed to ignore. Edmund, then in his sanatorium in Germany, disturbed her further by writing of the strong anti-British feeling there. With the support of *The Times* she organized a series of pamphlets setting out the British case. What she wanted, she wrote to a friend, was 'equal political privileges for all white races'.[24] This may shock now, but it simply echoes Cecil Rhodes, who had declared two years earlier (to the approval of Edmund's 1909 biographer)[25] that there should be 'equal rights for every white man south of the Zambesi'. It seems liberal compared to Mrs Humphry Ward's view that the Boers 'will have to learn to live peacefully with the people who financially run their country' for English rule was 'the natural discipline appointed for them by Providence'.[26]

British public opinion was fiercely divided over the Boer War, famously between the 'jingoist' supporters and a left wing almost as strongly opposed as it is now over Iraq. From India in 1899, Philippa commented on the enthusiasm among the soldiers – 'it must be frightfully hard', she wrote in her diary, 'for real soldiers to think that volunteers are going and they are not'. Some of the strongest anti-war feeling came from W. T. Stead, by then editor of the *Review of Reviews*. But whatever their politics, few could be happy about the 'scorched earth policy' used by Kitchener to end the Boer guerrilla warfare. Farms were burnt, crops destroyed, 100,000 white women and children rounded up into 'concentration camps' (the first use of the phrase) where at least 26,000 died of disease (largely measles and typhoid). Between 14,000 and 20,000 black farm labourers and their families died in a camp population of 120,000. Around 7,000 British soldiers were killed fighting, and a further 13,000 or so died of disease.

The British government, moved by the conditions in the women's camps reported by the reforming activist Emily Hobhouse, asked Millicent to go out in 1901 with two colleagues and join Jane Waterston and two other women there to investigate and suggest what might be done – an all female committee, for the first time, to report on the scandal exposed by a woman. 'These people will never ever forget what has happened', Emily Hobhouse had said, 'the children have been the hardest hit. They wither in the terrible heat and as a result of insufficient and improper nourishment ... To maintain this kind of camp means nothing less than murdering children'.

Before she left England, Millicent answered Emily Hobhouse in an article in the *Westminster Gazette* defending the government for 'no one can take part in war without sharing in its risks, and the formation of the concentration camps is part of the fortune of war'.[27] Jane Waterston's article in the *Cape Times* was even more defensive:

> We ordinary Colonial women who have been through the stress and strain of these last two years are not very favourably impressed by the hysterical whining going on in England at the present time ... This war has been remarkable for two things – first the small regard that the Boers from the highest to the lowest have had for their women kind, and secondly the great care and consideration the victors have had for the same, very often, ungrateful women.[28]

'Did ever a woman pen such nonsense?' was Emily Hobhouse's comment, dismissing Millicent and her colleagues as a 'Whitewashing Committee'.

On 22 July 1901, only a week after the investigating committee had been appointed, they sailed for the Cape in one of Skelton's Orient Line ships. As Emily Hobhouse had warned, 'one can't speak generally about these camps or the condition of the women therein. One is very different from another'.[29] There had certainly been some improvement by the time the committee arrived and got to work. Millicent had mixed reactions, and was ready to criticize many details of the organization and accommodation. Kitchener, the British Commander-in-Chief, was difficult to approach, but Edmund's friendship with Alfred Milner made it easier for her to be candid, so she wrote to Milner in November that 'we feel that in certain camps bad blunders have been made ... In every camp where there has been an exceptionally bad outbreak of disease, we think we see causes which more foresight and better organisation might have avoided'.[30]

Twenty-three years later, in *What I Remember*, Millicent seems to have dismissed some of the horrors from her memory, giving a jarringly rosy picture of what she found:

> The inhabitants of the camp were rationed free of cost to themselves with ample supplies of meal, meat, coffee, sugar, salt, and condensed milk ... In Natal potatoes, and sometimes fresh vegetables, were added, and later, on our recommendation, a supply of rice was given in all the camps ... the administration of the camps supplied clothing, including boots, full medical attendance and nursing, also education and religious services.[31]

These were the camps that had had a 26 per cent death rate.

Emily Hobhouse also looked back after 23 years, seeing things differently from Millicent:

> Her commission did not enter the camps till four and a half months after I left them. It was an interval of rapid whitewashing. They did not see the camps as I had seen them, but nevertheless found a grave condition of things: two-thirds of the people still lying on the bare ground, water supplies still needed, overcrowding. They had to cable for scores of nurses, had to dismiss several superintendents, to order an increase of fuel, and urge upon Kitchener the service of another weekly truck from the coast to provide rice etc. for the children.[32]

It was, she admitted, that extra food that helped check the appalling death-rate.

So, hostile as Emily Hobhouse was, and severely critical of the 'superficial' nature of the Report, she does give Millicent's committee credit for getting some things done: 'they do not shrink from condemning ill-chosen sites, dismissing incompetent superintendents, reforming entire hospitals, urging various improvements in food, fuel, water, recommending beds and ameliorating sanitation'.[33] And the editor of the Hobhouse letters admits that, whatever her political views, Jane Waterston 'tackled issues like sanitation and hygiene in the camps with impressive dedication and drive'.[34]

The committee's report blamed the Boers themselves for much of the distress: 'every superintendent has to wage war against the sanitary habits of the people', Millicent said, and she claimed that many Boer children would have died anyway if they had stayed on their farms:

> The heavy part of the death-rate in the camps is that of children under five. It is not because they are in the camp, but because war has exposed them to poisonous conditions of water and atmosphere, and has deprived them of food suitable to their tender age. More is being done for them in camp, ten times more in the way of skilful doctors and feeding and nursing than could have been done for them had they remained on their fathers' farms.[35]

Hobhouse denied this, insisting that Boer children in the camps were vulnerable because they arrived in such states of shock and exhaustion.[36]

Millicent did emphasize the need for better water supply and sanitary conditions and fresh food. It was not, she conceded, an easy matter to get really competent and kindly men to act as superintendents of the camps, and the camp at Mafeking came in for special criticism for failing to improve the food or isolate the sick: 'we found one or two really grossly incompetent men in charge and recommended their removal, but we did not come across one single instance of cruelty or even of harshness... All through the camps we found almost without exception that the schools were a great success'.[37]

The three questions she had asked herself, she wrote in the *Westminster Gazette*,[38] were, first, 'was the creation of these camps necessary from the military point of view?' Here she accepted the military argument that the farms had to be emptied both because they were used for military supplies of food and ammunition, and because they were a source of false information for British troops. Then 'are our officials exerting themselves to make the conditions of the camps as little oppressive as possible?' She thought so, and quoted Emily Hobhouse herself saying things were improving. And finally 'ought the public at home to supplement the efforts of the officials and supply additional comforts and luxuries?' Yes, she wrote, extra help was good in itself and also good in rebuilding good relationships.

She had tried to be fair, but feelings ran high and many had thought her prejudiced. When she came home Millicent had to face hostility. As she wrote to Dr Jane Walker (Elizabeth's colleague, and her own friend and neighbour): 'several pro-Boer people who used to be quite good friends of mine now cut me dead and turn their backs if I am coming towards them. I don't exactly like it; but I try to bear it with patience. It takes a many people to make a world'.[39]

The one good feature of the camps had been the schools. Philippa, accompanying her mother, was so moved by what she saw that she went back the following year to help to set up a system of public elementary education in the Transvaal – something that Edmund had always wanted. Millicent had earlier had great ambitions for Philippa – wanting her to shine in some new profession for women to be 'an astronomer, a physicist, a lighthouse designer or an engineer ... or train as a solicitor or an actuary'.[40] But now she was happy and proud at Philippa's decision to work for education, first in South Africa and later for the London County Council. Millicent had recovered from her appalling early views about free education for the poor, even if she still opposed mothers' pensions and family allowances.

Millicent spent a second six months in South Africa in 1903, visiting Philippa and touring round. Although Emily Hobhouse, distressed at the widespread poverty and hunger, was at that time writing home about the Boer 'disgust with the present administration',[41] Millicent managed to be impressed by how well the country was recovering and at signs that Boer and British were starting to work together. It was the hope that Edmund expressed in an epitaph on a war cemetery:

Together, sundered once by blood and speech,
Joined here in equal muster of the brave,
Lie Boer and Briton, foes each worthy each,
May peace strike root into their common grave,
And blossoming where the fathers fought and died,
Bear fruit for sons that labour side by side.[42]

That was fine, but Millicent's attitude to black South Africans – and to class structure – still fitted all too well with the attitudes of the time and place. In an article in the *Contemporary Review* she wrote:

Domestic work is done entirely by natives, who live in their own locations, distant from their employers' houses from about half a mile to two miles or perhaps more. These servants arrive at about 7.30 in the morning, and leave again at about 2.30 p.m. Everything required by their employers after that hour the latter must procure and do for themselves. This in itself almost paralyses social life.[43]

She goes on to talk of 'the plan of allowing the native servants to live in their own locations' – so inconvenient for their employers. And she approves of a scheme that has sent 'many hundreds of female servants' from England to South Africa.

The patriotism which blinkered her in South Africa blossomed in Millicent's great admiration for the Queen. Edmund knew this well. The day after the Queen's diamond jubilee he wrote to Agnes: 'in London yesterday must have been a wonderful day, and no people would take keener delight in the tributes to our Queen, and our national sense of pride and unity, than my own dear people in Gower Street'.[44] Millicent sent him her photographs of Jubilee crowds in Pall Mall and St James, and he published them in the *Cape Times Weekly*.[45]

Her admiration went beyond the excitement of the moment and led to one of her two excursions into biography, with her *Life of Her Majesty Queen Victoria* published in the diamond jubilee year,[46] which, Edmund loyally wrote to Agnes, 'seemed to have everything worth telling ... I was *very* much struck with the clever way in which she has got the essence of the period, politics etc, into the picture as a frame for what she says about the Queen herself'.[47] Her early radical views against hereditary monarchy or aristocracy[48] had faded with time, and the jubilee led her to celebrate the British constitution that, unlike the German, allowed a woman to inherit the throne. Carried away with enthusiasm, she praises the Queen's 'intellectual grasp', her 'mind and will', her 'courage and self-possession' – it is easier to agree with all that than with her assessment of the Queen as a mother. She also thoroughly approved of 'the stand the Queen made against the loose morals of the previous reign'.[49] But Millicent was well aware of the paradox that the Queen herself, while being an excellent example of a highly accomplished political woman, was strongly opposed to all aspects of women's rights:

> Several of the Queen's daughters, notably the Empress Frederick and Princess Alice, have shown the greatest sympathy with what is known in England as the women's movement. They have promoted by every means in their power improved opportunities of education and employment for women, and greater social liberty for them. The Queen, it must be confessed, has never shown that she sympathises with her daughters in their attitude on this question.

Millicent then clutches at all available straws to show that the Queen who had fumed about 'this mad wicked folly of woman's rights' was not entirely wrong-headed:

Though, on the whole, the Queen has been very far from giving encouragement, except by the magnificent example of her own life and character,
to the modern movement among women for sharing in political work and
responsibility, she testified her interest in their higher education by opening
in person, in 1887, the palatial buildings of Holloway College ... Another of
the modern women's movements which the Queen has promoted is their
entrance into the medical profession.

That encouragement for medical training for women had of course been
triggered when the Queen learnt of India's need for women doctors.

William Molesworth (1810–55), radical politician and founder of the
Reform Club, was chosen as the subject for Millicent's second biography, both because he had been one of Henry Fawcett's heroes and
because she admired him and felt his views were relevant to the current
problems of South Africa. She was in sympathy with his political creed –
'the ballot, free trade, national education, reform of the House of Lords,
religious equality, household suffrage, and better government for Ireland'.[50] Above all he was a spokesman for colonial self-government,
believing in extending Britain's colonies for trade and for emigration of
Britain's surplus population (though not as dumping grounds for
criminals), and in helping them to develop their own representative
institutions under British sovereignty. Molesworth wanted, Millicent
wrote, 'free government and every other adjunct of civilised life which
could help to make Colonial life attractive'.[51] Such views would be
entirely acceptable to someone who said she wanted equal political
privileges for all white races. She contrasted Molesworth with James
Stephen who, when at the Colonial Office 'looked with no friendly eye
on the various schemes for promoting emigration and colonisation,
because he wished to protect the aboriginal races of New Zealand and
Australia from white men's diseases and white men's sins', and for them
to have no contact with European civilization except through
missionaries.[52]

James Stephen, the father of Leslie and Fitzjames Stephen, seems an
odd choice for anti-hero. His father had been associated with Wilberforce in the abolition of the slave trade, and he followed the same
tradition by drafting the 1833 Bill for the abolition of slavery. He had in
fact much in common with the radical agnostic Molesworth, and like
him he came increasingly to believe in trusting colonial governors and
in helping colonies to become self-governing within the empire,
'relaxing the bonds of authority' as had been done in Canada. But

Stephen had less belief in increased colonization and more sympathy for indigenous peoples. For, anxious both to protect native civilizations and to promote Christianity, Stephen realized that even though it might be wonderful to convert heathens, 'if we acquire the whole of Africa it is a worthless possession'; settling in Natal, he wrote with foresight, would lead to 'the consumption of treasure, the waste of human life and a warfare alike inglorious, unprofitable and afflicting'. Criticizing him, Millicent was being carried away by her faith in Empire, her belief in spreading the British way of life.

Never detached and neutral, Millicent used her book as a platform for an outburst of patriotism. She supported Palmerston's view (although in this case differing from Molesworth) that any Englishman abroad was entitled to his country's support, and wrote with pride of Napier's appalling Abyssinian Expedition of 1868 when, in a so-called 'small war', an army of 32,000 marched to the rescue of a group of European hostages, with the loss of around 400 British and Indians and 1,000 Abyssinians: 'who is there that does not feel that it is worth something to be a British subject? That if he is wronged anywhere in the ends of the earth, Great Britain will see him righted? When Great Britain acts up to this character, every Briton repays the debt he owes his country with love and gratitude, and with his life if need be'.[53]

15

An Interlude of Schools

Classics for girls, mathematics, proper physical training, organized games, the wise but difficult combination of freedom and watchful care.

Julia Grant, St Leonards School, 1927

Attitudes to schools for middle-class girls had changed in the generation since Louie and Elizabeth had been sent off to the Miss Brownings. There were many new institutions to join Queen's College and Bedford College, recognizing the need to move beyond teaching conventional domestic skills and accomplishments, to offer a broad secondary education. The Home and Colonial School Society (founded twelve years before Queen's, and where Anne Jemima Clough had briefly studied), trained teachers, particularly infant-school teachers, according to Pestalozzi and Froebel beliefs; Charlotte Mason, who had trained there, started the Parents Educational Union (later the Parents National Educational Union) in 1887. The College of Preceptors, which aimed to improve the standards of teachers, was founded in 1846 and opened its examinations to women; in 1869 Frances Buss became one of the first two women on its council. Help came too from the London Schoolmistresses Association (meeting from 1866 to 1887 with Emily Davies as secretary), one of several associations set up round the country. The general feeling, expressed by the National Union for the Education of Women, founded in 1872, was 'to raise the social status of female teachers by encouraging women to make teaching a profession'.[1] In 1885 the first fourteen students joined Miss Hughes at her training college in Cambridge for women teachers.

Newnham and Girton were slowly followed by other higher education colleges for women, all on a small scale and at first by no means generally accepted – four women's colleges in Oxford, Westfield College and Royal Holloway College in London, and the London School of Medicine for Women. Once the movement started, though, it was bound to grow, nurtured by its own new demands. The new opportunities for further education for women that had been made well before the turn of the century brought an urgency to the problem of improved schooling. Miss Buss's North London Collegiate (1850), and Miss Beale's Cheltenham Ladies' College (founded 1853) stood out as beacons, but there was a need for these to be followed by successful imitators. Between 1869 and 1880 there were 61 new schools for girls.[2] The Girls' Public Day School Trust, which was set up in 1872 to provide 'a real and solid education', opened eleven schools in London and eleven scattered round the country – it was one of their schools that Millicent Fawcett had chosen for Philippa. At the same time the higher education colleges themselves helped by producing graduates who were anxious to teach. The Garrett contribution to girls' schools, involving various members of the family and their friends, lay mainly in initiatives that evolved into new boarding opportunities.

St Leonards School, St Andrews, set up in 1877 'to give to girls the education which their brothers have at the Public Schools', owed something to Elizabeth and to her influence on the daughters of John Cook, the professor of ecclesiastical history in St Andrews. In her student days at St Andrews Elizabeth's particular friend had been Harriet Cook, who died very young. It was two of her sisters who were prominent in starting the school. A third sister, Rachel, became one of the first three students at Hitchin and later, as the wife of C.P. Scott of the *Manchester Guardian*, a founder of Withington School for Girls in Manchester. Another Girton graduate, Frances Dove, headmistress at St Leonards for fourteen years, left to found Wycombe Abbey School (1896). A Newnham graduate started Roedean School in 1885.

One of the early supporters of St Leonards was Sir James Ramsay, who sent four daughters there, including Agnata, who was to distinguish herself so conspicuously at Girton in 1887 by beating all the men and becoming the only candidate to get a first class degree in classics – Montagu Butler (the 55-year-old Master of Trinity and brother-in-law to Josephine Butler) then married her, so he said, for 'her goodness, not her Greek and Latin'. Louisa Garrett Anderson went to St Leonards in 1886 at the age of thirteen, on 'one of the most delightfully unhappy days I have ever had, I think, for I cried on and off, nearly the whole day'.[3] There is a letter to her mother much later, in a jollier mood, describing a visit from Emily Davies to the headmistress:

> I don't think Miss Davies and Miss Dove seem great friends. They squash each other rather. Miss Davies is dry and snubs Miss Dove's theories to our joy. The other day Miss Dove announced that girls ought not to get letters at school, a short one once a fortnight was more than sufficient to keep

them posted in home events. Miss Davies: 'I never heard that letters were an evil before.' Dove: 'They occupy their minds and their attention away from school life.' Miss Davies: 'I should have thought that they might contain admonition to work.'[4]

Elizabeth was even more closely connected with the founding of St Felix School, Southwold (near Aldeburgh). It was a Newnham graduate this time, Margaret Gardiner, who had an ambition to start and run a school. Following Elizabeth's advice, she prepared herself first by teaching at St Leonards, and then by becoming headmistress of Withington School for Girls before opening her own school with seven pupils (some boarding) in West Hill, the Garrett Andersons' Aldeburgh house. It was a temporary arrangement until more permanent buildings could be found, and was not really convenient since everything had to be moved out so that the Andersons could use the house in the holidays. But the rambling house and fine garden was, an early pupil wrote, 'a particularly charming place'[5] and Margaret Gardiner could start her school 'where girls are treated like sensible creatures'.

Bedales, the influential progressive school, owed much to the family of the Derbyshire Garretts. It was a non-denominational school, started in 1893 by John Badley as a boarding school for boys aged nine to fifteen, run on unconventionally free and democratic lines, with a wide range of work and lots of arts and crafts. Garretts and girls' education came into the story partly because it claimed to be a 'family school' and families include girls, but mainly because Badley had married Edmund Garrett's forceful sister Amy. It opened, on an even smaller scale than St Felix, with only three pupils, one of them being Geoffrey Garrett, son of Amy's half-brother Frank. 'I wonder if the school List will ever get long enough to cover the School Bills and leave a margin!' Edmund wrote to Agnes in 1896, 'I feel it is such a big work and good work, and so fully practical too, that it would be ten thousand pities if it didn't come to *pay*, which is after all the security for permanence'.[6] It did grow, and girl pupils were added in 1898, so Bedales has been hailed as the first co-educational boarding school in England.

There had in fact been other, rather different, co-educational boarding schools. The Quakers ran several, such as Ackworth School (1779), Sidcot (1808), or Sibworth (1842), which had been co-educational from the start. Barbara Bodichon had founded and run the co-educational Portman Hall School (for young children) from 1852 to 1863. With Jessie White (who had hoped to become a doctor), Elizabeth

Whitehead (who as Mrs Malleson was to become the principal of the Working Women's College), and Octavia Hill as teachers, Portman Hall School was a fine example of the 'stage army' of women reformers. The 1911 *Encyclopaedia Britannica* also mentions that 'a private boarding and day secondary school on co-educational lines was instituted by Mr W. A. Case in Hampstead in 1865. A co-educational boarding-school was founded in 1869 by Miss Lushington at Kingsley near Alton, Hants'. Perhaps these did not succeed, but they show that the idea was around. At any rate, Bedales was probably the first undenominational co-educational secondary boarding school to survive.

Amy, who had studied music in Germany, was largely responsible for establishing Bedales' distinction in music. The *Pall Mall Gazette* interview with John Badley, written by Edmund, has a timeless ring in its criticism of the educational establishment:

> The points in which we faddists want reforms are – in a couple of sentences – the early specialization, which exerts its narrowing influence just as much on the modern sides as ever it did under the monopoly of the Latin grammar, and the all-pervading atmosphere of individual competition, with its machinery of marks and prizes and scholarships.[7]

Not that Bedales was unsuccessful academically. The 2005 Newnham College Roll Letter gives obituary notices of nine distinguished old students who were born in or before 1912; four of them had been at Bedales.

So in its early days, Bedales was very much a Garrett family affair. Edmund, in England and without a full time job, had time to write a pamphlet about the school, and to join Amy and their younger sister Elsie in the first school play – which had a backdrop painted by Roger Fry. In his autobiography Nigel Hawthorne wrote that there was no artistic or stage background in his family, but it is not hard to see something of both in his much-loved grandmother Elsie, with her painting and her enthusiasm for amateur dramatics.

The school went to the house rented by Agnes at Rustington for summer camps. Elsie, who had trained at the Royal Female School of Art, taught drawing and dressmaking at the school, and was to marry the science master Charles Rice; they left Bedales for a time for Charles Rice to become the first headmaster of King Alfred's School, a co-educational progressive school in Hampstead. Like her sisters, Elsie was active in the militant suffragette movement. Amy, a staunch feminist, used to invite all the Bedales girls to tea before they left, and 'urged them to work ceaselessly for women's rights, not to marry the first man who asked them and never to wear corsets'.[8] She was involved with both the National Union of Women's Suffrage Societies and the militant Women's Social and Political Union, managing to be on good terms both with Millicent and with Mrs Pankhurst. In 1912, too frail to take an active part in the protests herself, but sympathizing with the militant suffragettes and anxious to keep Bedales out of trouble, she secretly gave money to the fugitive Mrs Pankhurst. In spite of that frailty, Amy lived on until 1956, dying at the age of 93. John Badley died in 1967, aged 102. They had one son.

The more conventional boys' school, Framlingham College (founded 1864 as the Royal Albert Middle-Class School and College), had Garrett connections because it was near Aldeburgh. Newson's brother Richard was secretary of the committee, Richard's son-in-law Frederick Peck was the architect and other members of Richard's family, but not Newson, contributed. The split seems to have healed in the next generation, for Elizabeth and Skelton gave money to an appeal in 1886, Millicent and Elizabeth each presided at later prize-givings and their brother George, who became manager of the malting business at Snape, became a governor of the school. Framlingham did not help the cause of education for girls until it became co-educational in 1976.

16

The Campaign Trail

I, and I think the great majority of the men and women who are working for our cause, look upon it as one of the very greatest things that has ever happened in the history of the world ... It is the greatest step towards freedom which the human race has ever yet made, and it is the greater because it is not confined to any one nation or to any rank or class in society; it is the uplifting of our entire sex all over the world.

Millicent Fawcett, 1913

It was a grandiose claim, but it expressed Millicent's passionate belief. In the years leading up to the First World War she was totally absorbed by the great issue of women's suffrage, the issue that had always been the main theme that ran through her life, even if other problems had at times roused her sympathies and distracted her on the way.

One distraction – a problem that bordered on Elizabeth's field – arose both from Millicent's concern for her cousin Edmund's illness, and from friendship with Dr Jane Walker. Millicent became the chairman of the board of management of the East Anglian Sanatorium near her old home ground at Nayland in Suffolk, the first hospital of any sort founded and run by women to treat patients of both sexes. For over 30 years she was actively involved in organizing and fund raising. Edmund, back from South Africa and from an attempted cure in Germany, spent some time there recovering his strength under Jane Walker's care; and it was there that he fell in love with a fellow patient, Ellen Marriage, marrying her in 1903 to enjoy four happy final years of his sadly weakened life. One of Alice's daughters was there briefly and successfully, and Agnes had a month there for 'debility' in 1908.

Then Millicent, who tended to become concerned about any grievances that came her way, became distracted by time-consuming worries about Irish problems. She had learnt to distrust Gladstone when his 1884 Reform Bill ignored the question of women's votes, and she was even more indignant the following year when he came out in favour of Home Rule for Ireland. She had agreed with Henry years before when he had said that he would rather the Liberal Party should remain out of office until its youngest member had grown grey-headed than be inti-midated into supporting Home Rule.[1] Gladstone, Millicent thought, was now being intimidated. She did not approve of militancy in Ireland any more than she was to approve of it later in the suffrage movement. And the whole idea of Home Rule was upsetting to her creed of patriotism and British rule. So she became deeply involved with the Liberal Unionists, visiting Ireland, making speeches round Britain, and as a result becoming increasingly well known as a public figure.

Her patriotism was enthusiastic, but her support for the Liberal Unionists, her work in South Africa and her imperialist biographies are now almost forgotten, while her work for women's education, and above all for women's suffrage, will always be remembered. And her work in South Africa reinforced her arguments for the suffrage; as Ray Strachey wrote, 'If the representation of the Uitlanders was important enough for England to fight the Boers for, the denial of it to English-women became even harder to defend; and Mrs Fawcett lost no opportunity of driving this lesson home'.[2]

Not as wealthy as Elizabeth – who had a rich husband and a flour-ishing medical practice – Millicent could still afford to work for and support causes she believed in without the need to earn her own living. Henry left her £9,535 and the royalties from his books when he died in 1884; her father left £57,801 for his family in 1893, and her mother left £19,432 ten years later. There was no financial pressure, but plenty of pressure to achieve her ambition, and few domestic calls on her time. So a year after Henry's death she was ready to emerge from the shadows and take an active part in politics once more.

With her basic belief that if women had the vote many injustices could be tackled that were otherwise ignored, Millicent spoke out with endless energy for the rights of women and of children. For one thing, the vote was needed to help women fight the evils of the double stan-dards of Victorian morality – and she felt very strongly about morality. No longer afraid of damaging the suffrage cause by publicizing her views (as she had been in 1870 over the contagious diseases acts[3]), she actively supported W. T. Stead's famous pioneering effort at a jour-nalistic 'sting' against child prostitution. Back in 1866 the Pall Mall Gazette had opened a new approach to investigative journalism (and shot up its sales) when James Greenwood, brother of the then editor, had dressed as a pauper and spent a night in a 'casual ward' before writing about the horrors of workhouses. In 1885 the current editor W. T. Stead carried the idea further, to publicize the trade in young

girls. With the co-operation of the mother, and the agreed supervision
at all times of the Salvation Army to see that the child was protected and
cared for, he himself 'bought' a child and wrote a series of devastating
articles for his paper. In exposing the vulnerability of thirteen-year-old
girls under the existing state of the law he was deliberately stirring up
trouble. Less easily carried away by her emotions than Millicent,
Elizabeth did not approve: 'It cannot be necessary to go through Stead's
performance and to flood the world with sensational articles – disgusting and untrue. I myself believe that such things are done on some
scale or other, having seen children about the streets – or creatures
dressed up to represent children. But I cannot accept Stead's methods'.[4]

Unfortunately Stead's method did have one weak point – he had not
asked permission from the father before buying the child, and the
mother's permission was held to have no legal status (though later it
turned out that the child's parents were not married so the father had
no legal rights anyway). Stead, prosecuted for abduction, was sent to
prison for three months. 'I cannot find words to say how I honour and
reverence you for what you have done for the weakest and most helpless
among women', Millicent wrote to him. Full of righteous indignation,
she wrote too to the Queen's Private Secretary asking that Stead should
at least be treated as a first class prisoner. She spoke and wrote on his
behalf, for he had 'descended into the pit of infamy in order to be able
to compel the attention of all decent men and women to the hideous
crimes that were going on around them'.[5]

Never missing a chance to hammer home the way women's votes
could help tackle social ills, she appealed, in the *Englishwoman's Journal*,
for contributions to Stead's defence fund, as the only way women could
show their support: 'the taxpayers' money is being used to prosecute
those who have dared and done so much to protect the chastity of
English girlhood. It is true we women cannot help this; we have no
control, as long as we are unrepresented, over the manner in which the
taxpayers' money is spent'. The affair ended in triumph, for it led to the
raising of the age of consent to sixteen, and the founding of the National
Vigilance Association to protect women and children. Millicent became
involved in the work of the Association, as committee member or as a
vice-president, until 1926.

A later editor of the *Pall Mall Gazette*, the able and handsome Harry
Cust,[6] landed Millicent in a far less popular morality campaign. She
objected to his candidacy for parliament in 1894 on the grounds of a
sexual reputation which 'struck at the root of everything that makes

home and marriage sacred'. Her outspoken opposition temporarily checked his career, but at the expense of considerable bad feeling towards herself and some harm to the suffrage cause – the sort of harm that she had been so careful to avoid earlier. But she was always worried about the low moral standards accepted for men; she was active in a society formed to help vulnerable young girls arriving alone in London, and in 1899 she made a powerful speech on the white slave trade. In 1892 she hoped Thomas Hardy might write a moral story for working boys and girls. He refused, adding 'The other day I read a story entitled "The Wages of Sin" ... But the wages are that the young man falls over a cliff, and the young woman dies of consumption – not very consequent, as I told the authoress'.[7]

Millicent's worries about exploited children extended widely. She was horrified at stories of Indian girls as young as eight being forced into marriage; she argued against the exclusion of women from the courts when cases of assaults on children were tried; she was concerned for tiny children who were in need of care and education while supporting their families by working on the stage, particularly those touring in panto-mimes[8] – as wrong, she thought, as employing children in factories. But she was still opposed to special factory legislation or rules on equal pay for women, thinking that it might harm their chances of employment. And she seemed remarkably hard and unsympathetic when she sup-ported the matchmakers Bryant and May in 1898 in the notorious case of necrosis of the jaw ('phossy jaw') among women workers, on the doubtful grounds that the women were well looked after and anyway needed the work. Mrs Pankhurst, unsurprisingly, strongly supported the workers.

All this time Millicent continued to work for women's education, giving talks at schools, lecturing at Queen's College (Harley Street), at King's College Department for Ladies, and for the university extension movement, and lobbying for degrees for women at Cambridge. This side of her life was wonderfully celebrated in 1898, when St Andrews University gave her an honorary doctorate for her work for higher education, the first honorary doctorate ever given to a woman.[9] Dr Jane Walker wrote to Philippa that:

All the dignitaries of the University came first, followed by the Lord Rector and the recipients of the Hon. Degree: Buckle, Broadbent, the Chief Rabbi and others, and our dear Millie, who looked very nice. The colour of her hair showed up to perfection in the bright sunny day. She soon recognised

Agnes and me in the gallery and nodded to us ... When Millie's turn came the students all got up and cheered tremendously and waved their caps in the air, and the rest of the audience got up and cheered. Both Agnes and I had big lumps in our throats, and we felt so proud and happy and so glad to be there really to see it for ourselves.[10]

The climate had changed since the Senatus Academicus at St Andrews, 36 years earlier, had refused to accept Elizabeth as a student, returning her matriculation fee.

This personal boost for Millicent was particularly welcome, as the suffrage movement at that time had stalled. There seemed to be nothing but hopes and frustration. There had been no new parliamentary reform bill under discussion since 1884, only a succession of abortive efforts through Private Members' bills – a process that had begun back in 1870, when Jacob Bright's Bill had reached a second reading,[11] only to be dismissed by Gladstone in the committee stage. One after another, the Bills were mocked, or 'talked out'. A *Times* leader on the defeat of the 1897 Bill rehearsed all the old arguments: 'apart from a mere handful of ladies of masculine ambitions, the experience of every man is that the overwhelming majority of the best women of his acquaintance are perfectly content with the influence they wield in feminine ways, and have no wish whatever to mix themselves up in the dirty business of politics'.

The Bill was deliberately talked out by an irrelevant three-hour speech, which prompted Edmund to write consolingly from South Africa that 'the best silver lining visible just now to me is the fun Millie will make of the House of Commons burying itself with Verminous Persons to get out of its obligations to Women's Suffrage'.[12] So Millicent's policy was to keep the question of the suffrage as prominent as possible through endless campaigns of meetings and speeches and petitions. The Corrupt Practices Act of 1883, banning paid canvassing at elections, made both parties keen to recruit women as volunteers, and had the unforeseen effect of increasing the number of women involved in political activity, and even in the 'rough and tumble' of elections. But this influx of political women came with a baggage of political attachments that worried Millicent, for she was anxious to keep firmly outside both parties – particularly after her old attachment to the Liberals had been torn by Gladstone's conversion to Home Rule. For a time she supported the Liberal Unionists, but some notes she made in 1887 make her position clear: 'can best serve the various political movements in which I am interested by keeping clear of party associations. Not at all condemn others, but for me questions, e.g. on women and morality, come first and party second – a long way second'.[13]

It has often been pointed out that at this time, while members of the Liberal Party supported women's suffrage and their leaders were against it, support in the Conservative Party came only from the leaders. There were splits and groupings in the suffrage movement, and it was not until 1897 that the various suffrage societies, all with the same aims but with slightly varying philosophies, were united as the National Union of Women's Suffrage Societies (the NUWSS). Ten years later Millicent became the first elected president.

The strangest of public arguments opened in June 1889, when Matthew Arnold's niece Mary Ward (the novelist Mrs Humphry Ward) organized a protest in the *Nineteenth Century* against women's suffrage. Hating the idea of 'new women' with the overtones of aggressive feminism, she believed that parliament was already dealing adequately with past injustices – 'what *are* these tremendous grievances women are still labouring under?'[14] she wrote in a letter to her sister-in-law. Women, she thought, should stick to the work on offer in local government, for schools or for Boards of Guardians, for 'the emancipating process has now reached the limits fixed by the physical constitution of women':

> While desiring the fullest possible development of the powers, energies and education of women, we believe that their work for the State, and their responsibilities towards it, must always differ essentially from those of men ... It is not just to give women direct power of deciding questions of Parliamentary policy, of war, of foreign or colonial affairs, of commerce and finance equal to that possessed by men.[15]

A later passage could have been designed specially to irritate Millicent:

> We believe that women will be more valuable citizens, will contribute more precious elements to the national life without the vote than with it. The quickness to feel, the willingness to lay aside prudential considerations in a right cause, which are amongst the peculiar excellencies of women, are in their right place when they are used to influence the more highly trained and developed judgment of men.

It was not a unique view – four years earlier the wealthy philan-
thropist Angela Burdett-Coutts had told Millicent Fawcett that 'it would
neither benefit man nor woman to hazard the quiet but potent influence of good she now exercises in daily life, and to transform her into a
political agent'.[16] Mrs Ward managed to collect 104 signatures. Among
the many unlikely supporters of this unlikely women's movement were
the Dowager Lady Stanley of Alderley (to the bewilderment of Millicent,
who knew her as 'a constant, a generous, and an outspoken friend of
better education for women of all classes'[17]), Mrs T. H. Huxley, and
Beatrice Potter (later Beatrice Webb) who soon realized her mistake and
withdrew.[18] A form was attached, to be signed and returned to the
Nineteenth Century: 'the undersigned protest strongly against the proposed Extension of the Parliamentary Franchise to Women, which they
believe would be a measure distasteful to the great majority of the
women of the country – unnecessary – and mischievous both to
themselves and to the State'.

Millicent's answer appeared in both the *Nineteenth Century* and in
the *Fortnightly Review*. The article in the *Nineteenth Century* is a powerful attack on the protest, its inconsistencies, and the lack of understanding shown by the 104 signatories;

> It cannot be seriously argued that the means of making an intelligent choice
> between voting for this candidate or that, is not as much within the reach of
> women of education and property, as within that of their footmen,
> ploughmen, or other employees ... Among other inconsistencies of the
> protesting ladies, it should not be forgotten that many of them, as pre-
> sidents and vice-presidents of women's political associations, encourage the
> admission of women to the ordinary machinery of political life, although
> they say in this Protest that this admission would be dangerous to the best
> interests of society. If women are fit to advise, convince, and persuade voters
> how to vote, they are surely also fit to vote themselves ... We do not want
> women to be bad imitations of men; we neither deny nor minimise the
> differences between men and women. The claim of women to representa-
> tion depends to a large extent on those differences. Women bring some-
> thing to the service of the state different from that which can be brought by
> men. Let this fact be frankly recognised and let due weight be given to it in
> the representative system of the country.[19]

In the *Fortnightly*, Millicent makes it clear that there should be no
panic – she was anxious not to let the women voters outnumber the
men: 'there is not one single supporter of women's suffrage who wishes

women to be enfranchised except on the same conditions as entitle men to vote ... The women householders and property owners are much less numerous than the men householders and property owners'.[20]

Morality came into her argument too:

The majority of women electors will refuse to support men of notoriously bad character ... The thousands and thousands of homely folk whose good lives are needed to preserve a people from corruption and decay are women as well as men. And it is especially because women are accustomed to rely more on moral than on physical force that we who have been working for women's suffrage, believe that their admission to citizenship would add to the real strength and honour of England.[21]

But the activities of Mrs Humphry Ward and her followers had made it easier for Gladstone to retreat from the issue, arguing against a Private Member's Bill in 1892: 'in addition to a widespread indifference, there is on the part of large numbers of women who have considered the matter for themselves, the most positive objection and strong disapprobation'. If women had a vote, he went on, they might want to stand for parliament and then even to fill an office in the State:

I am not without the fear lest beginning with the State, we should eventually be found to have intruded into what is yet more fundamental and more sacred, the precinct of the family ... I have no fear lest the woman should encroach upon the power of the man. The fear I have is, lest we should invite her unwittingly to trespass upon the delicacy, the purity, the refinement, the elevation of her own nature, which are the present sources of its power.[22]

Mrs Humphry Ward had done a lot of damage. Millicent realized that she had to deal with a complicated character,

So constituted as to be able to believe at one and the same time that women were fundamentally incapable of taking a useful part in politics, but that she herself was an exception to the rule, for she took a deep interest in the whole political life of her country as it developed before her, and sought, both by speech and writing, often with considerable effect, to influence its direction.[23]

Rather like Queen Victoria. At any rate, Millicent understood Mrs Humphry Ward well, and made a show of enjoying the contest. It all helped to give the issue a high profile, and it was to rumble on until the suffrage triumph of 1917. The Anti-Suffrage League and the *Anti-*

Suffrage Review, fuelled by the antics of the militant suffragettes,[24] were founded in 1908, and the famous public debate between the two leaders took place the following year. The debate, Mrs Humphry Ward's daughter wrote, 'reached a high level of excellence, though it suffered from the usual fault which besets such tournaments – that the champions did not really *meet* each other's arguments, but cantered on into the void, discharging their ammunition and returning gracefully to their starting-points when time was called'.[25] But the truth was that Mrs Ward was mightily defeated, getting 74 votes to Millicent's 235. Later that year there was further humiliation for Mrs Ward when she tried arguing the anti-suffrage cause at Newnham and Girton.

The Anti-Suffrage League had a curious Indian offshoot. One argument used was that Indian men would never tolerate government by British women: 'the adoption of female suffrage in England would be a long step towards the disintegration of the British Empire in India, and should be steadily opposed by all who have imperial interests at heart'.[26] Millicent did, of course, have imperial interests at heart, and she recruited support from Lady Strachey, widow of the Indian administrator and her friend from early suffrage days, to show that this was nonsense. Neither of them had any doubt that the British – either men or women – were natural rulers.

The rise of Emmeline Pankhurst's militant movement was a more serious development. 'At the outset', Millicent wrote, 'they adopted the strictly orthodox and time-honoured method of asking questions of Ministers at public meetings'.[27] It might have seemed like a repeat of the old activities, just an effort to revive a stagnant cause. But there were fundamental differences, less patience, and a new philosophy. For one thing the questioners no longer came only from the frustrated middle classes. The Independent Labour Party was founded by Keir Hardie in 1895, and the demand for the vote, as Millicent too was well aware, was increasingly coming also from both working men and working women. Annie Kenney, the future militant leader, had started work in a cotton mill at the age of ten.

Emmeline Pankhurst, eleven years younger than Millicent, did have a middle-class background herself, in a highly political Manchester Liberal family with radical sympathies. No need for her to rebel against her upbringing. Some of her earliest memories were of the American Civil War and passionate arguments against slavery, although she was only three years old when the war began. At nine she and her small sister decided to campaign for the Liberals by parading at a polling-booth in

skirts and petticoats of Liberal colours (as Barbara Leigh Smith Bodichon had done for her father 40 years earlier); at fourteen her mother
took her at last to her first suffrage meeting. A natural suffragist,
marrying young and widowed when still young,[28] she might seem to
have much in common with Millicent. Like her again, she came to have
a distrust of political promises and political parties – Mrs Pankhurst
had joined the Labour Party, leaving it when the leaders seemed more
interested in full adult suffrage than in women's claims for votes on the
same terms as men. But the resemblance ended there for, as Mary
Stocks wrote, 'never were two women who served the same cause so
wholly unlike one another'.[29] They were far more different in their
approach than Emily Davies and Millicent had been over the introduction of women to Cambridge.

Boosted by the visit of the 82-year-old American campaigner Susan
B. Anthony in 1902, Emmeline's daughter Christabel declared that it was
time for begging to give way to action; the Pankhursts founded the
Women's Social and Political Union (WSPU) the following year.
Anxious to raise the profile of the whole campaign, and fed up with
polite promises from vaguely sympathetic politicians, Mrs Pankhurst's
faith was in 'Deeds, not Words'. In 1905, when yet another Private
Member's Suffrage Bill was talked out, she called the women in the
Strangers' Lobby to come out and protest – the first of a series of
outdoor protest meetings. And it was in the general election meetings at
the end of that year that the WSPU started their conspicuous campaign
of insistently asking whether the Liberal party would support votes for
women, with Annie Kenney and Christabel Pankhurst dominating the
scene. That was when the trouble started.

There was plenty to protest about. The Liberal Party came into power
in 1906 with a huge majority, including many who had promised
support for women's suffrage. But such promises had been given, in
the words of one Member of Parliament writing to *The Times*, 'lightly
and casually', regarding the question as 'academic, and not very
serious':[30]

Was woman suffrage one of the grounds on which men elected them? If
they cannot answer this question in the affirmative, then, however frankly at
the time they may have passingly expressed their partiality for woman
suffrage, they cannot properly allege that it was a real issue at the election;
and, until it has been put as a real issue, no such momentous and revolutionary change ought to be passed into law.[31]

One hopeful proposal after another was knocked down without mercy. In 1908 the Prime Minister (Herbert Asquith) said he would introduce a Reform Bill to extend the franchise, and would not oppose a possible amendment to include women; this faded into yet another failed Private Member's Bill. In 1910 hopes were raised by the Conciliation Bill, which would have enfranchised all women householders (about a million women); the Bill passed its Second Reading with a majority of 110, but had to be debated again after the 1911 general election, this time passing the Second Reading with a majority of 167. There it stuck. The next effort to introduce a Conciliation Bill failed, for Asquith, letting Millicent down as Gladstone had done before him, wriggled out and weaned supporters from the Bill by announcing that he would instead introduce a wider Bill extending the suffrage to all adult males; he added, after pressure, that he would not oppose an amendment to include women if it were tacked on later. As the *Saturday Review* commented: 'with absolutely no demand, no ghost of a demand, for more votes for men, and with – beyond all cavil – a very strong demand for votes for women, the Government announce their Manhood Suffrage Bill and carefully evade the other question!'

As it turned out, it was not possible to tack the amendment on – the Speaker ruled that such an amendment would alter the Bill so much that it would have to start all over again, so the whole Bill was withdrawn. All hope of help from Asquith had gone: 'the Speaker's *coup d'état* has bowled over the Women for this session – a great relief', Asquith wrote happily in a private letter.[32] His sympathies were made public when he told a deputation from the Anti-Suffrage League that inclusion of women's suffrage would be 'a political mistake of a very disastrous kind'.[33] *Punch* produced the following verse:

You speak, Mr Asquith, the suffragist said,
  Of the Will of the People wholesale;
But has the idea never entered your head
  That the People are not wholly male?

Disgusted with Asquith and the Liberals, Millicent became more determined to look for supporters wherever she could find them; at that time the Labour Party looked more promising.

This is not the place for a history of the militants, their demonstrations, the imprisonments, the forcible feeding. Protesting that 'men's blood-shedding militancy is applauded and women's symbolic militancy punished with a prison cell',[34] Emmeline Pankhurst claimed

Suffrage procession 1908 – Millicent is second from left

that double standards were applied in political life as in sexual morals, and urged her supporters on to ever more violence; she was particularly incensed by the comparatively tolerant approach to Ulster militants. Some say that without their militancy women would not have got the vote when they did; others, appalled, think militancy only roused hostility and was damaging a cause that had so far progressed firmly but courteously within the law. The Liberal statesman Herbert Samuel probably spoke for many when he wrote 'I was more than half-way towards becoming definitely a supporter of women suffrage when the suffragettes [i.e. the militants] stopped me';[35] Clementine Churchill, though 'ardently in favour of votes for women',[36] was horrified at the violence. The Garretts saw it all with mixed emotions. As Millicent emphasized, 'up to 1908, no physical violence was used by the Suffragettes, though much violence was used against them',[37] but, as she wrote to Lloyd George in 1910, she had 'not expressed or felt any sympathy with militant tactics since the time when the Women's Social and Political Union began to practise stone-throwing and other forms of personal violence'.[38] She disliked Mrs Pankhurst's style:

> I could not support a revolutionary movement, especially as it was ruled autocratically ... In 1908 this despotism decreed that the policy of suffering violence, but using none, was to be abandoned. After that, I had no doubt whatever that what was right for me and the NUWSS was to keep strictly to our principle of supporting our movement only by argument, based on common sense and experience and not by personal violence or law-breaking of any kind.[39]

Earlier she had been moved by the suffragettes' courage and their sufferings, visiting the first group in prison, writing to the King to ask that they should be given the privileges of first class prisoners. With Agnes, she gave them a much-publicized (and much-criticized) banquet as a gesture of support on their release in 1906 for, as she wrote, 'the action of the prisoners has touched the imagination of the country in a manner which quieter methods did not succeed in doing'. The increasing violence was another matter, though she did understand why it was happening:

> The physical courage of it all is intensely moving. It stirs people as nothing else can. I don't feel it is the right thing, and yet the spectacle of so much self-sacrifice moves people who would otherwise sit still and do nothing till the suffrage dropped into their mouths like a ripe fruit ... There is no doubt that the militant women are fighting this through in the spirit of a religious revival movement.[40]

When militancy intensified, she wrote to Dr Jane Walker:

> I can never feel that setting fire to houses and churches and letter boxes and destroying valuable pictures really helps to convince people that women ought to be enfranchised ... I consider all first-class social and professional work done by women, such as yours in your profession and outside your profession in helping numbers of men and women to be better human beings, is the finest kind of propaganda for Women's Suffrage.[41]

Challenged by the publicity generated by the WSPU, Millicent pushed her own movement even more into the news. The general growth of women's education and activities was bringing the NUWSS huge numbers of new members and sympathizers, and it was important to get money channelled to the old societies as well as the new. A weekly paper, the *Common Cause*, became the unofficial suffrage journal, reporting meetings and speeches and building up support. There was a series of processions, starting in 1907 when 3,000 took part in the 'Mud March' from Hyde Park to the Albert Hall; Lady Strachey joined Millicent at the head of the procession, and all sorts of friends and relations took part – the distinguished stewards even included Maynard Keynes.

The following year 15,000 made their way to the Albert Hall; Emily Davies, who had retired from Girton and was once again active for the suffrage cause, joined Millicent in leading the way in doctors' gowns. Millicent arranged meetings, spoke at meetings, spoke in the open air at Hyde Park Corner, wrote to the press, raised money, pestered ministers, led deputations to Herbert Asquith. Overwhelmed by suffrage business, she resigned from the Council of Newnham College – she had been a member for 28 years – and refused anything else that came her way. 'The cause is to you', her sister Alice wrote, 'what religion was to dear mother'.[42] The greatest peaceful demonstration was the pilgrimage of 1913, when women from all over the country marched to London, holding meetings as they went, ending with a gathering in Hyde Park and a service in St Paul's Cathedral. Millicent joined in wherever she could, and whenever possible she walked with the East Anglian group, with her old friends and neighbours. There was pleasure and a sense of achievement in all this, for as she wrote in *Women's Suffrage* at the time when the agitation was still in full swing: 'the long struggle to obtain the suffrage has been a great education for women, not only politically, but also in courage, perseverance, endurance, and comradeship with each other'.[43]

Ray Strachey has described Millicent's way of work:

> She refused to install a telephone in her house, or to employ a private secretary ... It was her habit, when she had an important speech to make, first to work it over at her desk, taking notes and arranging her ideas, and then to sit down somewhere else with a piece of needlework in her hands and go over it again carefully in her head ... She read the papers without the aid of Press-cutting agencies, and never allowed anyone to 'devil' for her. She still answered every letter personally and was punctual for every appointment ... When it was time to start for some engagement she would set off on foot, walking very fast, and glad of the exercise, and only when time pressed very hardly would she mount an omnibus.[44]

This personal discipline could be matched by a stern refusal to forgive anyone she felt had unfairly accused the suffragists. In 1928 she would decline an invitation with the words: 'Dame Millicent regrets that she does not feel she can accept the hospitality of XXX. She is ready to explain her reasons if desired. They relate to events which took place in 1912, and possibly Dame Millicent's recollection of these is more vivid than that of XXX.'[45]

But she was totally forgiving to Elizabeth when, once again, they disagreed for a while. In 1908, aged 72, Elizabeth joined the WSPU and, to the horror of her Aldeburgh neighbours, invited Mrs Pankhurst to stay with her at Alde House. Mrs Pankhurst went as a guest to Elizabeth's Scottish cottage too, and Elizabeth was active in speaking on her behalf. 'I am often asked, am I really in favour of militant methods. I always answer quite frankly, "Yes, I am".' It was only through the intervention of a friend of Millicent's (unknown to Elizabeth) that the police avoided arresting Elizabeth at a WSPU raid on parliament. In 1910 she led the 'Regiment of Portias', the group of educated and professional women, in the WSPU march. But Millicent's appeal to Elizabeth in December 1911 not to drift away into such a wrong-headed group brought an immediate response. By 1912, with the violence escalating, Elizabeth was one of those who signed a public letter of protest against militancy; her daughter Louisa though, by then a doctor herself, remained firmly with the militants.

Elizabeth marked her return to the fold at a meeting at the Albert Hall when she gave £100 to the NUWSS. It was an occasion full of family support: from the older generation, Millicent's sisters Agnes and Alice, her brother Sam, and her sister-in-law Louisa (George's wife) were there, with their cousin Edmund Garrett's widow Ellen; and, even without Louisa Garrett Anderson, many cousins from the younger generation – Philippa Fawcett, Alan Anderson, Marion Cowell, Dorothea Gibb (daughter of Louie, the eldest Garrett sister), and Sam's daughter Margaret, who was to become well known as the social reformer Margery Spring Rice. That was in February 1912, and the movement seemed to be surging ahead on all fronts. Millicent saw it almost as a crusade, 'immensely larger and more important than any merely national movement can be. The demand for the vote in England, USA, Sweden, Denmark, Hungary, etc., is part of this bigger movement which is gradually changing the status of women all over the world, even in the East'.[46]

Millicent was indeed in touch with the growing world-wide movement. It was encouraging that women's suffrage, which surprisingly had been adopted in the Isle of Man in 1881, reached New Zealand in 1893, and South Australia the following year. 'It is impossible to exaggerate the value to the movement here of the example of Australia and New Zealand', Millicent wrote.[47] A report on the results of women's suffrage in those States in the USA where it had been adopted was published in the *Nineteenth Century and After* in February 1914.[48] Delegates from seven countries met in Washington in 1902; eight, including Millicent, met in Berlin in 1904, eleven in Copenhagen in 1906, fifteen in Amsterdam in 1908, twenty (organized by Millicent) in London in 1909, then Stockholm 1911 and Budapest 1913. They were planning to meet again in Berlin in 1915.

17

Social and Medical

Where women walk in public processions in the streets the same as the men,
Where they enter the public assembly and take places the same as the men ...
There the great city stands.

Walt Whitman, 'Song of the Broad Axe'

Millicent put a portrait of Walt Whitman into her memoir because she thought he looked so extraordinarily like her father. So it seems appropriate to quote him.

Agnes, Millicent's close friend and companion, joined her in enthusiasm for the suffrage movement, but also spent much time in the latter part of her life on the perennial problem of providing affordable housing for single middle-class working women. In 1888 she became a director of the newly formed Ladies' Residential Chambers Ltd, and remained actively involved until she retired over 40 years later aged 86. Millicent, Elizabeth, Sam's wife Clara, and a Garrett uncle and aunt were at times among the shareholders in the company, which aimed to pay a dividend of 4–5 per cent. It was not quite the first venture of its kind; six years earlier a block of flats 'to benefit those of limited means' had been built in Oakley Street, Chelsea, and a further block of 'comfortable and cheap homes ... suitable for gentlewomen' had been opened at the beginning of 1888 in Lower Sloane Street – unimaginable now, in streets that have become among the most expensive in London.

There was no shortage of applicants for rooms in the Residential Chambers, so preference was given to those earning their own living or doing voluntary social work. Agnes' old master John Brydon was appointed architect, as he was for Elizabeth's New Hospital (also 1888) and for the Medical School (1896). Plans were drawn up for a block to be built on a site in Chenies Street, off Gower Street, and since things moved fast in those days, it was only a year later that Millicent officially opened the building.[1] Designed on something of a college system, each set of rooms had its own front door and space for a kitchen, while there was also a general kitchen and public dining room. Agnes was responsible for buying furniture, and fitting out the dining room and bathrooms, but it seems that her firm did not take on the decoration. The scheme was so successful that a similar block, York Street Chambers, Marylebone, was built three years later (with Thackeray Turner and Mrs Sidgwick's brother Eustace Balfour as architects) and the Chenies Street building was extended (by Brydon) from 22 sets to 37. The tenants included doctors, teachers, writers, artists, and various well-known names – there was the classical scholar Jane Harrison; the South African writer Olive Schreiner; Molly Thomas[2] when she was starting up the teacher training course at Bedford College, and Emily Penrose, Bedford's head.

Not everyone was happy. Emily Hobhouse, always ready to speak up when she thought there was an injustice, objected to paying the ten shillings a month dining room charge when she was away,[3] and sympathized with a colleague who announced 'I am leaving because of the irritating rules. They should avoid treating tenants as a cross between a pauper lunatic and a rebellious schoolgirl'.[4] Some left because rent and food were too expensive, while others criticized the communal food so sternly that the cooks were sent off for training. Still, it did clearly fill a need.

From 1896 the Garrett sisters at number two Gower Street were joined at number six by their friends the Wilkinson sisters, Fanny and Louisa. Fanny, pioneer woman landscape gardener, has left her mark all over London's parks and gardens, and in the plane trees and trees of heaven on London streets. She came into the Garrett story when she incorporated the grounds of the Fawcetts' old Vauxhall house into her new design for Vauxhall Park, and also when Elizabeth commissioned her to design the garden for the London School of Medicine for Women. In 1902, when Swanley Horticultural College became a women's college, Fanny became the first woman principal. The college had a Council of formidably intellectual women, including Eleanor Sidgwick, Anny Thackeray, Jane Walker, Skelton's medical sister Mary Marshall, and Elizabeth Garrett Anderson. Gardeners trained at Swanley worked for Elizabeth at Alde House, and for Jane Walker and Millicent at the East Anglian Sanatorium at Nayland.

Millicent wrote of Louisa Wilkinson giving 'help and affection' in Henry's first illness, in 1882. After training under Cobden-Sanderson she had struggled, with Millicent's help but without success, to be allowed into the book-binding classes of the Central School for Arts and Crafts – the bookbinders' union would not accept women. All the same, she managed to work for Douglas Cockerell, and her bindings were accepted for exhibition. Her connection with the Garretts led in 1900 to her marriage to Millicent's youngest brother George. Their only child did not survive.

At this time Elizabeth was still immersed in medical matters, though she was gradually to draw back to Aldeburgh. She retired from the staff of her New Hospital in 1892 when she was 55, two years after the opening of the new building, happy that Mary Scharlieb would be her successor; but she still acted as a consultant and remained on the managing committee. In the next eleven years, before leaving London, she continued to be Dean of the Medical School, adding to her duties by entertaining students, as well as taking on responsibility for the new buildings. And, confident in her authority as a doctor in fields that did not only concern women, she wrote influential articles on two of the major medical controversies of the day, vaccination and vivisection.[5]

Long ago, as a student in Edinburgh in 1863, Elizabeth had learnt about vaccinating the new-born. In the *Edinburgh Review* in 1899 she gave a history of smallpox and vaccination, and discussed the Royal Commission's recent Report on Vaccination and the various commentaries that had followed. Deaths from smallpox had fallen dramatically since Edward Jenner had introduced vaccination in 1798 – there were 32 years in the eighteenth century when at least 10 per cent of the total mortality in London was from smallpox, but not a single year was that bad in the nineteenth; even the 23,000 deaths in the smallpox epidemic in England and Wales following the Franco-Prussian war accounted for only 4.5 per cent of the total mortality that year.[6] She argued vigorously for vaccination and re-vaccination, attacking the 'large and impenetrable body of cranks'[7] of the anti-vaccination movement. There were many who objected to compulsory vaccination and refused to pay their fines, and others who, not understanding that it was vaccination that had brought smallpox under control, thought the risks of vaccination itself were greater than the risk of smallpox.[8] But, Elizabeth wrote, no one who had ever seen smallpox could oppose vaccination. She admitted that there were about 50 deaths a year in England and Wales from vaccination, but she reckoned this should improve with improved methods. (She was, after all, a friend of Monckton Copeman, the expert on new methods of vaccine preparation.) Isolation and better sanitation, proposed as solutions by the anti-vaccinators, were, she agreed, fine in themselves, but expensive, and totally inadequate as a protection against smallpox unless they were combined with vaccination. The article is, as might be expected from

Elizabeth, well backed up with facts and figures. In 1899, the year of this review, her New Hospital for Women opened a vaccination department.

Once more Millicent's unbending belief in personal independence led her astray, and she unfortunately joined the 'body of cranks'. Her article in the *Contemporary Review* in March 1899 strongly attacked compulsory vaccination. After an inadequate statistical argument against universal infant vaccination, she said she would so hate to see it enforced that she 'would rather see England pock-marked than without the personal independence which is the basis of everything worth having in our national character'. And anyway, she said more acceptably, compulsion was proving so impossible that the law was being brought 'into disrepute and contempt'. Over-impressed by haphazard reports and individual interviews, Millicent was confused about the efficacy of vaccination and the benefits of re-vaccination. She should have listened to her sister.

In 1901–2, while Millicent was in South Africa looking at concentration camps, which were full of measles and typhoid and dysentery but no smallpox, there was a minor outbreak of smallpox in London; 9,659 cases were admitted to smallpox hospitals, of whom 1,663 died. Elizabeth, in letters to *The Times*, used the mortality and vaccination statistics to drive home the need for re-vaccination. She reinforced this by more letters in 1903 and 1904, from her position as honorary secretary to the newly founded Imperial Vaccination League, showing how revaccination at school age would have saved lives, saved money, and saved the need for more smallpox hospitals. 'Smallpox', she wrote, 'is the one great cause of epidemic illness and of death which can be prevented if we choose to prevent it'.[9] It may have sounded an optimistic belief, and it took more than 70 years to eradicate the disease worldwide, but she has been proved right.

The scientific spirit of Victorian Britain had led to a great number of experiments on animals, and the nation's conscience had expressed itself in the Cruelty to Animals Act of 1876, an act (updated in 1986) that is basically still in force. Elizabeth's attitude to vivisection could be predicted. She was fond of animals – there were dogs, ponies and pet rabbits for her children – but logical and clear about the needs and limits of vivisection. As the Royal Commission that led to the Act had concluded: 'it is impossible altogether to prevent the practice of making experiments upon living animals for the attainment of knowledge ... the greatest mitigations of human suffering have been in part derived from such experiments'.[10]

Such experiments should therefore be controlled, inspected and only done under licence. Elizabeth agreed, condemning cruelty or any unnecessary pain and welcoming the use of anaesthesia in experiments. She also welcomed the development of inoculations, which had been made possible by testing on animals. (In 1895 Louis Pasteur had successfully used inoculation to prevent rabies developing in a human subject.) All this, she argued, was acceptable – far worse things were done for sport or fashion:

> It cannot be right to give pain to animals in order to improve their flavour as food, to make them more docile as servants, to furnish us with food, fur, feathers, and skins, or to give us pleasure in trapping, killing, or wounding them, to rid our fields and gardens of their depredations, and to do all this on a gigantic scale and often in most unskilful ways, if it is wrong to give a fractional part of the same amount of pain to animals, often of a lower grade of sensibility, in order to improve our knowledge of the laws of life and disease, and to search for new remedies.[11]

'Let us', she wrote, 'clear our minds of cant and look facts frankly in the face':

> A duke going to preside at a meeting against vivisection dines off animals who have been vivisected; he may even eat live oysters and the livers of geese in whom disease has been artificially induced. The ladies with him wear furs, feathers and ospreys. He drives to the meeting behind vivisected horses. In fact, the only form of vivisection he objects to is that which furnishes, not luxury, amusement, or vanity, but knowledge.[12]

Such knowledge, she argued, is worthwhile in itself and 'everything of solid value in medicine and surgery is based upon knowledge gained by the experimental method'.[13]

Like many doctors towards the end of a medical career, Elizabeth found herself increasingly interested in the history of medicine. Her presidential address to the East Anglian branch of the British Medical Association in 1896 was 'On the Progress of Medicine in the Victorian Era', and she developed this into a centenary article in the January 1903 issue of the *Edinburgh Review*: 'On the Progress of Medicine since 1803'. In a framework of reviewing ten books of medical history and biography she wrote an impressive account of how science was replacing guesswork and transforming medical practice. It all started, she said, when Edward Jenner proved the use of cowpox to protect against smallpox 'by a critical study of other people's observations, and by putting them to the test of experiment'. She explained the enormous importance of the discovery of anaesthetics, not only for the relief of pain, but also because great surgeons were no longer those 'who could amputate a limb in the smallest number of seconds', but were now able to work slowly and carefully. It had led to big advances in abdominal surgery; and there were two other spin-offs – since surgery was less horrific to witness, more women were willing to become nurses; and, as she had explained in her article on vivisection, research on animals had become more practical, for 'physiologists are not more cruel than other people' and 'very little of that which we now know for certain as to the action of drugs, of physiology, and of bacteriology could have been arrived at had we been without the aid of anaesthesia'.

Lister, who was preaching antiseptic surgery just when she qualified, had always been one of Elizabeth's heroes, so she gave plenty of space to 'the great glory of nineteenth century medicine, the revelation given to us by Pasteur and Lister as to the origin of many diseases through the admission of germs'. Many doctors, she said, would not accept the germ theory of disease, but the improved survival rate with antiseptic surgery gave overwhelming proof. She explained the work of Pasteur and of Koch in bacteriology, the discovery of various bacteria specific for different diseases and the possibility of various 'antitoxic serums'. And she wrote of 'excretory glands' (her name for glands that secrete hormones), of the malarial parasite and its complicated life-cycle in the mosquito, of X-rays and their possible future – always emphasizing that there was much more work to be done. She added, in a plea that sounds all too familiar:

> Original research on any large scale is impossible in the absence of big endowments ... If England is to keep up with the United States in research and its applications to pathology and medicine, large endowments must be forthcoming for Oxford and Cambridge, and for the University of London. Failing them we shall have to be content with admiring the work done in the best American universities, and with taking a second place ourselves.

For the *Encyclopaedia Medica*, which came out from 1899–1910 in fifteen volumes, Elizabeth contributed well-argued articles on vaccination, puberty, the menopause, and neurasthenia.

By this time Elizabeth Blackwell, Elizabeth Garrett's early role model, was retreating into vague ideas of health and hygiene and morality, firmly opposed to all animal experiments and sadly even refusing to accept Pasteur's work on vaccines and bacteriology. Fashionably, but unscientifically, she had become interested in spiritualism and in theosophy. She died in 1910, aged 89.

All her life, Elizabeth Garrett Anderson wrote weekly letters home to her parents, and later to her children when they were away at school. Astonishingly for such a progressively minded and busy person, she never had a secretary or a typewriter but used goose quills and cut them herself.[14] Newson died in 1893[15] and, not one to pass over the claims of his eldest child because she was a girl, made Elizabeth the eventual heir to Alde House and all its grounds. Her mother, outliving Newson by ten years, lived on at Alde House as the centre of the family, answering letters and keeping in touch with all her 75 descendants – children, grandchildren and great-grandchildren – with endless interest in their careers and activities. All opposition long forgotten, she subscribed to Elizabeth's hospital and school.

Elizabeth spent increasing time in Aldeburgh in the house Newson had given her earlier, before moving to Alde House when her mother died. She loved gardening – listing it as a recreation in *Who's Who* – and happily dug and planted as well as designing and directing. At times in the vacation she would add to her household by inviting needy students to stay. Skelton, thoroughly at home and accepted in Aldeburgh, was already an alderman, a trustee of the lifeboat and a Justice of the Peace, and he took over as mayor after Newson's death.[16] Nineteen-hundred and seven, the year of the Mud March and the year Florence Nightingale became the first woman to be awarded the Order of Merit, was also the year (after a campaign dating back to 1889[17]) of the 'Qualification of Women Act', making women eligible to be members of county and borough councils and even to be mayor. So it was almost to be expected that the first woman mayor in England would be Elizabeth Garrett Anderson in Aldeburgh. Newson would have been proud and delighted.

She was elected in 1908 (Skelton had died in 1907 and her brother George had finished Skelton's term) and took a thorough and energetic part in local affairs – paving, drains, dealing with rats (with fear of plague), water supply, electric lighting, new trees and shrubs. She encouraged home industries and classical music concerts, and designed herself an official black velvet hat. Elected for a second year, she was in office to proclaim the accession of George V in 1910, but was no longer mayor when the mock-Tudor shelter and public lavatory was put up in June 1911 in honour of George V's coronation – lamentably placed between the Moot Hall and the sea. There is a story that when she rented out Alde House for August and moved to the converted stable

Elizabeth as Mayor of Aldeburgh

block the vicar asked doubtfully whether it was quite suitable for a mayor to live in a stable. 'Why not?' she answered, 'Your Lord was *born* in a stable'.[18]

The stable might be acceptable, but the association with Mrs Pankhurst was harder to swallow. At that time Elizabeth was still a staunch member of the WSPU, going with Mrs Pankhurst to see Asquith to appeal for the Conciliation Bill. Her support for the violent methods of the suffragettes spoilt her chance of election as an alderman in 1910 and, it has been suggested, may well have been the reason why she never had any royal or official recognition. Millicent was made a Dame, though this was not until 1924, seven years after Elizabeth's death.

18

The Next Generation

The lines are fallen unto me in pleasant places; yea, I have a goodly heritage.

Millicent wrote that her mother would often quote those lines from Psalm 16 'with a happy smile'. The Garrett heritage, powerful in Millicent's own generation, was still strong in the next. We have seen five cousins, full of idealism and family loyalty and each from a different branch of the family, supporting Millicent's Albert Hall rally in 1912. Among them of course was Philippa Fawcett.

It is a pity that Philippa, Millicent's only child, never married, so the Fawcett line came to an end. In many ways Philippa was an ideal daughter, though perhaps rather overshadowed by her devoted but ambitious mother. Millicent's memoir gives a revealing picture of their good relationship and Philippa's obvious intelligence when little:

> 'If I told lies would you leave off loving me?' [Philippa asked] This was rather a poser, and I fenced. 'Well, no, not at once, of course: but if you went on telling lies and being cross, I should not love you so much, and gradually, perhaps, I should leave off loving you altogether.' Then she looked up, and said, 'Would you? Well, I should love you if you was ever so naughty.' I felt that she had thoroughly bested me, and that we had better have a game or run races on the Trumpington road.[1]

In 1890, three years after Agnata Ramsay had come top of the Cambridge classics tripos, another Girton student was bracketed with the senior classic, and at the same time Philippa triumphed in mathematics. As Millicent wrote to her colleagues on the suffrage committee: 'the news on Saturday made me very happy. You will know that I care for it mainly for the sake of women; but of course I also feel especially blessed in the fact that the thing I care most of all for has been helped on in this way by my own dear child'.[2]

It was convincing proof that, given good teaching, some women could achieve as much as some men – and it had happened in the best possible way. There was naturally much rejoicing, though in the middle of it all Richard Litchfield (Charles Darwin's son-in-law) wrote slightly caustically to his wife:

> It's a great triumph for Newnham, and I'm glad for the sake of the Fawcett-Anderson circle. I don't know what inferences may safely be drawn from a success of this kind, but it's at any rate curious to see those that are drawn. One thing that strikes me is this that so many say it's remarkable, extraordinary etc., a woman should have this success; and that the people who are loudest about the intellectual power of women use this language.[3]

The custom was to read out the results in the University Senate House, and Newson, who clearly had some idea what to expect, came from Aldeburgh for the ceremony with two of Alice's daughters, Marion and Christina Cowell, whose brother Philip was then an undergraduate at Trinity. Marion (the daughter who had been born in India and who seems to have inherited Alice's letter-writing skill) described it all in a long letter to her mother:

> It was a most exciting scene in the Senate this morning. Christina and I got seats in the gallery, and grandpa remained below. The gallery was crowded with girls and a few men, and the floor of the building was thronged by undergraduates as tightly packed as they could be. The lists were read from the gallery and we heard splendidly. All the men's names were read first, the Senior Wrangler[4] was much cheered. There was a good deal of shouting and cheering throughout; at last the man who had been reading shouted 'Women'. The undergraduates yelled 'Ladies', and for some minutes there was a great uproar ... A fearfully agitating moment for Philippa it must have been; the examiner, of course, could not attempt to read the names until there was a lull. Again and again he raised his cap, but would not say 'ladies' instead of 'women', and quite right I think. He signalled with his hand for the men to keep quiet, but he had to wait for some time. At last he read Philippa's name, and announced that she was 'above the Senior Wrangler'. There was great and prolonged cheering; many of the men turned towards Philippa, who was sitting in the gallery with Miss Clough, and waved their hats. When the examiner went on with the other names there were cries of 'Read Miss Fawcett's name again', but no attention was paid to this. I don't think any other women's names were heard, for the men were making such a tremendous noise; the examiner shouted the other names, but I could not even detect his voice in the noise. We made our way round to Philippa to congratulate her, and then I went over to Grandpapa. Miss Gladstone [daughter of the statesman, who, in spite of her father's

beliefs, became vice-principal of Newnham] was with him. She was, of course, tremendously delighted. A great many people were there to cheer and congratulate Philippa when she came down into the hall. The Master of Trinity and Mrs Butler [the former Agnata Ramsay] went up into the gallery to speak to her. Grandpapa was standing at the bottom of the stairs waiting for Philippa. He was a good bit upset.[5]

Newson was overcome with emotion at Philippa's success, but two years later, to his enormous pride, his grandson Philip Cowell was himself to become senior wrangler. To have two grandchildren top of the mathematical tripos is very rare even if not unique – Francis Galton, investigating evidence for inheritance of intellect, managed to find two cousins, grandchildren of James Alderson and his wife Judith (neé Mewse) from Lowestoft, twenty miles up the coast from Aldeburgh, as it happens.[6]

Taking Part II of the tripos the following year, Philippa was put in the first class, together with Geoffrey Bennett, the male senior wrangler

Philippa Fawcett in 1891, the year after she came first in the mathematical tripos

of her year. Bennett promptly became a Fellow of St John's College, with a university prize and a university lectureship, but such things were not then available for women. Philippa became a college lecturer at Newnham for the next seven years, while keeping closely in sympathy with her mother's political views. Her first public speech, in July 1893, was against Home Rule for Ireland. In 1899 she took a break for nine months, for the journey with Blanche Athena Clough (niece of Newnham's first Principal) as far as Japan and India. Then she was ready and well prepared to accompany her mother to South Africa.

After her successful work for South African education, Philippa came back to London, where she worked in the education service of the London County Council for 30 years, responsible for secondary schools, county council scholarships, and teacher training. Millicent must have been delighted when Philippa became the first professional woman on the Council's permanent staff, and had the same salary as a man. It was a distinguished career though Philippa never again hit the headlines. Her Newnham obituary describes her as shy, almost obsessionally tidy, with a liking for poetry, art, nature and needlework, and a passion for walking. Sharing the Gower Street house with Millicent and Agnes, Philippa seems to have been content to share their views and ambitions – rejoicing at the Diamond Jubilee, attacking Home Rule, and above all – though as a public servant she tended to take a back seat – supporting their campaign for the suffrage.

The other Garrett mathematician, Philip Cowell, had a mother who had considerable mathematical ability and perhaps might have achieved greatness herself, but special coaching and Newnham had not been on offer for Alice as it had been for Philippa. Alice had settled for a domestic life, emerging occasionally in support of her sisters and producing three daughters, including Agnes who went to Girton, as well as two sons. Philip (1870–1949) was to become a fellow of Trinity College, Cambridge, and an astronomer of distinction, winning the gold medal of the Royal Astronomical Society in 1911, but he seems to have been a reclusive and difficult character. There is no record of any involvement in social reform, though there is something of a Garrett connection in his work for tide tables, and in his attachment to Aldeburgh. He retired when he was 60 – supposedly clearing his desk and leaving at precisely the hour of his birth – and then lived at Aldeburgh, doing little but playing bridge and chess. His wife had died in 1924, and they had no children. Philip had, a friend wrote, 'certain deficiencies in his make-up that gave him the air of a clever and loveable child who required careful and sympathetic handling'.[7]

Not surprisingly, Elizabeth's children were made of tougher stuff as well as being clever. But in this progressive household there was still a deep-rooted conservatism – Louisa, admiring her mother as Philippa admired Millicent, became a doctor. Alan, who had got a scholarship to Eton in the year of Philippa's triumph, was taken into the Anderson family shipping business, together with Sam Garrett's son Ronald.

Louisa's illness when she was eleven, and the memory of young Margaret's death, had made Elizabeth into a surprisingly over-protective and anxious mother, constantly worried that Louisa was not eating enough, taking enough exercise, wearing warm enough clothes. So Louisa was sent for her health to board at St Leonards School, in St Andrews. She went on to the London School of Medicine for Women – like Philippa, she owed her training to her mother's pioneering work – and it was not until she qualified as a doctor that Elizabeth at last relaxed, admitting that Louisa was 'eating famously and looking younger'.[8] As a second-generation woman doctor, less cautious about upsetting entrenched sensibilities than Elizabeth had been, Louisa was outspoken from the start in her support for the suffrage, and became thoroughly involved in all the activities of a suffragette. In 1909 she was a founding member of the Tax Resistance League – emphasizing the role of women in the time-honoured opposition to taxation without representation.

She was active in the WSPU, helping her friend and colleague Dr Flora Murray run the nursing home for released hunger strikers, smashing windows, sentenced to six weeks in Holloway prison. In court she said the violence was a political protest, 'in reply largely to a speech made by Mr Hobhouse [whose windows she wrongly believed she had broken], in which he said he did not consider that the Suffrage agitation was supported by popular feeling because women were not doing the damage to property similar to that committed by men in the 1832 Reform riots'.[9] Letters to her mother from Holloway insist that imprisonment is a valuable experience, that she is well, and only sorry and worried because she is making Elizabeth miserable. Like most of the Garrett clan, Louisa always felt family ties very strongly – in a letter to her cousin Kenneth Anderson written in 1939, four years before she died, she wrote of how much her cousins had meant in her life.[10] Her other close tie was with Flora Murray; they are both buried in Holy Trinity Church, Penn; the inscription on Louisa's tombstone ends 'We have been gloriously happy'.

Since Louisa never married, it was left to Alan to carry on the Garrett

Anderson family. He did this very traditionally, not only joining his father's shipping business, but also following his mother's interests by becoming treasurer for the Royal Free Hospital. His contribution to the war effort, for which he was knighted, was in work for shipping and for wheat supplies. He was by this time a thorough establishment figure, and distinguished appointments flowed in – director of the London Midland and Scottish Railway, Deputy Governor of the Bank of England, Member of Parliament for the City of London. He had four children, his younger son Donald following him both into shipping and into voluntary work as treasurer of the Royal Free. Skelton's Anderson cousins and nieces formed a tribe to rival the Garretts, with an impressive number studying at Cambridge; perhaps the most distinguished of these was Adelaide Anderson (1863–1936), writer and factory inspector, who became a Dame in 1921, three years before Millicent.

The Garrett social conscience appears now and then in other familiar names. Two Garrett Smiths, children of Louie, the eldest Garrett sister, are listed as lecturing at the Working Women's College in Queen Square in 1879, where Elizabeth had demonstrated the dissection of frogs thirteen years earlier; Evelyn Gates, grand-daughter of Rhoda's brother Frank, appears in 1924 as the editor of the *Woman's Year Book*, listing opportunities then open to women; Edmund's widow Ellen worked for a time on the NUWSS paper the *Common Cause*. And then there was the prominent social reformer, Sam Garrett's daughter Margery Spring Rice. Her first excursions into public life were political – secretary of the League of Nations Society, honorary treasurer of the Women's National Liberal Federation. Then, moved by stories of poverty and overcrowding in North Kensington, she became involved in the North Kensington birth control clinic, work that led to a lifetime campaign for family planning, something that was still very little discussed.

Margery's aunt Elizabeth had avoided the subject. Early in her career, delivering twins, one stillborn, for Lady Amberley, Elizabeth had clumsily remarked that 'she supposed Amberley did not mind as he was so Malthusian'.[11] She learnt to be more tactful, but went to the other extreme. Although she must have been well aware of women worn down with constant pregnancies, and indeed of the facts of infanticide and criminal abortion, contraception was never mentioned at the London School of Medicine for Women – it was important to tread carefully, not to seem 'advanced', not to upset sensibilities. And Mary Scharlieb, a Catholic, was totally opposed to the idea. In Elizabeth's private practice it was different; when Mary Costelloe, mother of Millicent's biographer Ray Strachey, went to see her in 1888, she was shocked to be advised that 'there are plenty of other ways besides abstinence' to avoid having too many children.[12] And Elizabeth herself, with three children, and Millicent with one, probably used some form of contraception. The fact that her niece could be so much more outspoken shows how much the climate had changed in a generation.

Margery's influential book, *Working-Class Wives: Their Health and Conditions*, published in 1939, was reprinted by Virago in 1981 and is still available. Based on information from 1,250 working-class wives in different parts of Britain, it gave a worrying picture of poverty, loneliness, inadequate food and poor health, and recommended many measures that are now routine aims and features of the welfare state – minimum wages, day nurseries, family allowances, more housing at affordable rents, more clinics and health insurance, better social opportunities and holidays.

Living near Aldeburgh and loving music, Margery was a link between the Aldeburgh of the Garretts and the Aldeburgh of Benjamin Britten. Louisa Garrett Anderson, writing in 1939, said that Elizabeth had 'encouraged musical taste' in Aldeburgh at the beginning of the century by organizing classical concerts. Margery carried the musical theme further; she started the Suffolk Rural Music School, and she helped organize the Aldeburgh Festival in its early days, giving financial backing, suggesting programmes, putting up performers and guests.[13]

Margery had lost her first husband in 1916, in a war that took, Millicent wrote, ten members of the Garrett family – sons, sons-in-law, nephews and cousins. Among them were Alice's son Maurice Cowell, who had been manager of the malting business, and Sam's artist son Henry Fawcett Garrett, who was Millicent's godson, born a year after his uncle's death.

As well as bringing personal disaster, the war disrupted normal life on an unprecedented scale. And the mobilization of both men and women in the common cause was to make a deep and lasting change in social and political life.

19

The War

The great searchlight of war showed things in their true light, and they gave us our enfranchisement with open hands.

Millicent Fawcett, speech at Queen's Hall, March 1918

In 1914 patriotism was stronger than protest. As factories turned from ploughshares to swords, all organizations that had been working for women's rights put their old activities on hold and mobilized their members. It was done because it was felt to be the proper thing to do, not because it was politic; but, as it turned out, the impressive work that women did during the war made it hard to deny them the vote at the end of it. Women were showing what they could do rather than pro-testing because they were excluded. There was an amnesty for suffra-gette prisoners, and it was the end of militancy.

'Let us prove ourselves worthy of citizenship, whether our claim to it be recognised or not', Millicent wrote, only three days after war was declared.[1] There were, all over the country, around 50,000 members of 500 suffrage societies looking to Millicent as their leader. She guided them first to offer their services to local councils, to help where war had disrupted employment. Workshops were opened for some 2,000 women. As unemployment gave way to the need for women to fill the gaps left by the enlistment of so many men, the suffrage societies became at times virtually employment agencies both for traditional women's jobs and in new fields – the London society even changed its name to the London Society for Women's Service. Various needs were filled, from laundries and canteens for soldiers, to maternity centres and baby clinics; from bus conductors in London, to acetylene welders in aeroplane factories. A major challenge came with the rush of refugees from Belgium, and this was impressively tackled with a mixture of hostels and private hospitality. As Millicent herself emphasized, it was not only suffragists who took part: it became a movement of 'the great majority of women throughout the whole country, suffragist and non-suffragist, militant and non-militant'.[2]

Louisa Garrett Anderson dropped her tax-resistance activities to concentrate on the more important business of looking after the wounded.[3] She and Flora Murray, backed by the WSPU, organized a fully equipped hospital staffed entirely by women and took it out to Paris. Louisa has described how her mother, now ill and frail, came to see them set off:

> At Victoria station she heard the roll-call for the corps and saw the equipment which she had helped to provide – tons of lint and cotton wool, cases of instruments, with drugs and chloroform in wooden crates marked with the Red Cross and the superscription 'Women's Hospital Corps'. That such a service by medical women was possible was mainly due to her. She stood apart, old, bent and confused. Where were they going? To Russia, perhaps? Never mind: it was a great adventure and to the leaders she said: 'My dears, if you go, and if you succeed, you will put forward the women's cause by thirty years'.[4]

The Army Medical Corps and the British Red Cross had refused offers of help from women's hospital units, so Flora Murray and Louisa went with the blessing of the French Red Cross to treat French wounded and a few British cases in Paris. As Louisa wrote to her mother, 'this is just what you would have done at my age. I hope I shall be able to do it half as well as you would have done'.[5] She need not have worried – they seem to have run a model hospital, and she was glad to realize, after her track record of protest, that this time she was on the side of the angels. French medical women, envious of the training given by the London School, were able only to act as assistants and dressers.[6] Louisa and Flora set up a second hospital in Wimereux, near Boulogne, recognized this time by the British War Office, to treat British wounded; visitors and presents poured in – games, gramophones, Louisa's brother Alan with a carload of pheasants. Soon the Paris hospital was closed, and Wimereux absorbed all the staff. 'Give them the vote? If I had the chance I'd give 'em ten votes apiece', said one grateful patient.[7]

Later, with British support, Louisa (as chief surgeon) and Flora (as chief physician) ran the Women's Military Hospital in Endell Street, London (in the building reputed to be the original workhouse described by Dickens in *Oliver Twist*). It could take 500 patients and was, the *Daily Chronicle* wrote, 'a triumph not only for women in medicine, but for women in administration'.[8] There were 15 women doctors, and all the staff were women; Winston Churchill's niece was among the nurses. According to Flora Murray, 26,000 patients passed through the wards.[9] As well as working monstrously long hours in the hospital, Louisa found time to agitate for tetanus serum and to write articles in *The Lancet* on the treatment of septic wounds.[10] The revolutionary had turned into an establishment figure, awarded a CBE at the end of the war and becoming a Justice of the Peace for Buckinghamshire.

These hospitals were part of the huge contribution British women made to medical care all over Europe, as doctors and nurses if they were trained, as nursing auxiliaries if they were willing but ignorant. Dr Elsie Inglis, secretary of the Edinburgh branch of the NUWSS, was particularly prominent, organizing the Scottish Women's Hospitals, sending units to Belgium, Serbia, Russia and Corsica – an enterprise that was supported by fund-raising at Newnham and Girton and escorted by a Newnham don Elsie Butler as interpreter. 'Millicent Fawcett Hospitals' that worked for women and children and battled against infectious diseases were set up in Russia until they were forced to leave by the Revolution in 1917. The War Office sent 50 women doctors to Malta in 1916, and the Royal Army Medical Corps asked for 50 more for hospital work in Britain – altogether more than 400 women doctors worked for the army. Women – more than 18,000 of them – enrolled in the Voluntary Aid Detachments, 8,000 in the Territorial Forces Nursing Service, 10,000 in the Queen Alexandra's Military and Naval Nursing Service. They worked in Hospital Supply Depots, they ran convalescent homes.

But the path to medical training for women was still not clear. Nearly all the London teaching hospitals, which opened their doors a little during the war, shut them again when the exceptional needs were over. The male students of St Mary's Hospital, for example, protested in 1924 that the intake of women was not only 'the principal cause of dissatisfaction' but was also wrecking their chances in the Hospital Rugby Cup – so women were kept out once more. The old arguments were reappearing everywhere, and it was not until the National Health Service was set up in 1948, three years after Louisa's death, that women were generally welcomed to join men as clinical students. Changes then came so thoroughly that just over half a century later, the (female) President of the College of Physicians was worrying that more than 60 per cent of doctors qualifying in Britain were women.

'The war', Millicent wrote in her melodramatic way, 'revolutionized the industrial position of women. It found them serfs and left them free.'[11] When five million men volunteered for military service in the first eighteen months of the war, and at the same time there was urgent need for military equipment and for home-produced food, who else could fill the gaps? In March 1915 the trade unions grudgingly agreed to suspend the restrictions against employing women in skilled trades, as long as the women did not undercut the men, and on condition that the limitations would be restored after the war. Still, the agreement was worth accepting in the hope that things would in fact never move backwards. Mrs Pankhurst added her voice, encouraging women to come forward for munitions work. By August the *Engineer* was writing in surprise:

> There is a widespread idea that the only machines which women can work are automatic or semi-automatic tools with which it is impossible to make mistakes. This idea is being daily disproved ... In fact, it may be stated with absolute truth that women have shown themselves perfectly capable of performing operations which have hitherto been exclusively carried out by men.[12]

And they worked in countless other ways – as clerks in the Civil Service and in business, in the Land Army, in welfare schemes, in savings campaigns. Eventually there were even 150,000 women in the armed forces to help in every way they could short of fighting.[13] For the first time, women were employed in the Garrett Long Shop at Leiston, helping to make shells, shell-turning lathes and aeroplanes.[14]

An extra problem Millicent had to tackle was opposition from many pacifist officers of the NUWSS who felt that nothing should be done to support the war effort. Patriotic here as always, she stood up to them firmly, but her determination tore through the unity of the Council. Convinced she was right, and not wanting the women's movement to be branded as pro-German, Millicent was ready to act autocratically in what she saw as the defence of democracy. She had risked splitting the movement over her fierce opposition to Home Rule in the 1890s, she had upset many colleagues in her persistent crusade against Harry Cust on the grounds of morality in 1894–5, but her stand this time was far more serious and did bring a devastating split. It was, she wrote retrospectively, 'the only part of my work for Suffrage which I wish to forget'.[15] The crisis came in the Council meeting in February 1915, when she opposed a suggestion that there should be an international suffrage meeting in a neutral country and she declared herself 'heart and soul for the cause of Great Britain' against 'Prussian militarism', and that until the Germans withdrew from Belgium and France 'it is akin to treason to talk of peace'.

A collection of high-powered women, united only by their belief in the suffrage, were likely to differ strongly over their attitudes to the war. Millicent, in spite of her deceptively mild manner, was prepared to defy any opposition, and had to face the resignation of the honorary secretary and the parliamentary secretary of the NUWSS, and the editor of the *Common Cause*, followed by ten members of the executive. But her determination won through, and a special council meeting in June 1915 gave her a vote of confidence. So the NUWSS remained a patriotic supporter of the government, helping the government in turn to become more sympathetic to the cause of women's suffrage. Even Asquith seemed to be softening, in his speech on the death of the heroic nurse Edith Cavell (October 1915): 'in this United Kingdom and throughout the Dominions of the Crown there are thousands of such women', he declared, 'but a year ago we did not know it'. Millicent's comment was simply 'pathetic blindness!'[16]

News came from Canada that one state after another was giving women the right to vote. The federal vote there was granted in time for a general election in 1917, and in the province of Alberta a woman was elected. This was a good omen for Britain but, as Millicent herself admitted, the final push for the British government came because there was an urgent need for a new parliamentary register and voting qualification for men. It was becoming increasingly impossible to go ahead and organize that without dealing at the same time with the claims of women. The problem was that, under the existing rules, to qualify as voters men generally had to be householders occupying their property continuously for twelve months; with so many in the armed forces or moving to other parts of the country for national service, the register had become absurd. Something had to be done before the general election that would be held at the end of the war. The suffrage societies all round the country surfaced from their war work to make it clear that they would all support Millicent, that women must be included in the new Franchise Bill. Millicent wrote to Asquith, on behalf of the NUWSS emphasizing how 'women of all classes are eager to bear their full share of the work and the suffering demanded from the country' and that therefore 'we trust that you may include in your Bill clauses which would remove the disabilities under which women now labour'.[17]

More and more people came to agree. In August 1916, the editor of the *Observer* wrote: 'time was when I thought that men alone maintained the State. Now I know that men alone never could have maintained it, and that henceforth the modern State must be dependent on men and women alike for the progressive strength and vitality of its whole organization'.[18] Then the newspaper magnate Lord Northcliffe became converted, and asked the editor of *The Times* to give his support. Asquith softened a little further in a speech to parliament on the question of a new register: 'have not the women a special claim to be heard on the many questions which will arise directly affecting their interests? ... I say quite frankly that I cannot deny that claim'.[19] Millicent now felt that at last the Liberal Party was on her side.

A Speaker's Conference, with members from both houses and all parties, was set up in October to discuss many aspects of electoral

Asquith catching the suffrage bus

reform – votes for the armed forces, proportional representation, adult suffrage, plural voting, as well as votes for women. Before it could report, Asquith had given way to the far more sympathetic Lloyd George as Prime Minister. The proposals that emerged were to give the vote to women over the age of 30 if they were householders or the wives of householders. The age limit meant that they would not be on the same footing as men (who had to be 21, or even only eighteen if they had been in the fighting services),[20] but since there were about 1.5 million more women than men in the country, the argument was that the majority of voters would otherwise be women. Many of course objected to the exclusion of young women (who were playing a large part in the war effort), but Millicent felt that it was better to accept partial success, hoping to improve on it later, than hold out for everything at once and risk losing altogether: 'we are asking, and shall continue to ask, for the Suffrage for women on the same terms as it is, or may be, granted to men. But I do not think it is very wonderful if, at one stroke, Parliament should refuse to enfranchise the whole female population. Men in this country have never been enfranchised in this wholesale fashion'.[21]

So they agreed, and the new register gave the vote to about eight million women – about two thirds of the number of men voters. The proposals passed the Commons, and Lord Curzon's famous January speech, when he announced that he would not oppose the Bill in the Lords was, Millicent wrote, the greatest moment of her life:

> Ten minutes later the figures were given out, and the majority for Women's Suffrage was 63; and then there followed a scene of great enthusiasm in the halls outside. The suffragists who had been waiting in the precincts crowded round Mrs Fawcett, the friendly Peers came forward and shook her by the hand, and the police beamed with satisfaction. Members came out from the House of Commons to join the throng, and Mrs Fawcett made her way to the doors amid a tumult of joyous congratulations.[22]

Millicent added that the next month she saw the 'gorgeous ceremony' in the Lords when the royal assent was given.[23]

Furious with Curzon (who in 1912 had been President of the National League for Opposing Women's Suffrage), Mrs Humphry Ward started an angry correspondence in the *Morning Post*, though she nobly ended it with the words: 'amid my own disappointment I could not help thinking of Mrs Fawcett, who had been sitting beside me in the House of Lords, and feeling a sort of vicarious satisfaction that after her long fight she at least had gone home content'.[24] But her disappointment was deep. (My aunt Helen Bentwich, who was to be Millicent's host in Jerusalem when the 1928 Suffrage Act was passed, was in the Land Army in 1918, and happened to be billeted on Mrs Humphry Ward. When Mrs Ward returned from the debate, she remembered, 'she spent the evening in tears'.[25]) One by-product might have consoled Mrs Ward, who had always believed women should be involved in local government. The new register greatly increased the number of women who could vote in local elections too, with the result that many more women were soon elected onto Borough Councils.

Millicent presided at the great celebration rally of the suffrage societies in March at the Queen's Hall. They listened to the Leonora Overture no. 3 with its triumphant proclamation of freedom, and they sang Blake's 'Jerusalem' with the music written by Agnes' old friend Hubert Parry, a song that Millicent hoped would become the Women Voters' Hymn. 'Lively uproar of joy when Mrs Fawcett went on the platform', Parry wrote in his diary, 'The sound of "Jerusalem" when the audience joined in was tremendous'.[26] Elizabeth had not lived to join the celebrations. She had died in December 1917, after three distressing years of increasing vagueness and weakness.

As soon as the war was over Millicent was in Paris, telling the Peace Congress of various aspects of women's concerns (including the horrors of the white slave trade), making sure women could serve the League as delegates or officers, and becoming an enthusiast for the League of Nations Union. It was satisfying after the war, too, to work with Sam on a committee to allow women into the legal profession. The Sex Dis-qualification Removal Bill was passed in 1919, and the next year the first seven women invited to be Justices of the Peace included Mary Scharlieb, Mrs Humphry Ward (who accepted but did not live to sit as magistrate) and, following her father's tradition, Millicent herself.

'It is very blessed to have peace', Millicent wrote to Jane Walker when, seven months after the Armistice, negotiations finally ended in June 1919, 'we heard it this morning at breakfast-time at Alde House, and we all jumped up and kissed each other'. It reads like an echo of the old Aldeburgh days, when Newson came in at breakfast-time to announce the fall of Sebastopol.

Campaigning in the first post-war election, Lloyd George asked Millicent to preside in the Queen's Hall over his meeting for women voters. She was happy and proud to do so. It was just over 50 years since Millicent, with Louie, Elizabeth, and Agnes, had heard John Stuart Mill pleading for women to be given the vote on the same terms as men, and Henry Fawcett had supported him. Looking back, Millicent summed up the achievements of those 50 years, the municipal suffrage, the girls' schools, the opening up of the universities and the medical profession, the revolution in the legal status of women. Justifiably proud, Millicent, now 71, refused to stand for parliament herself, and decided it was time to resign as President of the National Union.

She was right to resign, for her great work was done and in her old age she was becoming in some ways increasingly out of touch. She could not bring herself to accept plans for mothers' pensions or for family allowances, as these went against the deep-rooted Fawcett belief in personal responsibility. But she kept up her interest in women's rights – and her firm handwriting – to the end of her long life. 'Every year's experience of the voting power of women brings home to us the tremendous value of what we won in 1918', she wrote to her cousin Amy, 'it is a wonderful piece of good fortune for me to have lived to see my dream come true'.[27]

20

Epilogue in Palestine

Jerusalem the Golden

Friends and admirers marked Millicent's retirement with a present, a cheque to be used any way she liked, but not to be given away. She asked permission to share it with Agnes, so that they could spend it on visiting Palestine. She had always loved travel. She had been to Rome with Elizabeth, to Egypt and Athens with Jane Walker, and now, just when she had money and time to spare, Palestine was emerging from the 'blighting control of the Turk'[1] and was shortly to be under the control of the British Mandate. This was the time to see Jerusalem.

They set off in February 1921 – train to Trieste, boat to Alexandria, train to Cairo, and finally by night, the military railway to Jerusalem. Dawn showed them the anemones and cyclamen of a Mediterranean spring, and they were overwhelmed by their first sight of Jerusalem. It was everything they had hoped for, with the ancient walls, the Temple area, the Mosque of Omar, and the Mount of Olives beyond, leading to the Dead Sea and the mountains of Moab.

Neither of the sisters was conventionally religious, but they knew their Bible well, and they had a great sense of tradition and love of ancient sites. They walked round the walls of the Old City, moved by its history from biblical times to the Crusaders and to the recent drama of Allenby. They became well aware of the mixture of races, with different ideals, standards, outlooks and religions, which made government difficult then and threatened more problems for the future. But Millicent was impressed by the hopes of the Balfour Declaration in November 1917, and had faith in the League of Nations and the British Mandate. Why were so many people so worried, she wondered: Jews were such a small minority of the population (83,000 Jews and 73,000 Christians out of a total of 750,000) and, in those early days before the rise of Fascism, there was no reason to think there would be great immigration. And anyway, as she pointed out, the Declaration, after saying that there should be a national home for the Jewish people in Palestine, added that 'nothing shall be done which may prejudice the civil and religious rights of non-Jewish communities in Palestine'.

Agnes and Millicent saw the holy places of all three religions, they were entertained at Government House, they admired the new water supply brought by the British administration, and they set off boldly in a little Ford car to tour Galilee. The tyres punctured, the car stuck in the mud, but the flowers and the biblical scenes gave endless pleasure. They made friends with all sorts of people, staying in Haifa for a week with the Christian missionary Effie Newton, and enjoying the company of the Jewish artist Amy Drucker, whose painting of a street scene in Jerusalem was to make the frontispiece of Millicent's book. They visited schools where Jew, Christian, and Moslem learnt together – one was the British High School for Girls, with a headmistress who had been a pupil of Dorothea Beale at Cheltenham. They were duly impressed by visits to Jewish agricultural colonies at Rehovoth and Rishon-le-Zion, and Millicent was particularly moved by an enthusiastic group of suffragists at Rishon, who overwhelmed her with flowers and speeches. She addressed a Jewish suffrage meeting in Jerusalem, stressing that there should be equality for women of all races; Lady Samuel (the High Commissioner's wife) told her 'she liked what I had said and that it needed saying'.[2]

There had been so much to see that one of the first things to do on getting back to England was to plan the next visit. So they were off the following spring to Beirut, across Lebanon to Baalbek, then to Damascus, and so through Tiberias and Nablus back to Jerusalem. Here they learnt more about the suffering in the war, how 200 children out of the 700 at one school had died of starvation, how the Turks had used the British Ophthalmic Hospital as a munitions dump and had then blown it up; they heard of the outbreaks of disease, and they saw crowds of orphans. But they were happy to be back, to be welcomed and to visit much that they had missed before. Again, their sightseeing included agricultural colleges and colonies and various philanthropic initiatives from both Jews and Christians. And since it was April, they witnessed the Christian Easter, the Moslem Nebi Musa, and the Jewish Passover.

Once Agnes and Millicent had the habit of visiting Palestine in the spring it was hard to stop, and they were back again in 1927 and 1928. It was in February 1927, when Jerusalem was surprisingly full of snow, that they alarmed their friends with their adventures. Helen Bentwich, there as the wife of the Attorney General, wrote home to her mother:

Dame Millicent Fawcett and Miss Garrett came to lunch. They are wonderful old ladies. They came out again, resolved to see Trans-Jordan. Their
niece Dr Louisa Garrett Anderson turned up, and they went off, spending
the night in Jericho. They tried to go to Jerash, but it was flooded and they
went to Amman. They tried to leave Amman, but got in the snow near the
Circassian village Swaley, and had to return. They stayed at Amman till
Monday – in the very primitive local hotel – and then went by train on the
Damascus line, stayed two nights at Tiberias, and returned here by car –
looking very well and full of life. Everyone was expecting them to be nearly
dead.[3]

Even the imperturbable Millicent described it in a letter to her daughter
as 'quite an adventure'.[4]

The following year they stayed with the Bentwiches in Jerusalem:

I had Dame Millicent and her sister here – terribly energetic, at 83 and 85,[5]
and having their cold baths every morning ... Miss Garrett is a little vague
and wandering, but Dame Millicent is as clear as ever, and full of good
stories of bygone days and political life. She was greatly excited yesterday at
a telegram which came for her saying that the Suffrage Bill had a large
majority for the second reading.[6]

This was the Bill that, at last, was to give women the vote on the same
terms as men. 'The two dear octogenarians were so happy', Helen
Bentwich wrote, 'that they joined hands and danced round the room'.[7]

Notes

Chapter 1

1. V. B. Redstone and F. Garrett, *The Garretts of Suffolk* (1916), privately printed, Ipswich.
2. Agnes to Frank Garrett, 7 June 1916; John and Elizabeth Dunnell (neé Gayford) were both born in Dunwich, Suffolk.
3. J. Pipe, *Port on the Alde* (1976), Snape Maltings, p. 3, quoting from W. White, *History, Gazetteer & Directory of Suffolk* (1844).
4. J. Pipe (1976), p. 27
5. Still existing, but now divided into several parts; the row of terrace houses has been converted into the Brudenell Hotel.
6. M. G. Fawcett, *What I Remember* (1924), p. 33.
7. Most of these were done by J. M. Christie in 1888, but there is one in the same tradition painted by E. G. Cotman in 1899 (6 years after Newson died) which must have been commissioned by George Garrett; Millicent writes of the Barham portrait in *What I Remember*, p. 18.
8. M. G. Fawcett (1924), p. 32.
9. M. G. Fawcett (1924), p. 36.
10. L. G. Anderson, *Elizabeth Garrett Anderson* (1939), p. 29.
11. R. A. Whitehead, *Garretts of Leiston* (1964), p. 11.
12. R. A. Whitehead (1964), p. 13; he quarrelled so badly with his son John that they remained not on speaking terms (Alice's letter to her father on Richard's death, 31 July 1866).
13. R. A. Whitehead (1964), p. 17.
14. Population of Leiston was 1177 in 1841, 2242 in 1871; at around the turn of the century there was a workforce of 2000 (Suffolk Record Office).
15. N. Mitchison, *Revaluations, Studies in Biography* (1931).
16. *Illustrated London News*, 21 June 1851, p. 587.
17. A hundred years later it was all over, and in 1984 the Long Shop became a museum of industrial archaeology.
18. Exports to Russia were hit disastrously by the Russian Revolution, and the repudiation of foreign debts in 1919.
19. M. G. Fawcett (1924), p. 14.

20. R. A. Whitehead (1964).
21. One of these brothers was Rhoda's grandfather (see family tree p.ii).
22. The Cambridge degree exams.
23. M. G. Fawcett (1924), p. 10.
24. L. G. Anderson (1939), pp. 48–9.

Chapter 2

1. The odd assumption that state schools should be co-educational, and private (fee-paying) schools generally single-sex, persisted and often still persists.
2. J. Barker, *The Brontës* (1997), p. 65, letter from Charlotte Brontë to her sister Emily, 8 June 1839.
3. In a paper to Social Science Congress 1862.
4. L. G. Anderson, *Elizabeth Garrett Anderson* (1939), p. 30; Elizabeth Blackwell, who was the first English woman to qualify as a doctor (though with an American degree) was luckier with her intelligent Miss Major; Miss Major later married Elizabeth Blackwell's uncle and opened a school in New York.
5. M. G. Fawcett, *What I Remember* (1924), p. 38.
6. *Women's Penny Paper*, 18 January 1890, p. 145.
7. This was the impressive pair immortalized in the rhyme (written anonymously about 1884):
    Miss Buss and Miss Beale
    Cupid's darts do not feel.
    How different from us
    Miss Beale and Miss Buss.
8. Barbara Bodichon, painter, feminist and one of the founders of Girton College, Cambridge, was the wealthy daughter of the radical Benjamin Leigh Smith; she was a first cousin of Florence Nightingale, who refused to acknowledge her because of her illegitimate birth.
9. P. Hirsch, *Barbara Leigh Smith Bodichon* (1998), p. 243.
10. H. Martineau 'Middle-Class Education in England – Girls', *Cornhill Magazine* (Nov. 1864) vol. X, p. 559.
11. A test started in 1858 to give a standard to boys' schools.
12. R. Strachey, *The Cause* (1928), p. 135.
13. R. Strachey (1928), p. 168; 'Lecture to Ladies on Practical Subjects' (1855).
14. E. Davies, *The Higher Education of Women* (1866; repr. 1988), p. 153.
15. W. Gérin, *Elizabeth Gaskell* (1976), p. 281.
16. M. G. Fawcett, *What I Remember* (1924), p. 50.

17. Alice in India to Agnes, 15 February 1869.
18. On 29 February 1868, Alice wrote 'So Judy has gone to school – will you give me Miss Buss's address?' So perhaps at 15 Josephine was at North London Collegiate.
19. J. Howarth, introduction to E. Davies, *The Higher Education of Women* (1866; repr. 1988), p. xvii.

Chapter 3

1. White's *Directory of Derbyshire* (1857).
2. M. G. Fawcett, *What I Remember* (1924), p. 48.
3. E. Crawford, *Enterprising Women* (2002), p. 25.
4. E. Crawford (2002), pp. 25–6.
5. Alice to her mother, 28 September 1863.
6. See Chapter 1, note 1.

Chapter 4

1. F. P. Cobbe, *Essays on the Pursuits of Women* (1863), p. 220.
2. L. Goldman, *Science, Reform and Politics in Victorian Britain* (2002), p. 2.
3. R. A. Whitehead, *Garretts of Leiston* (1965), p. 21.
4. Described in Elizabeth Crawford's biographical note (in *Enterprising Women*) as 'successively linen draper, maltster, and artist'.
5. J. Manton, *Elizabeth Garrett Anderson* (1965), p. 44.
6. L. G. Anderson, *Elizabeth Garrett Anderson* (1939), p. 39.
7. M. G. Fawcett, *What I Remember* (1924), p. 41.
8. Ray Strachey came from a powerful line of woman suffragists; her American grandmother made her first speech for women's suffrage in 1882; M. Carey Thomas, who became President of Bryn Mawr, was her mother's cousin. See B. Strachey, *Remarkable Relations* (1981), p. 55.
9. A. I. Thackeray, 'Toilers and Spinsters' in the *Cornhill Magazine* (March 1861), pp. 322–31.
10. L. G. Anderson (1939), p. 43.
11. L. G. Anderson (1939), p. 42.
12. J. Manton (1965), pp. 53–4.
13. L. Goldman (2002), p. 121.
14. Letter from EG to J. S. Anderson, 8 December 1870, in Women's Library.
15. Letter from EG to Emily Davies, 15 June 1860, in Women's Library.
16. F. Nightingale, *Notes on Hospitals* (1859), p. 4.

17. F. Nightingale, 'Site and Construction of Hospitals', in the *Builder* (28 August 1858).
18. F. Nightingale (1859), p. 15.
19. EG to Emily Davies. 28 June 1860 in Women's Library.
20. Agnes to EG, 17 August 1860 in Women's Library.
21. M. Wollstonecraft, *A Vindication of the Rights of Women* (1792).
22. B. Abel-Smith, *A History of the Nursing Profession* (1960), p. 18, quoting Haddon, 'Nursing as a Profession for Ladies', in *St Paul's Monthly Magazine* (Aug 1871), p. 461.
23. E. Davies, 'Medicine as a Profession for Women' (June 1862), paper read at the Social Science Congress, reprinted in C. A. Lacey (ed.), *Barbara Leigh Smith Bodichon and the Langham Place Group* (1987), pp. 411–12.
24. E. Garrett (1866), 'Hospital Nursing', a paper read at the National Association for the Promotion of Social Science; reprinted in C. A. Lacey (1987), pp. 445–6.
25. L. G. Anderson (1939), p. 56; Newson Garrett to EG, 8 July 1860.
26. Presumably some relation, since Russell Gurney's grandfather was a physician called William Hawes.
27. L. G. Anderson (1939), pp. 57–8.
28. J. Manton (1965), p. 278.
29. J. Manton (1965), p. 75.
30. EG to Emily Davies, 16 July 1860 in Women's Library.
31. M. G. Fawcett (1924), p. 42.

Chapter 5

1. S. Jex-Blake, 'Medicine as a Profession for Women', in J. Butler (ed.), *Women's Work & Culture* (1869).
2. D. Rubinstein, *A Different World for Women* (1991), pp. 9–10.
3. EG to Emily Davies, 21 August 1861 in Women's Library.
4. R. Strachey, *Millicent Garrett Fawcett* (1931), p. 14.
5. E. Crawford, *Enterprising Women* (2002), p. 23.
6. J. Glynn, *Prince of Publishers* (1986), p. 202.
7. H. Cowell, 'The Conservative Reascendancy Considered', *Blackwood's Magazine* (August 1854).
8. J. Manton, *Elizabeth Garrett Anderson* (1965), p. 134 fn.
9. L. G. Anderson, *Elizabeth Garrett Anderson* (1939), p. 34.
10. E. Crawford (2002), p. 27.
11. *Women's Penny Paper* (18 January 1890), p. 145.
12. October 1916, Louisa Garrett Anderson to her mother, in Women's Library.

13. M. G. Fawcett, *Janet Doncaster* (1875), pp. 34–5.
14. E. T. Cook, *Edmund Garrett* (1909), p. 166.
15. M. G. Fawcett, *What I Remember* (1924), p. 27.
16. R. Strachey, *Millicent Garrett Fawcett* (1931), p. 17.
17. M. G. Fawcett (1924), p. 52.
18. J. S. Mill, *The Subjection of Women* (1869), ch 3.
19. Clementia Taylor and Peter Taylor MP, supporters of women's suffrage.
20. D. Rubinstein (1991), p. 15.
21. J. Manton (1965), p. 182.
22. D. Rubinstein (1991), p. 16.
23. R. Strachey (1931), pp. 26–7; Barbara Bodichon herself thought her husband 'the handsomest man ever created', though she admitted to another friend that some people think him 'ugly and terrific'. See P. Hirsch, *Barbara Leigh Smith Bodichon* (1998), p. 126.
24. L. G. Anderson (1939), p. 125.
25. Louie's fifth child, a boy, had died in 1863; it seems, from a letter of Alice's, that Rhoda too was helping to look after the children.
26. L. G. Anderson (1939), p. 180.

Chapter 6

1. E. Blackwell, 'Letter to Young Ladies Desirous of Studying Medicine', *Englishwoman's Journal* (Feb 1860).
2. EG to Emily Davies, 7 August 1860, in Women's Library.
3. EG to Emily Davies, 5 September 1860, in Women's Library.
4. EG to Emily Davies, 12 October 1860, in Women's Library.
5. D. Rubinstein, *A Different World for Women* (1991), p. 19.
6. M. Seacole, *Wonderful Adventures of Mrs Seacole in Many Lands* (1857; repr. 2005), p. 71.
7. My husband remembers his medical student aunt at work dissecting a brain on the dining room table as late as the 1930s.
8. EG to Emily Davies, 14 October 1860, in Women's Library.
9. EG to Jane Crow, 9 October 1860, in Women's Library.
10. J. Manton, *Elizabeth Garrett Anderson* (1965), p. 90.
11. EG to Emily Davies, 12 December 1860, in Women's Library.
12. L. G. Anderson, *Elizabeth Garrett Anderson* (1939), p. 77.
13. L. G. Anderson (1939), p. 80.
14. EG to Emily Davies 7 June 1861, in Women's Library.
15. *The Lancet* (6 July 1861).
16. *The Lancet* (3 August 1861).

17. M. G. Fawcett, *What I Remember* (1924), p. 51.
18. John Keats qualified this way, as number 189, in 1816.
19. EG to Emily Davies, 21 August 1861, in Women's Library.
20. J. Manton (1965), p. 124.
21. J. Manton (1965), p. 156.
22. M. E. Bell, *Storming the Citadel* (1953), p. 57.
23. *The Lancet* (5 July 1862).
24. J. Manton (1965), p. 127.
25. J. Manton (1965), pp. 130–1.
26. *The Lancet* (30 May 1863).
27. *Spectator* (8 November 1862).
28. *British Medical Journal* (22 November 1862).
29. EG to Louisa Smith, in Women's Library, undated but 1863.
30. Alice to her mother, 5 June 1863.
31. L. G. Anderson (1939), p. 108.
32. In the same way, Emily Davies refused the suggestion that London University might offer special external exams for women, less difficult than matriculation: 'We are really obliged to Convocation for their kind intentions in offering us a serpent when we asked for a fish, tho' we cannot pretend to believe that serpents are better for us'. See B. Stephen, *Emily Davies and Girton College* (1927), p. 103, and R. Strachey, *Millicent Garrett Fawcett*, (1931), p. 142.
33. B. Stephen (1927), p. 78.
34. I. Ross, *Child of Destiny* (1950), p. 226.
35. Alice to her mother, 19 May 1865.
36. B. Stephen (1927), p. 80.
37. *Beccles and Bungay Weekly News* (10 October 1865).
38. E. Davies, *The Higher Education of Women* (1866; repr. 1988), p. 78.
39. Licentiate of the Society of Apothecaries; her name appeared on the Medical Register a year later.
40. B. Stephen (1927), p. 115; for much the same reason, Millicent steered clear of the apolitical Social Science Association, never speaking there except once (in 1868) to read a paper for her husband; the Association, founded in 1857, had, though, admitted women as members from the start.

Chapter 7

1. E. Crawford, *Enterprising Women* (2002), p. 28.
2. E. Crawford (2002), pp. 28–9.
3. Alice to her mother 6 November 1866.

4. Alice to her mother 9 May 1869.
5. *Women's Penny Paper* (18 January 1890), pp. 145–6.
6. Alice to her father 10 April 1872.
7. Alice to her mother 28 December 1869.
8. Alice to her mother 4 January 1870.
9. P. Hirsch, *Barbara Leigh Smith Bodichon* (1998), p. 164.
10. M. Lutyens, *Edward Lutyens* (1980), p. 25.
11. A. I. Thackeray, 'Toilers and Spinsters', in the *Cornhill Magazine* (March 1861), p. 320.
12. J. Boucherett, 'On the Choice of a Business', *Englishwoman's Journal* (Nov 1862).
13. Richard Garrett's son-in-law, Frederick Peck, architect for Framlingham College, Suffolk.
14. A. Callen, *Women Artists of the Arts and Crafts Movement* (1979), p. 26; 'Art-work for Women', *Art Journal* (1872), p. 102.
15. EG to JSA, 3 January 1871, in Women's Library.
16. R. Strachey, *Millicent Garrett Fawcett* (1931), pp. 59–60.
17. E. Crawford (2002), p. 173; 'Some Practical Women', *Woman's World* (1890).
18. A. Callen (1979), p. 171.
19. *Women's Penny Paper* (18 January 1890), pp. 145–6.
20. R. & A. Garrett, *Suggestions for House Decoration* (1876), introduction.
21. The Garrett style has been well described in E. Crawford (2002), ch 4.
22. The surviving furniture, and the ceiling in Gower Street painted by the sisters, are documented and illustrated in E. Crawford (2002), pp. 178–203.
23. *Women's Penny Paper* (1890), pp. 145–6.
24. A. Callen (1979), p. 172.
25. See Chapter 17 in this volume.
26. The house, with some Garrett furniture is now owned by the National Trust. Beale was a solicitor whose wife supported the New Hospital for Women; he became President of the Law Society in 1908, ten years before Sam Garrett.
27. G. Shaw, *The Garrett Papers* (1984), p. 62.
28. C. L. Graves, *Hubert Parry: His Life and Work* (1926), vol. 1, p. 149, quoting Parry in 1874.
29. C. L. Graves (1926), vol. 1, p.163, quoting Parry in 1875.
30. C. L. Graves (1926), vol. 1, p.165, quoting Parry in 1876.
31. E. Crawford (2002), p. 199.
32. She was a children's writer; their mother was an enthusiast for women's suffrage.

33. E. Smyth, *Impressions that Remain* (1923), vol. ii, pp. 7, 12 and 57.
34. C. L. Graves (1926), vol. 1, p. 206, quoting Parry in 1879.
35. E. Crawford (2002), p. 185; Maud Parry's diary entry.
36. M. Conway, *Travels in South Kensington* (1882), p. 169.
37. See Chapter 8 in this volume.
38. D. Rubinstein, *A Different World for Women* (1991), p. 59.
39. R. Strachey, *Millicent Garrett Fawcett* (1931), p. 60.
40. E. Smyth (1923), vol. ii, p. 8.
41. Jane Lewis (ed.), *Before the Vote was Won* (1987), pp. 159–73; R. Garrett, 'Electoral Disabilities of Women' (3 April 1872).
42. E. Crawford (2002), p. 201.
43. Agnes kept the house until 1899, then rented a smaller house in Rustington for a further five years.

Chapter 8

1. C. A. Lacey (ed.), *Barbara Leigh Smith Bodichon and the Langham Place Group* (1987), p. 412; E. Davies, 'Medicine as a Profession for Women', paper read at the Social Science Congress (June 1862).
2. *The Lancet* (13 December 1862).
3. *The Lancet* (7 October 1865).
4. Elizabeth Blackwell's American ladders were pulled up too – Geneva College stopped taking women students, and her sister Emily had to go to two different colleges to achieve her medical course – see J. Boyd, *The Excellent Doctor Blackwell* (2005), pp. 135 and 146.
5. E. Crawford, *Enterprising Women* (2002), p. 54.
6. Including the 31-year-old John Hughlings Jackson.
7. *The Lancet* (7 July 1866).
8. E. Crawford (2002), p. 54; EG to her mother.
9. E. Crawford (2002), p. 50; EG to her mother.
10. E. Crawford (2002), p. 58; 'During the second half of the nineteenth century 60 other specialist hospitals were founded in London, most owing their existence to groups of ambitious medical men or enterprising individuals seeking to carve out for themselves a specialist practice'.
11. L. Goldman, *Science, Reform, and Politics in Victorian Britain* (2002), p. 117.
12. Mother of Bertrand Russell.
13. E. Crawford (2002), p. 51.
14. Alice to EG, 18 February 1868.
15. Alice to her mother, 27 August 1869.
16. *The Lancet* (18 June 1870).

17. Alice to her mother 11 July 1870.

18. Among the others who followed the Paris route was Professor Ayrton's wife Matilda, MD 1879.

19. *Pall Mall Gazette* (25 January 1870).

20. *The Times* (22 March 1870).

21. Heckford had meanwhile been in India, where Alice 'was sorry not to like him better for Lizzie's sake'. He had, she reported, 'expected to make about £1000 a year to begin with', but failed to get patients.

22. C. Dickens, *All the Year Round* (19 December 1868).

23. EG to JSA, 20 August 1870, Women's Library.

24. EG to JSA, 20 August 1870, Women's Library.

25. *The Lancet*, 24 October 1870, p. 615.

26. B. Stephen, *Emily Davies and Girton College* (1927), pp. 120–1.

27. Alice to her father 29 November 1870.

28. J. Russell, *The Amberley Papers* (1937), vol. 2, p. 386.

29. B. Stephen (1927), p. 124.

30. B. Stephen (1927), p. 124.

31. Alice to her mother 4 January 1871.

32. *Punch* (10 December 1870).

33. Alice also remained on the Board for three years.

34. E. Crawford (2002), p. 159.

35. *Blackwood's Magazine* (June 1874).

36. See Chapter 12, pp. 121–2.

37. *The Lancet* (7 January 1871).

38. *The Lancet* (28 January 1871).

39. *Women's Penny Paper* 18 Jan 1890.

40. EG to Millicent Fawcett, 25 December 1870, Women's Library.

41. Millicent told of speaking in East Suffolk in 1865 about this law, and having to give up when an old farmer protested 'Am I to understand you, ma'am, that if this Bill becomes law, and my wife had a matter of a hundred pound left her, I should have to arst her for it?'

42. EG to JSA, 28 December 1870, Women's Library.

43. EG to JSA, 21 January 1871, Women's Library.

44. Alice to her mother, 1 February 1871.

45. Alice to her father, 7 February 1871.

46. EG to JSA, 21 January 1871, Women's Library.

47. L. G. Anderson, *Elizabeth Garrett Anderson* (1939), p. 187; EG to Millicent, undated.

48. EG to JSA, 3 January 1871, Women's Library.

49. EGA to her father, 17 February 1871, in collection of Alice's letters.

Chapter 9

1. R. Strachey, *Millicent Garrett Fawcett* (1931), p. 26.
2. R. Strachey (1931), p. 27.
3. D. Rubinstein, *A Different World for Women* (1991), pp. 15–16 (quoting from undated letter).
4. R. Strachey (1931), p. 36.
5. Alice to her father 21 February 1867.
6. S. Collini, in L. Goldman (ed.), *The Blind Victorian* (1989), p. 43.
7. L. Stephen, 'Henry Fawcett', in the *Dictionary of National Biography*.
8. Hampstead Heath, Wimbledon Common and Epping Forest owe much to Fawcett.
9. Alice to her mother, 9 May 1872.
10. H. Spencer, *Social Statistics* (1868), pp. 173 and 175.
11. M. G. Fawcett, *The Women's Victory – and After, 1911–18* (1920), p. 166.
12. R. Strachey (1931), pp. 43–4.
13. M. G. Fawcett, *What I Remember* (1924), p. 82.
14. M. G. Fawcett (1924), pp. 70–82.
15. D. Rubinstein (1991), p. 19.
16. From evidence in Alice's letter to her mother (January 1869), their sister Josephine seems to have taken it, and (according to a letter of 28 March) to have passed though not with honours, and then gone on to the Cambridge senior exam.
17. G. Sutherland, *Faith, Duty and the Power of Mind* (2006), p. 93.
18. C. Blake, *The Charge of the Parasols* (1990), p. 97.
19. G. Sutherland (2006), p. 80.
20. J. Russell, *The Amberley Papers* (1937), p. 260; Lady Amberley's diary 24 February 1869.
21. L. Huxley, *Life and Letters of Thomas Henry Huxley* (1900), vol. I, pp. 211–12, letter from T. H. Huxley to Sir C. Lyell, 17 March 1860.
22. M. R. Bobbitt, *With Dearest Love to All* (1960), p. 63.
23. D. Rubinstein (1991), p. 24.
24. Alexander Macmillan had been a friend of Fawcett's at Cambridge, and was already his publisher.
25. In her next article (*Fortnightly Review* November 1868) she changed those figures to 1,192 boys and eighteen domestic girls; and she added that Dulwich College, originally meant for both sexes, now had only boys.
26. Alice to her mother, 28 March 1869.
27. Other Garrett subscribers to the Girton building fund, at times, were

Newson Garrett and Herbert Cowell (husband of Alice); Elizabeth was still helping Girton financially as late as 1912.

28. *The Times* (10 October 1868).

29. G. Johnson, *University Politics* (1994), p. 11.

30. Later, as Mrs Humphry Ward, she was to cross swords with Millicent (see Chapter 16).

31. R. Strachey, *The Cause* (1928), p. 149.

32. M. G. Fawcett (1924), p. 73.

33. D. Rubinstein (1991), p. 27.

34. B. Stephen, *Emily Davies and Girton College* (1927), p. 255.

35. Alice to her mother, 14 May 1868.

36. E. Crawford, *Enterprising Women* (2002), p. 136.

37. H. Fawcett and M. G. Fawcett, *Essays and Lectures on Social and Political Subjects* (1872), p. 222. Lecture given at Newcastle 13 November 1871.

38. E. Darwin, *A Century of Family Letters* (1915), vol. 2, p. 245.

39. E. Darwin (1915), p. 172.

40. There were to be many institutions and buildings named for Millicent and for Elizabeth.

41. Rather like Millicent at Cambridge, Mrs Humphry Ward became secretary of the 'Lectures for Women' at Oxford which led to the foundation of Somerville, and she was on the original Council; but unlike Millicent she did not connect the need for education with the need for the suffrage.

42. *Fortnightly Review* (April 1874).

43. *Fortnightly Review* (May 1874).

44. Elizabeth Garrett earlier (see Chapter 4, p. 28).

45. P. Deane, 'Henry Fawcett: The Plain Man's Political Economist', in L. Goldman (ed.), *The Blind Victorian* (1989), p. 106.

46. Letter from Alice to her mother 11 July 1870.

47. M. G. Fawcett, *Political Economy for Beginners* (1880, 5th edition), pp. 112–13.

48. H. Fawcett, 'Pauperism, Charity and the Poor Law', *British Quarterly* (April 1869), reprinted in *Essays and Lectures* (1872), p. 89.

49. J. A. V. Chapple and A. Pollard (eds), *Letters of Mrs Gaskell* (1966), p. 669.

50. *Opinions of Women on Women's Suffrage*, Central Committee of the National Society for Women's Suffrage (1879).

51. *Life of Her Majesty Queen Victoria* (1895), and *Life of Sir William Molesworth* (1901) (see Chapter 14). Also, M. G. Fawcett and E. M. Turner, *Josephine Butler* (1927) for the Association for Moral and Social Hygiene.

52. *Women's Suffrage: A Short History of a Great Movement* (1912); *The Women's Victory – and After, 1911–18* (1920).

Chapter 10

1. Letter, 11 February 1876, Women's Library.
2. M. G. Fawcett, *What I Remember* (1924), p. 74.
3. Alice to her mother, 27 June 1867.
4. R. Strachey, *Millicent Garrett Fawcett* (1931), p. 46.
5. J. Russell, *The Amberley Papers* (1937), pp. 324–5.
6. A. Hochschild, *Bury the Chains* (2006), p. 137.
7. See Chapter 7, pp. 64–5.
8. Alice to her mother 20 April 1870.
9. J. Lewis (ed.), *Before the Vote was Won* (1987), pp. 100–17.
10. *Irish Times* (19 April 1870).
11. Alice to her mother, 4 June 1872.
12. In her article on 'Communism' for the *Encyclopaedia Britannica*, 9th edition.
13. Reprinted from *Macmillan's Magazine* (September 1870 and March 1871).
14. H. Fawcett and M. G. Fawcett, *Essays and Lectures on Social and Political Subjects* (1872), pp. 262–91 (written in March 1871).
15. Fawcett and Fawcett (1872), pp. 230–61 (written in July 1871).
16. R. Strachey, *The Cause* (1928), p. 214.
17. Fawcett and Fawcett (1872), p. 52; 'Free Education in its Economic Aspects' (reprinted from *The Times* 14 December 1870).
18. Fawcett and Fawcett (1872), p. 43; 'The General Aspects of State Intervention', lecture given by Henry Fawcett at Cambridge 1872.
19. M. G. Fawcett, review of *The Woman Socialist* by E. Snowden in *Economic Journal* (1907).
20. Fawcett and Fawcett (1872), 'Pauperism, Charity and the Poor Law' (repr. from *British Quarterly* April 1869), pp. 76, 90.
21. R. Strachey (1928), p. 234.
22. *The Times* (9 June 1873).
23. *The Times* (12 June 1873).
24. *The Times* (5 August 1873).
25. M. G. Fawcett (1924), p. 59.
26. D. Rubinstein, *A Different World for Women* (1991), p. 52, quoting from *Women's Union Journal* (July 1881), pp. 67–8.
27. R. Strachey (1931), p. 77.
28. M. G. Fawcett, 'Mr Fitzjames Stephen on the Position of Women' (July 1973), p. 15 (reprinted from the *Examiner*).
29. N. Annan, *Leslie Stephen* (1984), p. xii.
30. R. Strachey (1931), p. 92.
31. D. Rubinstein (1991), p. 21.

32. M. G. Fawcett (1924), p. 109.

33. L. Goldman, *The Blind Victorian* (1989), p.18 (Fawcett correspondence with Gladstone 18 April 1872).

34. R. Strachey (1931), p. 99.

35. R. Strachey (1931), p. 94.

36. J. Lewis (ed.), *Before the Vote was Won* (1987); reprinted from *Pall Mall Gazette* (14 January 1884).

37. Hubert Parry to Alice Leith, 8 November 1884, Women's Library.

Chapter 11

1. Trinity College Dublin did not admit women medical students until 1904.

2. E. M. Bell, *Josephine Butler* (1962), p. 47.

3. J. Russell, *The Amberley Papers* (1937), vol. 2, p. 20; a note in Lady Amberley's diary for 8 March 1867 read 'Miss Garrett came to see us and prescribed for A [Amberley] and Baby but sent the medicines to me as she does not profess to attend men'.

4. Sixteen years earlier, Elizabeth Blackwell had opened her New York Infirmary for Women and Children, with her sister Emily and one other woman doctor. See J. Boyd, *The Excellent Doctor Blackwell* (2005).

5. J. Manton, *Elizabeth Garrett Anderson* (1965), p. 230.

6. M. Todd, *The Life of Sophia Jex-Blake* (1918), p. 186.

7. M. Scharlieb, *Reminiscences* (1924), p. 138.

8. Including Skelton Anderson's sister Mary, who finally qualified in Dublin 1880, after a degree in Paris.

9. Her father, Dr Thomas Jex-Blake, was a proctor of Doctors' Commons.

10. Sophia never learned. In 1890 two of her Edinburgh students successfully sued her for wrongful dismissal; they were awarded £50 damages and she had to pay costs.

11. L. Huxley, *Life and Letters of T. H. Huxley* (1900), vol. 1, p. 417; *The Times* 8 July 1874).

12. M. Todd (1918), p. 423.

13. *The Times* (5 August 1873).

14. *The Times* (23 August 1873).

15. J. Manton (1965), p. 248.

16. J. Manton (1965), p. 240.

17. M. Todd (1918), pp. 424–5.

18. L. G. Anderson, *Elizabeth Garrett Anderson* (1939), p. 226; *Standard* (16 January 1878).

19. J. Manton (1965), p. 259.

20. EGA to JSA, 4 August 1878, Women's Library.

21. M. B. Bell, *Storming the Citadel* (1953), pp. 137–8.

22. L. G. Anderson (1939), p. 263.

23. M. B. Bell (1953), p. 141.

24. EGA to her father, 6 May 1883, Women's Library.

25. I am indebted to Victoria Rea, archivist of the Royal Free, and Professor Neil McIntyre for this information. Louisa Garrett Anderson says that Mary Scharlieb was left in charge; but Scharlieb came to London only in 1887, so her time in charge must have been in 1887 when Elizabeth and Skelton went on another (unspecified) holiday.

26. E. Crawford, *Enterprising Women* (2002), p. 60.

27. E. Crawford (2002), p. 61.

28. J. Manton (1965), p. 286.

29. M. Scharlieb, *Reminiscences* (1924), p. 135.

30. EGA to MGF, 22 October 1890, Women's Library.

31. *RIBA Journal* (1894), pp. 235–37, book review.

32. *Christian World* (14 April 1892).

33. G. Shaw (ed.), *The Garrett Papers* (1984), p. 64, n. 11.

34. *The Times* (11 December 1896).

35. I. Ross, *Child of Destiny* (1950), p. 260.

36. EGA to MGF, 10 June 1895, Women's Library.

37. UCL Hospital website, www.uclh.nhs.uk/GPs and healthcare professionals, accessed 17 April 2007.

Chapter 12

1. E. Pankhurst, *My Own Story* (1914), p. 57.

2. EGA to MGF, June 1867, Women's Library.

3. E. Crawford, *Enterprising Women* (2002), p. 246; *Women's Suffrage Journal* (1 May 1871).

4. E. Crawford (2002), p. 247.

5. R. Strachey, *Millicent Garrett Fawcett* (1931), p. 253.

6. D. Rubinstein, *A Different World for Women* (1991), pp. 187–8.

7. J. Manton, *Elizabeth Garrett Anderson* (1965), p. 129.

8. J. Manton (1965), p. 295.

9. L. G. Anderson, *Elizabeth Garrett Anderson* (1939), p. 190.

10. R. Strachey, *Millicent Garrett Fawcett* (1931), p. 88; Henry Fawcett and Henry Sidgwick had both given up fellowships rather than sign the 39 Articles.

11. Alice to her mother, 4 April 1872.

12. Alice to her mother, 11 May 1870.

13. G. Shaw (ed.), *The Garrett Papers* (1984), p. 7.

14. E. Crawford (2002), p. 202, quoting Maud Parry's diary.
15. F. E. Garrett, 'Isis Very Much Unveiled: The Story of the Great Mahatma Hoax', *Westminster Gazette* (29 October – 8 November, 1894). (Mme Blavatsky's book expounding theosophy was called *Isis Unveiled*).
16. G. Shaw (1984), p. 108, letter 2 September 1897.
17. R. Strachey (1931), p. 133.
18. E. Crawford (2002), p. 41; in the next generation, Louie's daughter Dorothea and one of Alice's daughters were members of the University Club for Ladies.
19. E. Crawford (2002), p. 203.
20. E. Crawford (2002), p. 41, quoting Elizabeth Garrett Anderson, 'An Address on Medical Ethics', 1896.
21. C. L. Graves, *Hubert Parry: His Life and Work* (1926), vol. 1, p. 198.
22. M. G. Fawcett, *What I Remember* (1924), p. 106.
23. L. G. Anderson (1939), p. 196.
24. R. Strachey (1931), p. 358.
25. L. G. Anderson (1939), pp. 193–4.
26. L. G. Anderson (1939), p. 193.
27. See Chapter 8, p. 74.
28. Alice to her mother, 26 September 1870.
29. Alice to her mother, 9 October 1870.
30. EG to her father, 12 Sept 1870, Women's Library.
31. L. G. Anderson (1939), pp. 140–1.
32. L. G. Anderson (1939), pp. 141–2.
33. Smallpox killed between 60,000 and 90,000 Frenchmen in that war, and French refugees spread the epidemic round Europe.
34. J. Manton (1965), p. 278.
35. N. Mitchison, 'Elizabeth Garrett Anderson', in *Revaluations, Studies in Biography* (1931), p. 189.
36. L. G. Anderson (1939), p. 269.
37. E. Sharp, *Unfinished Adventure* (1933), pp. 124–5.

Chapter 13

1. G. Orwell, *The Road to Wigan Pier* (1937; repr. 1989), p. 115.
2. Alice to her father, 1 July 1867.
3. Alice to her father, 6 January 1866.
4. Alice to her mother, 3 July 1865.
5. Newson Dunnell Garrett to his father, 3 October 1869.
6. The idea of 'trade' always worried his father, who later thought Sam would

be better as a solicitor than in the Brewery. Alice disagreed. Letter to her mother, 11 June 1872.

7. Alice to her mother, 1 February 1870.
8. Alice to her father, 10 June 1870.
9. It was Edward Cowell who introduced his East Suffolk friend Edward Fitzgerald to the Persian verses of the Rubaiyat. In proper East Suffolk tradition, Professor Cowell's father is described as 'merchant and maltster'.
10. Newson Dunnell Garrett to his parents, 22 December 1861.
11. Alice to her mother, 18 June 1863.
12. Alice to her mother, 8 November 1867.
13. Alice to her father, 6 May 1866.
14. Alice to her father, 21 February 1867.
15. Alice to her mother, 7 February 1868.
16. Newson Dunnell Garrett, 8 December 1867.
17. Alice to her mother, 4 May 1868.
18. Alice to her mother, 24 June 1870.
19. Alice to Agnes, 15 February 1869.
20. Alice to her mother, 26 April 1870.
21. Alice to her brother Sam, 14 June 1894.
22. J. Manton, *Elizabeth Garrett Anderson* (1965), p. 286.
23. E. Crawford, *Enterprising Women* (2002), p. 90.
24. J. Manton (1965), pp. 289–90.
25. *The Queen*, 5 July 1890
26. F. Murray, *Women as Army Surgeons* (1920), p. 236.
27. D. Rubinstein, *A Different World for Women* (1991), p. 100.
28. MGF letter in Women's Library.
29. D. Rubinstein (1991), p. 268.

Chapter 14

1. E. G. Rice and R. H. Compton, *Wild Flowers of the Cape of Good Hope* (1950). Elsie's twin, John, eventually emigrated to Australia.
2. H. Hall, *Common Succulents* (1955), illustrated by Elsie Garrett Rice.
3. FEG to W. T. Stead, 24 October 1889, Churchill College Archives.
4. E. T. Cook, *Edmund Garrett: A Memoir* (1909), p. 86, quoting letter in *Cape Times* (25 June 1895).
5. G. Shaw (ed.), *The Garrett Papers* (1984), covering the period 1896–8. The replies have not survived.
6. F. E. Garrett wrote up the Jameson Raid in *Story of an African Crisis* (1897).
7. G. Shaw (1984), p. 45.
8. N. Hawthorne, *Straight Face* (2002), p. 22.

9. FEG to W. T. Stead, Churchill College Archives.

10. G. Shaw (1984), p. 107, 2 September 1897; p. 124, 30 March 1898; p. 126, August 1898.

11. E. Crawford, *Enterprising Women* (2002), p. 255.

12. G. Shaw (1984), p. 87.

13. E. T. Cook (1909), p. 99; F. E. Garrett, *In Afrikanerland* (1891; a *Pall Mall Gazette* 'Extra' reprinting articles from the magazine).

14. E. T. Cook (1909), p. 101; F. E. Garrett (1891).

15. E. T. Cook (1909), p. 103; F. E. Garrett, *Cape Times* (2 October 1895).

16. G. Shaw (1984), p. 94.

17. G. Shaw (1984), p. 69.

18. G. Shaw (1984), p. 65.

19. E. T. Cook (1909), p. 147.

20. *Westminster Gazette* (31 July 1906).

21. E. T. Cook (1909), p. 192, memorandum circulated in 1906.

22. FEG, 12 December 1899, Churchill College Archives.

23. M. G. Fawcett, *What I Remember* (1924), pp. 149–50.

24. R. Strachey, *Millicent Garrett Fawcett* (1931), p. 186.

25. E. T. Cook (1909), p. 139.

26. J. Sutherland, *Mrs Humphry Ward* (1990), p. 197; Mrs Humphry Ward to her father, 14 September 1899. Beatrice Webb wrote in retrospect that everyone seemed to have forgotten the 'vast majority of Kaffirs, five or six million in number, among whom this variegated white minority had intruded itself'. K. Muggeridge and R. Adam, *Beatrice Webb* (1967), p. 163.

27. *Westminster Gazette* (4 July 1901).

28. J. Waterston article in *Cape Times* (24 July 1901), quoted in R. van Reenan (ed.) *Emily Hobhouse: Boer War Letters* (1984), p. 452, n. 15.1.

29. R. van Reenan (ed.) (1984), p. 86.

30. R. Strachey (1931), p. 201.

31. M. G. Fawcett (1924), p. 159.

32. R. van Reenan (ed.) (1984), p. 425.

33. E. Hobhouse, *The Brunt of the War* (1902), p. 292.

34. R. van Reenan (ed.) (1984), p. 453, n. 15.1.

35. R. van Reenan (ed.) (1984), p. 448, n. 21, Report of the Ladies' Committee.

36. R. van Reenan (ed.) (1984), p. 424.

37. M. G. Fawcett (1924), pp. 159 and 163.

38. *Westminster Gazette* (4 July 1901).

39. R. Strachey (1931), p. 203.

40. R. Strachey (1931), p. 205.

41. R. van Reenan (ed.) (1984), p. 195.

42. M. G. Fawcett (1924), p. 166.
43. M. G. Fawcett, 'Impressions of S. Africa in 1901 and 1903', in the *Contemporary Review* (November 1903), pp. 647–8.
44. G. Shaw (1984), p. 98.
45. G. Shaw (1984), p. 99.
46. M. G. Fawcett, *Life of Her Majesty Queen Victoria* (1897).
47. G. Shaw (1984), p. 97.
48. D. Rubinstein (1991), p. 31.
49. R. Strachey (1931), p. 139, MGF letter, May 1888.
50. M. G. Fawcett, *Life of Sir William Molesworth* (1901), pp. 116–17.
51. M. G. Fawcett (1901), pp. 158–61.
52. M. G. Fawcett (1901), p. 160.
53. M. G. Fawcett (1901), p. 296.

Chapter 15

1. Christina de Bellaigue, 'Teaching as a Profession for Women before 1870', *Historical Journal* 44/4 (2001), pp. 971–85.
2. G. Sutherland, 'The Movement for the Higher Education of Women', in P. J. Waller (ed.), *Politics and Social Change in Modern Britain* (1987), p. 92.
3. J. Manton, *Elizabeth Garrett Anderson* (1965), pp. 293–4.
4. L. G. Anderson, *Elizabeth Garrett Anderson* (1939), pp. 266–7.
5. E. Crawford, *Enterprising Women* (2002), p. 164.
6. G. Shaw (ed.), *The Garrett Papers* (1984), pp. 77–8.
7. *Pall Mall Gazette* (5 October 1892).
8. R. Wake, *Bedales School* (1993), p. 47.

Chapter 16

1. R. Strachey, *Millicent Garrett Fawcett* (1931), p. 125.
2. R. Strachey, *The Cause* (1928), p. 288.
3. In 1898 she was prepared to attack the continued use of the Contagious Diseases Acts for the army in India.
4. R. Strachey (1931), p. 111.
5. *Englishwoman's Review* (15 October 1885), p. 455.
6. Generally assumed to be the natural father of Diana Manners (Lady Diana Cooper).
7. C. Tomalin, *Thomas Hardy* (2006), p. 232.
8. M. G. Fawcett, letter to *The Times*, 5 February 1889.

9. Millicent had to wait till 1918 for a doctorate (from the University of Birmingham) for her leadership of the women's movement.

10. R. Strachey (1931), p. 183.

11. There was a Bill every year in the 1870s except 1875; one Bill passed its second reading in 1885, others were defeated in 1892 and 1897.

12. G. Shaw (ed.), *The Garrett Papers* (1984), p. 100.

13. R. Strachey (1931), p. 122.

14. J. Trevelyan, *Life of Mrs Humphry Ward* (1923), p. 227.

15. *Nineteenth Century* (June 1889), pp.781–9.

16. Angela Burdett Coutts to MGF, 19 November 1885, Women's Library.

17. *Nineteenth Century* (July 1889), p. 88.

18. B. Webb, *Our Partnership* (1948), pp. 360–3; according to her niece Kitty Muggeridge, Beatrice Potter 'admitted candidly that she had been anti-feminist simply because the fewer women there were in her field the higher her rarity value'. K. Muggeridge and R. Adam, *Beatrice Webb* (1967), p. 117.

19. *Nineteenth Century*, (July 1889), pp. 89, 96.

20. *Fortnightly Review*, xlv, new series (1889), pp. 562–3.

21. *Fortnightly Review*, xlv, new series (1889), pp. 564, 567.

22. J. Lewis (ed.), *Before the Vote was Won* (1987), p. 446, letter (for publication) written to Samuel Smith MP, 11 April 1892.

23. M. G. Fawcett, *What I Remember* (1924), p. 123.

24. The word 'suffragette' was used for the militants; Millicent's followers were known as 'suffragists'.

25. J. Trevelyan (1923), p. 234.

26. B. Caine, *Bombay to Bloomsbury* (2005), p. 49, quoting 'Woman Suffrage and India' (pamphlet no. 26 of the Anti-Suffrage League).

27. M. G. Fawcett (1924), p. 177.

28. Millicent married at 20 and was widowed at 37; Emmeline married at 21 and was widowed at 40.

29. M. Stocks, *Commonplace Book* (1970), p. 71.

30. R. Strachey (1931), p. 247, referring to Dr John Massie.

31. *The Times* (19 February 1907).

32. R. Jenkins, *Asquith* (1964), p. 250.

33. R. Strachey (1928), p. 322.

34. E. Pankhurst, *My Own Story* (1914), p. 168; men who actively supported the militants, such as my uncle Hugh Franklin, were certainly also punished in prison cells.

35. H. Samuel, *Memoirs* (1945), p. 130.

36. *The Times* (4 February 1909).

37. M. G. Fawcett (1924), p. 183.

38. R. Strachey (1931), p. 217.
39. M. G. Fawcett (1924), p. 185.
40. R. Strachey (1931), p. 223.
41. R. Strachey (1931), p. 268.
42. R. Strachey (1931), p. 230.
43. M. G. Fawcett, *Women's Suffrage: A Short History of a Great Movement* (1912), p. 11.
44. R. Strachey (1931), p. 229.
45. R. Strachey (1931), p. 235.
46. R. Strachey (1931), p. 240.
47. M. G. Fawcett (1912), p. 43.
48. Some countries were slower – women in Kuwait voted for the first time in 2006; in Saudi Arabia the struggle goes on.

Chapter 17

1. Damaged by bombing in 1941, it was restored and is still there, owned by Camden Council.
2. Later Molly Hughes. When she married, of course she not only moved out but her job ended; she went back to teaching only when her husband died.
3. E. Crawford, *Enterprising Women* (2002), p. 210.
4. E. Hobhouse, 'Women Workers how they Live, how they Wish to Live', *Nineteenth Century* (March 1890).
5. E. G. Anderson, 'History and Effects of Vaccination', *Edinburgh Review* (April 1899); 'Ethics of Vivisection', *Edinburgh Review* (July 1899).
6. *Edinburgh Review* (April 1899), p. 251.
7. *Edinburgh Review* (April 1899), p. 356.
8. Some, objecting to compulsory vaccination, were even prepared to go to prison; a baby in Kent was christened Anny Antivaccinator Austin (personal commumication from Dr J. C. Burne).
9. *The Times* (15 September 1903).
10. Quoted by EGA in *Edinburgh Review* (July 1899), p. 148.
11. *Edinburgh Review* (July 1899), p. 161.
12. *Edinburgh Review* (July 1899), p. 163.
13. *Edinburgh Review* (July 1899), p. 166.
14. L. G. Anderson, *Elizabeth Garrett Anderson* (1939), p. 265.
15. There is a particularly fine wall tablet in his memory in Aldeburgh church.
16. EGA's brothers George (died 1929) and Sam Garrett (died 1923) had already each served terms as mayor; Josephine's great-grandson, Christopher Wood, became mayor in 1985, 100 years after Newson.

17. E. Crawford (2002), p. 258. Edmund Garrett, recently down from Cambridge, had been to the early meetings of the Society for Promoting Women as County Councillors.
18. J. Manton, *Elizabeth Garrett Anderson* (1965), p. 337.

Chapter 18

1. M. G. Fawcett, *What I Remember* (1924), p. 137.
2. R. Strachey, *Millicent Garrett Fawcett* (1931), p. 145.
3. H. Litchfield, *R. B. Litchfield* (1910; privately printed), p. 210.
4. The top performer in the examination for the Cambridge mathematical degree was known as the senior wrangler.
5. M. G. Fawcett (1924), pp. 143–4.
6. F. Galton, *English Men of Science* (1874); and *Oxford DNB*. They were Robert Woodhouse, senior wrangler in 1795, who became Lucasian Professor of Mathematics (Newton's chair), and Edward Hall Alderson, senior wrangler in 1809, who became a judge (and blotted his distinguished copybook by criticizing George Stephenson's engine designs, thus helping to defeat the first bill to authorize the Liverpool and Manchester Railway, and delaying the project for several years).
7. G. A. Wilkins on Philip Cowell in *Oxford DNB*.
8. J. Manton, *Elizabeth Garrett Anderson* (1965), p. 329.
9. Newspaper report, in Women's Library.
10. Louisa Garrett Anderson to Kenneth Anderson, 1939, Women's Library.
11. He did mind; see J. Russell, *The Amberley Papers* (1867), p. 85.
12. B. Strachey and J. Samuels, *Mary Berenson* (1983), p. 38.
13. S. Dunkley on Margery Spring Rice in *Oxford DNB*.

Chapter 19

1. M. G. Fawcett, *The Women's Victory – and After, 1911–18* (1920), p. 88, quoting R. Strachey in the *Common Cause* (7 August 1914).
2. M. G. Fawcett (1920), p. 96.
3. E. Sharp, *Unfinished Adventure* (1933), pp. 165–8, described her experiences when she continued to refuse to pay taxes (because women were not represented in parliament) and was therefore declared bankrupt.
4. L. G. Anderson, *Elizabeth Garrett Anderson* (1939), p. 275.
5. LGA to EGA, Women's Library.
6. E. M. Bell, *Storming the Citadel* (1953), pp. 107 and 161.
7. E. Sharp (1933), p. 119.

8. *Daily Chronicle*, 25 April 1916, Women's Library.

9. F. Murray, *Women as Army Surgeons* (1920), p. 146.

10. *The Lancet* (3 June, 12 August and 2 September 1916).

11. M. G. Fawcett (1920), p. 106.

12. M. G. Fawcett (1920), p. 110–11, quoting the *Engineer* (20 August 1915).

13. The last surviving woman to have served in that war, Alice Barker who repaired aircraft as a member of the Royal Flying Corps, died in 2006 aged 107.

14. R. A. Whitehead, *Garretts of Leiston* (1965), p. 196 says there were a thousand of them, a 'turbulent multitude' which 'disturbed Leiston days and nights for nearly four years'.

15. D. Rubinstein, *A Different World for Women* (1991), p. 216.

16. M. G. Fawcett, *What I Remember* (1924), p. 229.

17. M. G. Fawcett (1924), pp. 232–3.

18. M. G. Fawcett (1920), pp. 132–3, quoting the *Observer* (13 August 1916).

19. M. G. Fawcett (1920), p. 133, quoting Asquith's speech on 14 August 1916.

20. M. G. Fawcett (1924), p. 241.

21. M. G. Fawcett (1924), p. 242, quoting from the *Common Cause* (9 February 1917).

22. R. Strachey, *Millicent Garrett Fawcett* (1931), p. 321.

23. But it seems that she did not stay to the end, for Ray Strachey wrote that she herself 'skooted off in the car to tell Mrs Fawcett, who hadn't stayed so long' and found her 'sitting up in a dressing gown by the fire', quoted in B. Strachey, *Remarkable Relations* (1981), p. 273.

24. M. G. Fawcett (1924), p. 248.

25. N. and H. Bentwich, *Mandate Memories* (1965), p. 115.

26. D. Rubinstein (1991), p. 242.

27. MGF to Amy Badley, 11 June 1923, Women's Library.

Chapter 20

1. M. G. Fawcett, *Easter in Palestine* (1926), p. 10.

2. M. G. Fawcett (1926), p. 87.

3. J. Glynn, *Tidings from Zion* (2000), p. 154.

4. R. Strachey, *Millicent Garrett Fawcett* (1931), pp. 341–2.

5. In fact 81 and 83; Millicent died the next year, 1929; Agnes was the last of the family to die, aged 90, in 1935.

6. J. Glynn (2000), p. 163.

7. N. and H. Bentwich, *Mandate Memories* (1965), p. 115.

Index